Driving Through Cuba

By the same author

THE ELEVENTH SUMMER
AUGUST IN JULY
WORK AND PLAY

DRIVING THROUGH CUBA

AN EAST–WEST JOURNEY

by

Carlo Gébler

To Julian Evans

AN ABACUS BOOK

First published in Great Britain by
Hamish Hamilton Ltd 1988
Published by Sphere Books Ltd 1990

All pictures by the author

Printed and bound in Great Britain by
Cox & Wyman Ltd, Reading

ISBN 0 349 10113 2

Sphere Books Ltd
A Division of
Macdonald & Co (Publishers) Ltd
27 Wrights Lane, London W8 5TZ
A member of Maxwell Pergamon Publishing Corporation plc

Contents

Acknowledgements

André Deutsch, 1968, *Inconsolable Memories*, Edmundo Desnoes; Collins, 1966, *A Precocious Autobiography*, Yevgeny Yevtushenko; Institute for Food and Development Policy, 1984, *No Free Lunch: Food and Revolution in Cuba Today*, Medea Benjamin, Joseph Collins and Michael Scott; Monthly Review Press, 1968, *The Economic Transformation of Cuba*, Edward Boorstein; Cassell, 1987, *The World of Yesterday*, Stefan Zweig (© Atrium Press Ltd., first published in 1944 by Bermann-Fischer Verlag zu Stockholm; *When Irish Eyes Were Smiling*, B. Feldman and Co. Ltd./EMI; *Too-ra-loo-ra-loo-ral (That's an Irish Lullaby)*, Shannon. Finally, I am indebted to Hugh Thomas's *Cuba, or the Pursuit of Freedom*, (1971) and grateful to Eyre and Spottiswoode and the author for permission to use material from his work. No study of Cuba would be possible without this encyclopaedic history. In Cuba, it was our Baedeker.

In addition, I would like to thank: Quinten Manby, my Spanish teacher, for his advice on the Spanish in the manuscript; Jason and Victoria Hartcup for their advice on American cars of the Fifties; Noll Scott and Patricia Smith; Marge Zimmerman: Lynn Geldof; John and Jenny Armit; Maureen and Jim Darrock; Robert McElroy; Michael Klein; Chiz Dubé; J. E. Meachem, librarian at the *Daily Telegraph*; Desmond Fennell; John Plummer; Jeffrey Rawle; R. J. Hines and Anna C. Urband, United States Navy; Madeleine Avramoussi; Georgia Garrett; George Barker; all my friends in Cuba; and finally Iain Bruce for financial assistance.

Foreword

The poet George Barker wrote (in the Introduction to his *Essays*), 'satirical poems love their enemies', meaning that, implicit in the satirist's work there is carried a sense of how wonderful the subject could be but for the fact it is deformed by the problems under attack. Why else would the satirist bother unless this was so? I would like to take this a step further and say the same is true of the critical travel writer.

Carlo Gébler

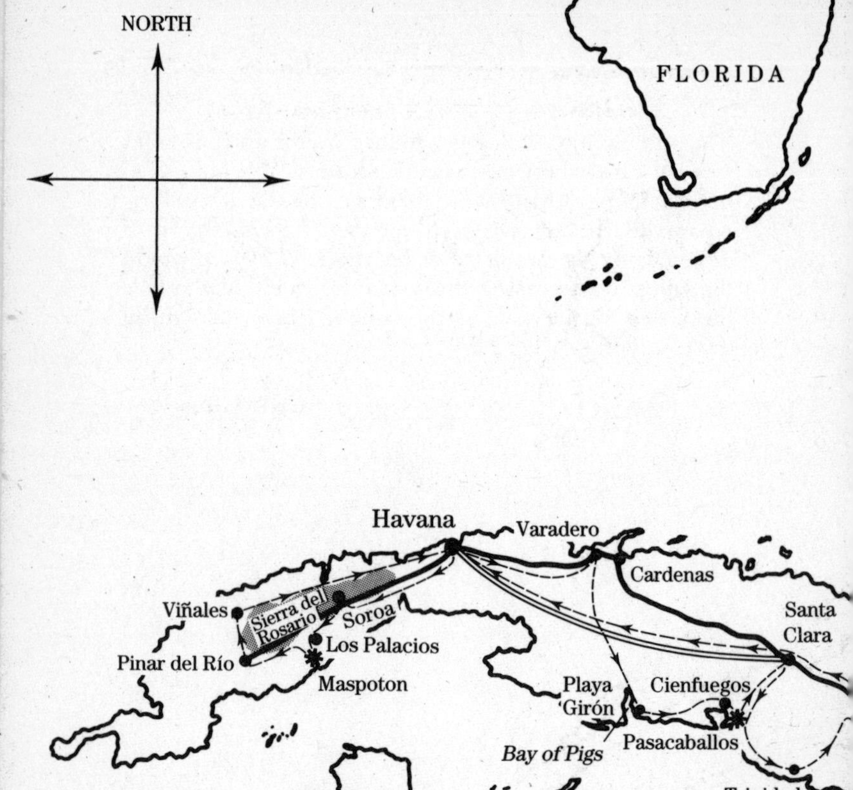
NORTH
FLORIDA
Havana
Varadero
Cardenas
Viñales
Sierra del Rosario
Soroa
Los Palacios
Pinar del Río
Maspoton
Santa Clara
Playa Girón
Cienfuegos
Pasacaballos
Bay of Pigs
Trinidad
CUBA
Caribbean
0
100 mls

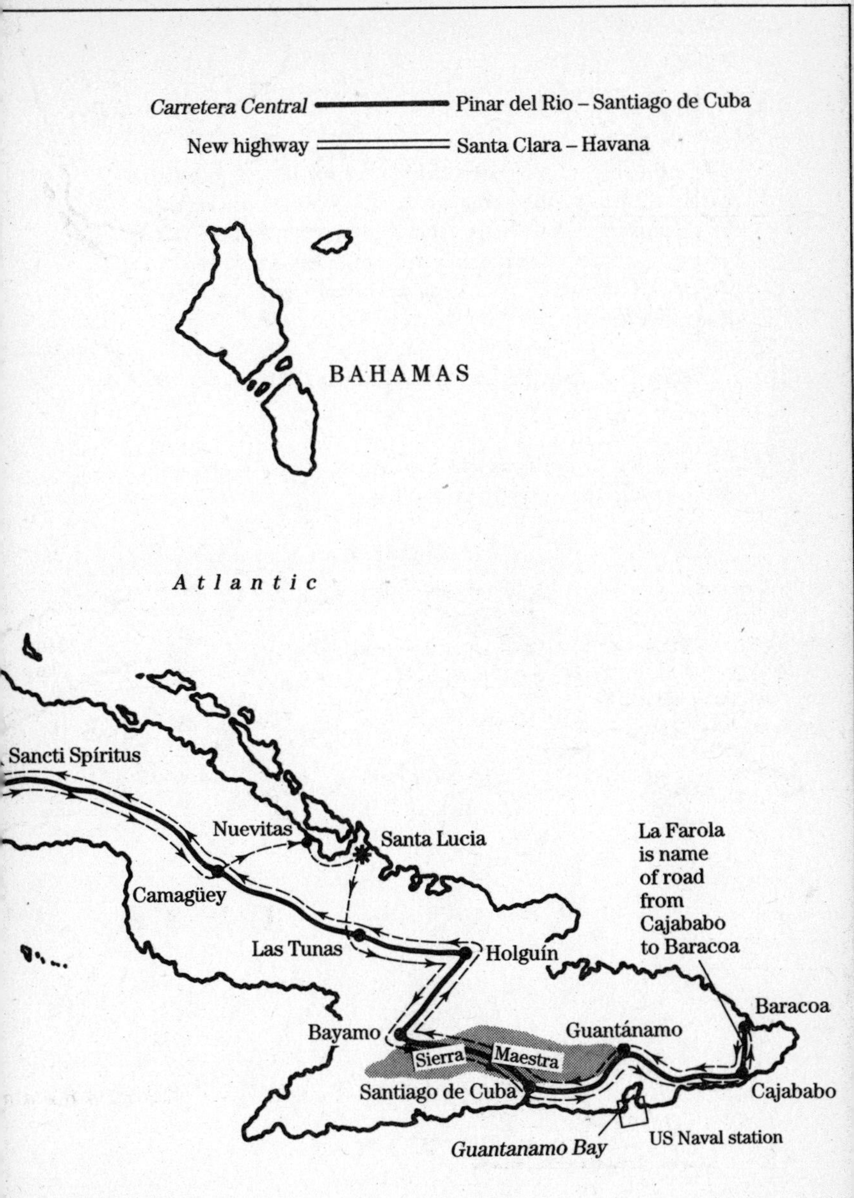
Carretera Central
Pinar del Rio – Santiago de Cuba
New highway
Santa Clara – Havana
BAHAMAS
Atlantic
Sancti Spíritus
Nuevitas
Santa Lucia
Camagüey
Las Tunas
Holguín
La Farola is name of road from Cajababo to Baracoa
Baracoa
Bayamo
Guantánamo
Sierra
Maestra
Santiago de Cuba
Cajababo
Guantanamo Bay
US Naval station

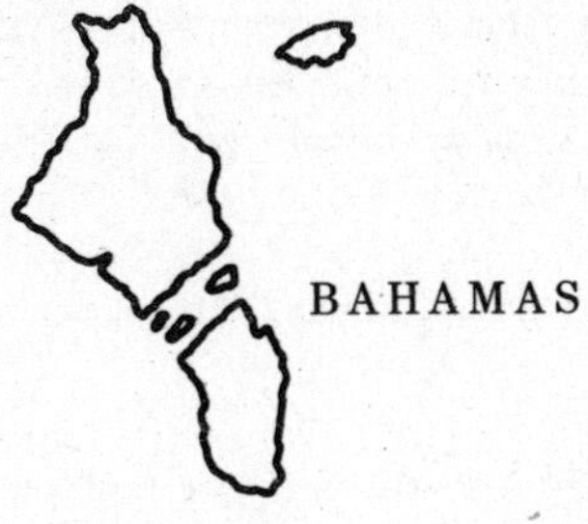

'Why is it that men's shoes, which are made with the same materials and by the same methods as before the revolution, soon lose their heels; and that women's shoes often become unusable after being worn for one day; and that the Coca-Cola now tastes unpleasant and contains all sorts of impurities?'

Che Guevara, then Minister of Industry, 16 March 1962

'When good Americans die they go to Paris; when good Cadillacs die they go to Havana'

Popular American saying

1

Memories

Cuba. I was eight years old when I realised it existed. We were living in a suburb in south London. One evening, on the black-and-white valve television set, there was a picture of something fuzzy, seen from high up in the air. It was a Soviet missile launching site. During the following days, the television appeared to be on almost continuously. I hadn't a clue what was happening but the island registered as an important place.

The Sixties rolled on. Cuba became famous, along with Israel, for having girl soldiers who wore mini-skirts. I went away to boarding school and for my special history project chose Cuba, and painstakingly typed this up in my first Easter holidays.

The History of Cuba

by

Carlos Gébler [sic]

When Christopher Columbus sailed to the Caribbean he was looking for the Orient because Europeans wanted the spices which grew there. During his journeyings he found

> Indians who spoke of a large island called 'Colba'. They said it took many days to sail around it in a canoe. Columbus thought they were talking about Japan, which he called Chipangu. He plotted his course and arrived on the north coast of Cuba on October 27th, 1492. In his earliest letters he described the island as fertile, productive and magnificent . . .

My facile work of plagiarism continued in this vein for five thousand words.

In 1973 I went to university. I joined the Film Society and one gloomy evening went to see a new Cuban film called *Memories of Underdevelopment*. It made a tremendous impression on me. I immediately went and found the book on which the screenplay was based.

Inconsolable Memories by Edmundo Desnoes was incomparably better than what was a very good film. The book is the diary of an unnamed narrator. He is the sometime owner of a chichi Havana furniture store who has always wanted to write but never has. It's 1962. The Fidelistas have been in power three years. Cuba is advancing relentlessly towards socialism. He has lost the business; there are shortages of everything; rationing is imminent; every other building in the city is being re-named after a luminary from the Marxist-Leninist gallery of heroes. His bourgeois family, and in particular Laura, his bourgeois wife, desert him for the lusher pastures of Miami. In their luxurious flat, she leaves behind her extensive collection of stockings and cosmetics. He spends much time contemplating these and thinking how much he hates her in particular and his class in general. He has stayed on because the revolution has it in for them. Yet he has had, and has, no place in the revolution. He's just a marginal observer; powerless. Result: angst.

He starts an affair with a working-class girl. It goes wrong, because, whereas he, being bourgeois, has a free and easy attitude to relationships, Elena has not and wants marriage. When he won't, her family initiate rape proceedings but at the trial it turns out she's a casual prostitute. He's let off but feels like a shit. More angst. He starts an affair with the maid, Noemi, more or less on the rebound. One day they are lying together in bed when President Kennedy speaks from the radio: 'I have directed . . . initial steps to be taken immediately . . . a strict quarantine on all offensive military equipment . . . It shall be the policy of this nation to regard any nuclear missile launched from Cuba as an attack by the Soviet Union on the United States, requiring full retaliatory response on the Soviet Union . . .'[1] It is the missile crisis or, as the Cubans euphemistically called it, the Caribbean crisis: what I had been watching in mysterious images on the television when I was eight years old.

Inconsolable Memories was a wonderful book. I carried it round in my pocket for weeks, re-reading it endlessly. I decided, vaguely, that one day I would have to go to Cuba. Three published novels finally gave me the opportunity.

It was early in November when I went to the Cuban embassy. Sitting in the waiting room I could remember scenes from the novel as if I had read it only the day before: Elena in one of the departed Laura's dresses, meandering around the apartment, nervous and insolent: the narrator visiting Ernest Hemingway's house outside Havana where visiting Soviets, the new colonialists, were having themselves photographed in front of the writer's hunting trophies; a butterfly in Vedado, the American district in downtown Havana, fluttering along, oblivious of impending nuclear annihilation.

I enquired about three-month visas, for myself and my family, explaining we wanted to go for such a long time because I wished to write. 'A wife called Tyga and a daughter called India,' said the official nodding his head. 'The visas should be no problem but do you have enough money to stay for three months? That's what we want to know.'

I asked him about the possibility of an exchange with someone in Havana, my flat in London for theirs. 'Perhaps I could advertise in a Cuban national newspaper,' I suggested carelessly

---

[1] Edmundo Desnoes, *Inconsolable Memories,* translated by the author.

and probably nearly scuppered the whole trip. He looked nervous and laughed.

'No,' he said, 'that is not possible in our economy.'

I was to find out, later, that on one level this dialogue anticipated the entire character of the trip. For the next three months almost my sole preoccupation would be in trying to function in and understand an economy which was alien. My perspective on what I saw was very limited. I was only one observer and I took my own cultural baggage with me. I saw the country from behind a car windscreen. Travelling with my family, I was a tourist of the revolution.

2

A Story of Invasion

There were Indians in Cuba long, long before Columbus got there, and the island may have been inhabited from as early as 3,500 BC. The earliest dwellers were Pre-Ceramic tribesmen, the Siboney and Guanahacabibes. They may have been indigenous as no one knows how they got there. Little is known about their way of living except that they dwelt in caves along the coast all over the island.

At about the beginning of the twelfth century, Ceramic peoples arrived from South America. They sailed north in two waves, the later of which is dated at about the mid-fifteenth century. These Taino Indians mostly lived in the areas where they landed in eastern Cuba, subsequently called Oriente. When Columbus arrived in 1492, he sent two emissaries inland to greet the Japanese emperor because he thought he had arrived in Japan. But instead of the Imperial court the emissaries found a village with round huts which had roofs made out of palm leaves, inhabited by a people who slept in *hamacs* and who played a game like baseball called *batos*.

The Taino were a clever people. They used the *guaican* fish to hook and catch other fish. They plotted the path of the sun and the moon on the walls of their dwellings. They cultivated root vegetables, manioc and yucca, as well as tobacco.

The Spanish nobleman Diego de Velázquez was given the right to colonise Cuba on behalf of Spain and to distribute land and Indian slaves among Spanish settlers. In 1512 he established his first city at Baracoa (where Columbus had been) and by 1515 he had established another six cities. These were Bayamo, Sancti Spíritus, Trinidad, Puerto Principe (now Camagüey), Santiago de Cuba and Havana (then called Batabanó). At this time there were about 100,000 Indians on the island. By 1540 their numbers were down to about 40,000, a decline caused in part by diseases introduced by the Europeans to which they had no immunity, in part by being worked to death in the goldmines, and by fighting the Spanish. By 1570 there were no Indians left. Only their name for the island, Cuba, has survived.

The Spaniards did not find much gold in Cuba. But they did find an abundance in Mexico and South America. After Velázquez's colonisation Cuba, and particularly Havana, became a port of passage for the Spanish fleet on its way backwards and forwards from the New World to the Old.

During the sixteenth and seventeenth centuries the economic success of Cuba rested on cattle, timber (the island was covered in forests) and tobacco. Because the Indians had been extinguished there was an appetite for cheap labour, which was satisfied with slaves. England and France were already slave-trading to supply their colonies—Jamaica and Haiti—which were the Caribbean's main sugar producers—and they also supplied Cuba. The island grew rich but its wealth was monopolised by the Spanish crown. Smuggling boomed.

In 1762 the English captured Havana. During the year they were in occupation about 700 merchant ships entered the port, whereas under Spanish rule the average was about fifteen a year. Much of the trade was to the thirteen English colonies to the north. Obviously the potential of Cuba was not being exploited. But then, after a year, the British were forced to leave. The impetus which the island needed finally came in 1791. Inspired by the French Revolution, the black slaves in the French colony of Haiti revolted and their masters, white French sugar planters, fled to Cuba. They brought with them their expertise. World demand for sugar was growing. Slave-traders loaned these new arrivals and Cuban landowners money for capital improvements. Forests were cleared for cane. By the start of the century, sugar was the foundation of the economy. Slaves flooded in and, later in the century, Chinese indentured labourers. By 1841 there were, it has been estimated, 436,495 black and mulatto slaves in a total population of 1,007,624, who constituted 43.5 percent of the population. The tradition of trading northwards, established during the British occupation, had persisted, and around this period about fifty percent of Cuban sugar was being sold to the United States.

Spain still governed Cuba. Her governors were corrupt and repressive. Cuba provided taxes to the Spanish crown, yet the new Cubans were allowed no say in their island's government. The resentment this caused did not go so far as offering support to Spain's South American colonies when they revolted under the leadership of Bolivar, however. They did not want a civil war which would have been economically disastrous. The century advanced, and with it so did the movement towards the abolition of slavery all over the world. Many Cuban sugar planters began to hope the US would insulate them from this horrible change and annex the island. The US was now Cuba's largest market, which was another reason why the idea of absorption into the Union seemed so attractive.

Then came the American Civil War. Now it was no longer possible for Cuba to maintain its slave system. The concepts of abolition and independence became entwined. In 1868 Carlos Manuel de Céspedes, a landowner in Oriente province in the eastern end of the island, freed his slaves and armed them for battle. Rebellion followed. Other leaders were Máximo Gómez and Antonio Maceo. The fighting went on for years. The United States withheld recognition of the state of belligerence.

In February 1878, the Cubans were offered an armistice by Spain, the treaty of Zanjón. It did not offer independence. Maceo and his fellow generals refused to sign (Céspedes was dead by then) but others did. Fighting was temporarily renewed and Maceo left Cuba with his brothers. An uneasy peace followed. Slavery was finally abolished in 1886. The slave owners were not compensated.

The years 1880 to 1890 saw a tremendous surge of US investment. Railways were built and the famous 'centrals'—self-contained sugar factories for grinding cane—were created. In 1890 there was a reduction in the tariff between the two countries. Cuba was now providing the US with only ten percent of its total imports. None the less there was money to be made in sugar.

The leader of the second Cuban revolution was José Martí. Born in 1853, he had been jailed because of his anti-Spanish attitudes by the time he was eighteen. Eventually he went into exile in the United States where he worked as a journalist. Although the US offered him a safe haven, he believed US domination of his country would be as dreadful as Spanish domination currently was.

In 1895, Martí returned to Cuba with the Maceo brothers and others. He landed on the southern tip of Oriente province. The peasants who joined their forces were called *mambises*. This was an African word meaning 'children of vultures' but in Spanish it meant 'the dregs'.

Martí was surprised and killed near Bayamo shortly after his arrival. This left the Cuban revolutionaries without a leader of stature, but the war ground on. It was observed in the US with great interest. Some in the government urged annexation, while the press was largely pro-rebel—an odd attitude—explained not by altruism but by fierce circulation wars. Randolph Hearst, the US newspaper proprietor, sent his ace cartoonist Frederic Remington to Cuba. Remington could not get to the front and wired Hearst, 'Everything is quiet. . . . There will be no war. I wish to return.' Hearst replied, 'You furnish the pictures and I'll furnish the war.' The Spanish general, Weyler, established military zones around the island into which he herded or concentrated almost the entire population, to stop them supplying the rebels.

Then in 1896 Weyler banned the export of tobacco and bananas, and prohibited the export of coffee and sugar without prior authorisation. This was intended to bankrupt those businessmen abroad who supported the rebels. In the US McKinley was campaigning for the presidency and declared he was not 'indifferent' to war.

Late in 1896 both Antonio Maceo and his brother José were killed by the Spanish. Theodore Roosevelt, Assistant Secretary of the Navy, urged US intervention. In 1897 came a new administration in Spain which seemed reconciled to Cuban autonomy. Weyler resigned in protest. Newly elected President McKinley ordered a 'watch and wait' policy. But with rumours of danger to US citizens in Havana, the USS *Maine* was dispatched to Havana harbour.

On 15 February 1898 the *Maine* mysteriously blew up. It has never been resolved whether this was an accident or, if not, whether the ship was sunk by rebels who wanted to bring America into the war or by US agents who wanted to give their government a pretext to enter the war. Whatever the cause, the result in the north was hysteria. McKinley offered to buy Cuba for $300 million. The Queen of Spain offered office to any political party in the Cortes prepared to accept McKinley's proposals, but none was prepared to accept the responsibility of being seen to be the party who lost Cuba. The US Congress declared war on Cuba on 25 April 1898.

From the start the Spanish knew they were going to lose, and the United States knew they were going to win. Neither was eager for a long war and both wanted honour, but the war did not supply much of either. There was only one major engagement, when US troops, including Theodore Roosevelt's regiment of Rough Riders, charged up San Juan Hill near Santiago de Cuba in the east of the island. The invaders lost 223 men here and about the same again in other engagements, but far more died from malaria and yellow fever. Press coverage of the conflict began to emphasise this rather more than the glory of the situation. The Spanish forces surrendered on 17 July 1898.

The United States immediately established a temporary

government. It was argued that the Cuban people did not want to be separated from the US.

Congress in Washington passed the Platt Amendment. This gave the US 'the right of intervention for the preservation of Cuban independence and the maintenance of stable government'.

The Cuban flag was finally raised on 20 May 1902. The US governor withdrew. Estrada Palma became the first president. There was at the time about one hundred million dollars of US capital invested in Cuba in tobacco, railways, utilities and sugar.

The governments and presidents of Cuba from 1902 to 1959 were generally corrupt and inefficient. The life of most Cubans was spoilt by poverty. The US continued to be the force in the land. In 1925 a US-owned electric company with Cuban interests contributed half a million dollars to the campaign expenses of Gerardo Machado who was running for president. He won, extended his term of office, and instituted a reign of terror. US investments continued to grow and Cuba still sold a considerable amount of its sugar to the US under the quota arrangement.

In 1933, Machado fell and Fulgencio Batista, an army sergeant, staged a revolt with fellow NCOs and took over the army. A new constitution was introduced which did away with the Platt Amendment, as well as establishing various democratic rights. In 1940 Batista became president. In 1944 he ran for a second term of office and was, very much to his surprise, defeated. He retired for a while and then, in 1952, seized power. He suspended the constitution and started his second term of office as president.

One of those who was determined to oppose the government of Batista was Fidel Castro. He was born in 1927 in Oriente. His father was a landowner. He was educated privately and studied law at the University of Havana. On 26 July 1953 he and others attacked the Moncada army barracks in Santiago de Cuba during the carnival, when they assumed all the soldiers inside would be drunk. The intention was to start a revolution which would lead to the overthrow of Batista. The attack failed. Many of the attackers were rounded up and tortured to death. Castro escaped but was captured a week later. He was tried and found guilty.

Imprisoned on the Isle of Pines until 1955, Castro was released under an amnesty proclaimed by Batista. He went to Mexico and met Ernesto 'Che' Guevara, an Argentine doctor. They raised funds, trained a small force of men and set sail for Cuba in a US pleasure yacht called the *Granma* on the night of 24–25 November 1956, with eighty-two men on board. Only fifteen, including Guevara and Castro survived the landfall in Cuba. Somehow, members of Bastista's forces knew they were coming, and they were waiting.

From this core there slowly developed a revolutionary force in the Sierra Maestra mountains north of Santiago de Cuba. The brutality and corruption of Batista's regime drove many Cubans to support the rebels. The largest of the national anti-Batista movements was called '26 July', its name coming from the date of the attack on the Moncada Barracks. On 1 January 1959 Batista fled to the Dominican Republic. The Fidelistas marched into Cuba's cities and have since been the dominant force in the land.

On 6 March that year, all rents in Cuba were reduced by fifty percent. On 17 March, all beaches were declared open to the public. Under the first Agrarian Reform, land that had been owned by supporters of Batista was confiscated and the amount of land which any private individual could own was limited to a maximum of a thousand acres. The rich began to leave.

In February 1960 the Soviet Union agreed to sell cheap petroleum to Cuba. On 7 May Cuba and the Soviet Union resumed relations. In the US fears increased that the new Cuban government was Communist. The Soviet petroleum arrived in June. The US- and foreign-owned refineries refused to process it. On 29 June the Texaco refinery in Santiago de Cuba was expropriated. The following day, the Esso and Shell refineries in Havana went the same way. On 28 June the House of Representatives had passed a bill enabling the US to reduce or abolish the Cuban sugar quota, and on 6 July President Eisenhower announced a massive reduction. The Soviet Union agreed to take up the slack. On 2 September Fidel Castro made his 'Declaration of Havana' before a large crowd in the city, denouncing the US for 'open intervention for more than a century in the affairs of Latin America'. More nationalisations of US- and large Cuban-owned businesses followed. In January 1961 Cuba and the United States suspended diplomatic relations.

On 17 April 1961 some 1,297 US-trained and -financed Cuban exiles landed at Playa Girón on the south-east coast of Cuba at the mouth of the Bay of Pigs. The intention was to form a bridgehead and start a revolution against the government. The invasion was repelled in seventy-two hours. Following the débâcle, the US closed her market to Cuban goods, and in June 1961 she banned all exports to Cuba.

In 1962, relations between the two countries reached an all-time low when the United States protested at the deployment of Soviet nuclear missiles in Cuba. They never recovered and since the missile crisis Cuba has remained firmly aligned to the Soviet bloc.

Travelling around Cuba I was to discover that this history, dry and abstract, took on a life which I hadn't expected. The past is inescapable there: ubiquitous, and alive.

3

Going

On our last weekend in London, the three of us went along to a house in Brixton. We knocked and after a few moments, through a hole in the door where there had once been a Yale lock, there came a finger which hooked around the wood. A key turned inside and the door juddered back to reveal John, a man with sticking plasters on his thumbs. He had worked for two years at *Prensa Latina,* the Cuban press association in Havana.

In the freezing front room, we sat around eating raw fish. John said, 'They love children in Cuba. Your daughter will open every door.' He gave us a map and then he told us a Cuban joke.

Reagan, Gorbachov and Castro were each allowed to ask Jesus a question.

'How will my Star Wars initative go?' asked Reagan.

'Fine,' replied Jesus, 'but you won't see the fruits of it in your lifetime.'

'And what about my campaign for more openness in the Soviet Union?' asked Gorbachov.

'It'll be fine,' said Jesus, 'but you won't see the fruits in your lifetime.'

'And how about my rectification campaign?' asked Castro, referring to the campaign he had initiated to root out inefficiency and corruption in his country.

'It'll be fine,' said Jesus, 'except you won't see the fruits in your lifetime and I won't see them in my lifetime either.'

We left at three o'clock. Outside the street was cold and dead still with that deadly, Sunday stillness. We went to Regent's Park where footballers scrambled on muddy pitches and a few flakes of snow, shaped like grains of rice, fluttered down from the grey sky.

One task remained before we left England. I scoured various bookshops and finally, I found it: *Cars of the Fifties* from the Consumer Guide series published in Illinois. Knowing I like American cars, a friend had mentioned the most interesting fact so far on Cuba. During Batista's dictatorship, it had probably imported more Cadillacs than any other nation in the world (as well as all the other US makes).[1] What was more, because of the US blockade, no new cars had come in since then (apart from a few Ladas) and the Cadillacs and the Buicks and the Dodges and the rest of them were still being driven around. There was one in particular I was hoping to find.

The Eldorado Brougham, a Cadillac, was a pillarless sedan (with both doors open there was no column supporting the roof to impede the view of the interior) and a brushed aluminium roof. Its most unusual feature was its suspension system. There was an air spring at each wheel, with a domed air chamber, rubber diaphragm and pistons. A central air compressor fed the domes and by a system of valves and solenoids, the system continuously adjusted to the load and road conditions. Hence the Brougham was unbelievably smooth when it travelled. Visually, with its tailfins, sculpted exhausts and sweeping lines of chrome, it was one of the most extraordinary if exaggerated cars of the Fifties.

The Brougham went into production in 1957. After two years, during which only 704 were built, the model was re-

---

[1] Hugh Thomas makes the same point in *Cuba, or the Pursuit of Freedom*.

styled. In 1959, ninety-nine were assembled in Detroit, and one hundred and one the following year. I didn't imagine any of these later models had made their way to Cuba, so what I was hoping for was a '57 or a '58.

★

At Heathrow Airport, a fat young American was throwing all his possessions onto the floor and threatening to undress. His eyes were bright blue through his tears. Something to do with his girlfriend.

We were flying to Cuba via Prague because, perversely, the roundabout route was the cheapest.

Our aeroplane was a Soviet Tupolev Tu–134A. Inside it smelt of cheap scent. Battleship grey was the dominant colour. The padding in the seats was skimpy, the portholes tiny, and the amount of leg room even more of a joke than it usually is.

Besides frugality, everything was also out of fashion. In the safety booklet, the woman in the illustrations had an hourglass figure which accentuated her bosom, curling, cutesy eyelashes, which flicked up at the ends, and overlong legs tapering to miniscule feet. She was a sexpot figure from a *New Yorker* cartoon of the Fifties. Curiously, there was no safety drill.

We landed smoothly at Prague and cruised along the tarmac. Hares ran in the snow beside us and nibbled at the grass which showed through.

In the dreary departure lounge we sat for several hours at the bar. There was a large red neon advertisement reading 'Havana Club, El Ron de Cuba'.

At four, our flight was called. This time the jet was an Ilyushin Il–62. It was bigger than the Tupolev, but just as grey. Instead of scent it smelt of sweat. The passengers all seemed to be Czech holiday-makers. One was a midget with exquisitely fine hands.

We took off again. Again, no safety drill. But there was the same booklet with the same sexpot. Air travel is all repetition. Over the tannoy the captain began to speak.

'Welcome,' he said in English, 'we shall be flying to Havana,

Cuba, via Montreal, Canada . . .'

There was no mention of this on the ticket.

Everyone was given a meal. The unrecognisable meat left a furry feeling inside the mouth. It was put aside after the first forkful. All around, middle-aged Czech ladies, still in their fur hats and with their coats buttoned up, clicked open their handbags and put away the roll, butter, cheese, salt and pepper sachets, plastic cutlery and refresher towel.

Outside the portholes it was black. The cabin lights were dimmed. On the other side of the aisle from us there was a huge jelly of a woman who tilted her seat back and covered her face with the antimacassar. Soon she and the whole cabin had fallen asleep. Above the noise of the engines, intestines could be heard rumbling.

During the long night hours I read *Our Man in Havana* for the first time. The central character in the story is Wormold, a British vacuum-cleaner salesman resident in Havana in the Fifties during the reign of an unnamed dictator. Wormold is recruited by British intelligence but for want of any hard information to pass on, he begins to invent it. Amongst his most fertile creations are the missile sites from which rockets with nuclear warheads could be launched. The novel was a work of clairvoyance, since it was first published in 1957.

I was back with the missile crisis which had caused Cuba to register in the very first place.

The direct origins of the crisis were two. First, the US-sponsored invasion of Cuba by Cuban exiles in 1961, popularly known as the Bay of Pigs invasion: it had been successfully repelled, but who was to say there wouldn't be a second? There were lots of angry Cuban exiles in Miami and, misinterpreting Kennedy, they were making noises to the effect that a new invasion was imminent. From where Fidel Castro was placed, an invasion seemed likely.

The second factor was US nuclear strategy. In the early Sixties President Kennedy and Secretary of State for Defense McNamara, sought to maintain numerical superiority of nuclear weapons. In the event of their striking first, they wanted to have enough to take out all known or suspected Soviet bases and still have reserves left with which to threaten Russian cities and what was left of the Soviet nuclear capability. In the event of the Soviets striking first, the US plan was to have as much or more left over as the Soviets had struck with in the first place. The policy was known as 'counterforce'. In November 1962, the US had about 200 Intercontinental Ballistic Missiles (ICBMs) to a Soviet number of between fifty and seventy-five. It was the US intention to have a thousand of them by 1964 when the programme would be complete.

The solution to the apparently unconnected problems of nuclear imbalance and the threat of invasion to the first socialist state of the Americas was the inspired idea of placing missiles with nuclear warheads in Cuba. Who actually came up with the idea, whether it was Castro or Khrushchev or a third party, isn't clear.

In the summer of 1962 the sites were levelled and the missiles started to trickle in. Kennedy issued an ultimatum. The missiles in situ all had to go. To back this up a US naval 'quarantine' (the word being thought less offensive than blockade) was thrown up to stop, search and if necessary disable (rather than sink) all Soviet ships en route to the Caribbean carrying nuclear weapons.

The Soviet response revealed an administration in confusion. A letter from Khrushchev to Kennedy proposed a complete withdrawal and a UN inspection, in return for a promise never to invade Cuba. This was quickly followed by a second letter from the Kremlin (not from Khrushchev), which offered to remove the Cuban sites if the US would do the same in Turkey.

Meanwhile, Cuba mobilised, and Fidel Castro fulminated about 'the satiated shark, the US' and 'Cuba, the little sardine'. All US commands were put on a DEFCON 2 footing, the last step before DEFCON 1, war. This was scheduled to start, unless the Soviets gave the US satisfaction, on Monday, 30 October 1962. The Soviets were doubtless in the same state of preparedness as the US.

Then, suddenly, it was over. Khrushchev's letter was

probably written second but arrived first. Kennedy decided to ignore the second and answer Khrushchev's. This was apparently his brother Robert's idea. (Hugh Thomas, in his history, *Cuba, or the Pursuit of Freedom*, called it a 'brilliant, rather feminine suggestion'.) Khrushchev agreed. The missiles would go in return for the promise not to invade Cuba. Castro, when he heard the news, reportedly swore, kicked the wall and broke a mirror. He must have wanted the missiles. But the matter was in the hands of others.

There was an ironic coda to the story. Out came the missiles but, because the Cubans refused to allow UN observers, the US did not in the end have to give the formal promise never to invade Cuba. Thus the US and Cuba were left back where they had started: feeling paranoid about one another. Twenty-five years later, they were still just as paranoid and our loopy passage north was one tiny example of it. All flights to and from the island are prohibited from using US airspace. The Ilyushin couldn't make the trip from Prague in one go. It was flying across the Atlantic against the prevailing winds. The stop in Canada was to refuel.

*

From the air Montreal was lit up with lights of every colour, stretching in every direction. The Czechs gasped and cameras clicked. There was a sound of rushing wind and we landed.

Because the aeroplane was refuelling, we were all disembarked. We were brought to the airport in a futuristic coach, which again set cameras clicking, and left to wait in a transit lounge. Everyone, including ourselves, swarmed into the *Tabagie*. The different goods we bought seemed to sum up our enormous economic distance. The Czechs bought what they didn't have: woollen hats, electric razors and enormous bars of Swiss chocolate. We bought a padlock called a 'Little Trojan' for our blue holdall to protect what we had. Cuba was a Third World country and, therefore, as Westerners, we thought we ran a high risk of being robbed.

It was the middle of the night. We sat without speaking in the middle of the hall, India clutching the newly purchased 'Little Trojan'. Beyond a partition, out of sight but not out of earshot, an oompah band was playing a medley of Gallic tunes. One by one the Czechs wandered up to the partition clutching their bars of Lindt and with their '*Montréal Je t'adore*' hats pulled onto their heads, and squinted through. When the midget came up wearing a hat which read 'I love skiing', somebody fetched him a chair so he could see too.

Four and a half hours from Montreal, we landed in Havana. It was about two o'clock in the morning, local time. Stepping out onto the top steps was to enter a sea of heat.

By the entrance to the arrivals building, crowds waited behind glass. They had come not to meet passengers but to watch the spectacle of disembarkation.

The next part of the journey was like the London Underground at rush hour crossed with Kafka. A small, hot arrivals lounge crowded with people, two guides in powder-blue suits shouting at the Czechs who were very over-excited, policemen everywhere strutting about in their blue uniforms with pistols gleaming in their holsters, an hour's wait for the luggage to arrive on the antiquated carousel, and the discovery at the tourist desk, a small corner in the middle of this bedlam, that there was no record of our hotel booking, made and pre-paid in London.

This was worse than it sounds, because five nights' pre-paid accommodation is a condition of entry into Cuba. We argued in our appalling Spanish for some while and eventually the exhausted looking Cubatur girl said, 'Go to your hotel, they'll probably be expecting you.'

But first there was a currency declaration form to be filled in. Obviously, it was important to have some cash unaccounted for, free for the black market. But what if I was discovered? I decided I could always put my bad arithmetic down to fatigue. I declared half what I had and approached Customs, Tyga and India trailing behind. A large, fat, black lady official, wearing thick coats of magenta-coloured eye shadow, took the form without looking at it, scribbled an 'X' on each of our bags and waved us through.

★

The journey from an airport to its city is rarely beautiful but never forgotten. The taxi took us along avenues, wide and straight, with others leading off them at right angles and palm trees along the middle. There were factories where machinery thumped; petrol stations where solitary attendants sat on the forecourts; and bungalows with concrete porches and flat roofs, whose owners were often to be seen sitting in the cool of their gardens although it was the middle of the night. Occasionally, buses like illuminated aquaria, with people crammed inside, sailed past. I also spotted several old Chevrolets and a Pontiac Bonneville. Apart from some red flags hanging limply from lamp posts, all the indications were that we had arrived in a Hispanic Miami of the Fifties.

The hotel was the Colina in Vedado. The district was developed from the Twenties onwards and architecturally it was heavily influenced by North American styles. The hotel lobby was all marble, with a swirling counter and square pillars, and furnished with extraordinary ox-blood-coloured, leather cube sofas. They must have been one of the last pieces of Americana to have entered the country before the embargo.

We were expected. The clerk filled in a registration card for each of us. Then we struggled with our luggage to the lift and found a notice attached to the call button: 'Broken'. We were on the third floor and the service stairs were tortuous. Off our bedroom there was a bathroom, but no water would come out of the taps. The cellophane wrapping in which the lampshades had arrived from the People's Republic of China hadn't been removed and smoked faintly because of the heat of the bulbs. The shutters would not close. We lay down and listened to the lorries grinding around the corner below. A few birds far away started to sing and chirp.

4

The Capital

In Moscow, after the triumph of the Bolsheviks, churches became museums of atheism. In Algiers, after the triumph of the FLN, the prancing equestrian statue of Marshal Bugeaud, the French conqueror of Algeria in the 1820s was replaced with one of Abd-el-Kader, his wily old adversary. In Cuba there have been the same little sarcasms. Thus the presidential palace, synonymous with the loathsome *ancien régime*, has become the Museum of the Revolution.

It was the very first place we went to in Havana. The palace was a handsome but not particularly imposing nineteenth-century colonial building. It was closed for refurbishment, and would be for some time, we gathered. However, the outdoor exhibition of relics from the revolution, in the little park at the front of the palace, was not.

The principal exhibit, high in the air and encased in glass, was the *Granma*, i.e., the North American abbreviation for grandmother. In this ugly, fifty-eight-foot-long US motor yacht, Fidel Castro and eighty-two others sailed from Mexico—where they had been in exile—to Cuba in 1956 to start the revolution. It was the revolutionary symbol from which the national newspaper took its title, and if the yacht had been called the *Apple Pie* or *Alabama Rose* then doubtless, today, that would be the name of the *Órgano Oficial del Comite Central del Partido Communisto de Cuba*. The equivalent of the *Granma* in the Christian hierarchy of relics would be the Holy Cross.

Scattered below and around it were objects of lower status. These included Fidel's green Land-Rover station wagon, with *Commandancia General Sierra Maestra* written in red on the side door, which he'd first used early in the revolutionary campaign, when his forces had been in the mountains in the eastern end of the island; the red van with the words 'Fast Delivery' painted on the side, peppered with holes, used for the assassination attempt on Batista's life in 1957; one of the grey launches, with a skull and crossbones painted on the prow, used during the US-sponsored invasion at the Bay of Pigs in 1961; and a turbine from the U-2 spy plane downed during the missile crisis in 1962.

On the public address, against a background of stirring martial music, was a mocked-up roll-call of those who had participated in the attack on Batista in the presidential palace, just a few yards away. A leader figure called out their names and the actors replied, their voices trembling with passion. The tape was on a loop and went round and round.

I walked around the revolutionary exhibits taking notes, the cod roll-call booming above my head. I was particularly interested in the red 'Fast Delivery' van which had a Dinky toy quality which modern vans no longer have. As I was scribbling, a tall black came over wearing a navy blue double-breasted blazer, with officialdom written all over him.

'What are you doing?' he asked.

He seemed quite friendly, not cross or officious.

I pointed to the explanation board. There was one beside each exhibit.

'I write down the words I don't understand and later on I'll look them up in my dictionary,' I said. Meanwhile I was thinking: How strange. Take a notebook out in a museum, and immediately they want to know what you're doing. It wouldn't happen in the Tower of London.

'Yes, they are very hard words,' he said quite sweetly.

*

We left and went to begin our exploration of the city, starting with Old Havana.

To get an idea of the geography of the place here is a mental picture. Havana is on the northern coast of Cuba near the western end of the island. At the right-hand end of the city is the port of Havana. This is a landlocked bay which can only be reached by a narrow waterway. Old Havana comes next, lying on the western side of the harbour. The Museum of the Revolution is in central Havana, basically the nineteenth-century part of the city. To the left lies Vedado where our hotel, the Colina, was situated. Vedado is the new, twentieth-century part of the city. Of course it isn't as programmatic as I've suggested. Spanish colonial houses with fluted columns and white-washed walls, North American high-rise buildings of stressed concrete and glass, and Soviet-style monoliths (usually housing government departments) are all mixed in together.

Havana was founded not by Diego de Velázquez directly but by one of his colleagues, Panfilo de Nárvaez, in 1515. It was originally on the south coast, probably near what is called Batabanó. But with the discovery and conquest of Mexico, the Spaniards needed a port. Thus they moved the city north to its present site beside the enormous waterway of the Bay of Havana. 1519 is the date usually given for this move, but uncertainty attaches to it, as the city's archives were destroyed in a raid by pirates in 1538.

Havana grew, and attracted plunderers. After 1538 it was burnt again in 1555, and in 1588 it was menaced by Sir Francis Drake. The Spanish authorities then built the Castillo del Morro on the east bank of the channel leading into the harbour and the Castillo de la Punta on the Havana side. A great chain was stretched between the fortresses, and at night was raised to keep ships out.

Thus protected, the city prospered. There were 4,000 inhabitants by the end of the sixteenth century, which made it large by New World standards. A hundred and fifty years later, there were 70,000 inhabitants, about equal to the population of the whole of the rest of the island. Enter the British, who occupied the city from 1762–63. It was a prosperous year for Havana. When the Spaniards returned, however, instead of encouraging the sort of energetic trading which the occupiers had stimulated, they re-imposed their monopolies and set about building further fortifications. Lacking a legitimate outlet, smuggling and illicit trading developed, especially in rum and molasses. Gambling and prostitution developed.

In the nineteenth century, sugar and the slave trade created enormous amounts of capital. Down came the city walls in 1863 and the city went westwards. Theatres, plazas, public buildings were constructed in the area called Central Havana. Water was brought in by aqueduct, there was a railway station and rail network connecting the city to the rest of Cuba, and gas lighting was introduced. Havana was regarded as the most beautiful city in the Caribbean.

In the twentieth century the city continued to develop, now in the direction of Vedado and beyond. It had wonderful hotels and extraordinary casinos, restaurants and nightclubs. But it was also filled with slums where most Havanians lived lives of unmitigated poverty and squalor. One example which sums up the life on the underside of the city has been used by almost every historian and commentator without losing its impact. It is that in the 1950s the Havana City orphanage still had a drop chute with flaps over the top to facilitate the abandonment of babies by those who couldn't afford to bring them up.

After we left the Museum of the Revolution, we walked due east. This brought us into the oldest part of the city. Except for a few winding pockets, Old Havana, like most New World cities, was laid out on a grid system, with most of the streets being about the width of a carriage. The houses are mostly of eighteenth- and nineteenth-century construction. The dominant architecture was pre-baroque, a more than usually ornate baroque, and neo-classical. With the development of the Malecón, the boulevard running along by the sea, in 1902, and later the tunnels on the far east and west sides of the city, Havana's far-flung suburbs became accessible. Those who could afford it moved out of Old Havana, and the district was left to decay. Governments failed to expand the ancient water system, the sea air ate into the buildings. After the revolution, decay continued because of the state policy of allocating resources primarily to the countryside, which it perceived as more deprived than the cities. This positive discrimination may have backfired, because now the old city is in a terrible state, with parts of it beyond restoration.

We found ourselves in Cuarteles Street. I don't know if it was a carriage-width wide, but I had that sense of being hemmed in that every old city arouses in me, and the sky seemed far away. The houses were tall and dilapidated. The paint on every one of the enormous, handsome doors was flaking and peeling. The wrought-ironwork in front of the huge ground-floor windows was pitted and pock-marked with corrosion down the whole length of the street. The façades were crumbling and cracked, with lumps of masonry coming away, and some of the buildings looked as if they were in danger of collapsing. Through empty doorways were glimpses of dirty staircases with rickety banisters, crumbling tiles and fuse-boxes surrounded by tangles of wire. Behind the iron bars of her window, a woman spooned yoghurt from a glass. A boy with a shaven head played marbles in the gutter. The twists of paper in the little globes of glass were bright in the street. A bicyclist sailed by, cheekily asking if we wanted to change money. An old woman with a pail of rubbish fiddled with her door. In her room behind, a gigantic picture of Fidel hung from the wall.

We rambled on to the Plaza de la Catedral. It was a big square of museums, obviously newly developed. Tourists sat on the kerbstones looking at their maps and guidebooks. There was a febrile atmosphere of the type common to all centres for the consumption of culture. We made off as quickly as possible to Empedrado, which had the distinction of being the first street in

Havana to be paved. Here, a party of Canadian tourists streamed from the Bodeguita del Medio, a restaurant made famous by Ernest Hemingway. They were all clutching souvenir placemats printed with the menu. Further on, in a dilapidated alley, under lines of washing, was parked a cream-coloured 1955 convertible Pontiac Star Chief with enormous red-leather seats. Two girls sat smoking in the front, with packets of Popular, the Cuban cigarette, on their bare brown legs. This seemed a more real Havana than the Hemingway shrine we'd just passed. But it was the shrine and similar places which were going to earn the dollars to pay for the preservation and restoration of Old Havana.

We came to a small square with a statue of Cervantes. A teacher with a whistle and a stopwatch supervised a relay race involving coloured wooden blocks laid out on the pavement. There was an old street sweeper in trousers with enormous flares which flapped as he swept swollen cigar butts onto a metal scoop.

On Paseo de Martí, an old black man sat on one of the stone benches, dry-shaving with an old-fashioned razor. The Hotel Siboney was half demolished or else it had half fallen down. We ambled off under the laurel trees along the walkway running down the middle of the street. Once this was a haunt of tarts, but now all that remained of its past were the green lampstands in the shape of griffins.

At the bottom of the Paseo de Martí we turned west onto the Malecón and walked along by the sea, passing the Hotel Deauville and the memorial to Antonio Maceo, turning eventually onto 23rd Street, or La Rampa. Now we were in Vedado. Some nineteenth-century, two-storey, Spanish-style houses with pantiled roofs remained, most of them peeling and ramshackle. But the dominant influence was clearly the United States. It was obvious not just from the buildings, which ranged from art-deco apartment blocks with swept corners to the old Havana Hilton, or from the fact the streets were laid out in a block grid, and designated either by letters of the alphabet or numbers, but from details as well: the abandoned fire hydrant, tilting and rusting on a street corner; the empty lot with the neon sign of an automobile and '*Parqueo*' written below; the forlorn glamour of the walkway with the candy-stripe cover stretching from the kerbside to the entrance of the sometime plush restaurant.

Afterwards, I wrote in my notebook, 'The Americans have got right into the unconscious here.'

5

The Beach

The next morning, when I woke up, the sun was shining behind the half-closed shutters. Pulling open the drawer of the bedside bureau, I saw a telephone directory lying there. Idly I started leafing through, expecting names which were African, French and Chinese, a summary of the racial history of the country, but they were all disappointingly Spanish. I put it away and made a telephone call to a friend of a friend.

We were invited to the beach for the day and met Eleanor in the foyer. She was about forty years old and had a long face. She was a journalist.

Outside Eleanor had a black Volga, the Soviet motor industry's equivalent to the Oldsmobile. There were no number plates but an enormous cardboard sign stuck to the windscreen announcing, 'Number plates coming'.

She drove us all slowly down the street. No longer unfamiliar, Vedado, with its mess of colonial houses, Gaudi-inspired apartment blocks and skyscrapers, suddenly looked fake; fake like the buildings in Californian cities. One good strong wind and the whole lot would blow into the sea, I thought.

At the end of the street, some half dozen blocks away, was the sea. We turned onto the Malecón, the wide highway which runs parallel, carrying Havana's traffic from east to west, and drove out of the city.

Santa Maria was about twenty-five miles from Havana. Because it was Sunday, the beach was crowded.

We spread our towels on the white, coarse, spotless sand. It was an overcast day but the heat of the sun seeped through the cloud. The ocean was an inky blue.

One of the most memorable passages in *Our Man in Havana* is the description of the city as a conveyor belt for the manufacture of beauty. Even the most cursory glance around showed this to be true. What was also remarkable, as Greene had also said, was the racial mix. On the beach the colour of the people stretched from purest white with blue eyes and blonde hair to deepest black with olive eyes and curly hair and with every possible shade and combination of features in between. A sense of the island's racial history and its diversity wasn't to be culled from the telephone directory, but was to be seen at first hand on the sand by the edge of the sea.

A young man splashed out of the foam in front of us and stopped a few feet away.

He took a comb from the side of his tiny trunks and carefully started grooming his hair.

A girl came out of the ocean and led him past us. She wore a swimsuit with an enormous open 'V' from between her breasts to just above her groin.

The couple went up to a crowd of young people. They sank down and he put his head on her lap. She took the comb and started on the thick black hair—first his head, then his chest.

Looking around the group, it was evident that everyone had paid close attention to their own appearance, especially the girls. Bikini, lipstick, handbag, jewellery, shoes: everything was matched.

'Cuban girls are lovers of glamour,' Eleanor said. 'They melt down toothbrushes to make pendants, horrible, lumpy, green blobs, and from the cardboard inner linings of bottle tops, they make earrings.'

Someone in the group had a ghettoblaster, with plastic bags around the base to protect it from the sand. It was tuned to a radio station in Miami, only eighty miles away to the north. From the speakers drifted the voice of Paul McCartney, followed by details of an accident in the Miami suburb of Coral Gables. A young black of fifteen or sixteen asked me to sell him some dollars. I said no and he slid away, diffidently wiping the sand off that had stuck to his body.

We ate in a restaurant overlooking the sea, flaky salty fish with the texture of mullet, and drank Hatüey beer. There were no salads or vegetables, barring potatoes.

'The lorry with them didn't come this morning,' the waitress explained.

Eleanor told the story of Rosa, a young student who was having an affair with a foreigner. The relationship was frowned upon at the university by the tutors, and so Rosa started carrying around the Cuban constitution. Whenever any criticisms were levelled, she would brandish it and say, 'Tell me . . . where it is written, it is forbidden to love a man who isn't Cuban . . . ?'

'If the government wants more tourists,' I said, 'fraternisation is inevitable.'

'It will be discouraged,' said Eleanor.

'By whom?'

She pointed at the policeman in the corner in a tight blue uniform. He was eating a large, pink ice-cream.

'Cubans can be called to account for what they are doing,' she added mysteriously.

We got back to Havana late in the afternoon. As we were coming from the old part of the city towards the Hotel Colina, I noticed a piece of graffiti. It was on the corner of a building opposite the university steps. It said '*Batista Asesino*', a phrase that needs no translation. It had obviously been the work of a student radical in the 1950s but could it be original after so many years?

'Is it genuine?' I asked.

'Yes, it is.'

'Are you sure?'

Oh yes, it's genuine.' There was a pause and then she continued, 'Of course, they touch it up every year, just the same.'

6

Fifteen Cents Here, Fifteen Cents There

Fulgencio Batista, best known to the world as the man Castro licked, was born in north-east Cuba, supposedly in the village of Veguitas, in 1901. His father was a sugar worker, and both parents were mulattos—of European and Negro blood. He had a varied education and did many jobs before joining the army at the age of twenty. Apart from a short spell as a civilian teacher of stenography, he stayed in the services for twelve years, rising to become a sergeant stenographer in 1933.

This was the year the dictator Machado fell. The new president was the US choice, Carlos Manuel de Céspedes, who could be relied upon to protect American commercial interests. Céspedes did not have the support of the people, but opposition to him was centred not around the radical students (by tradition a potent force in Cuban politics) but around those who had been among Machado's closest supporters in the army—the NCOs. Self-interest rather than principle was at the root of their opposition. They were frightened their wages were going to be cut (money was very tight at the time) and terrified they were going to be the victims of a purge because they'd happily served under the hated Machado. Thus at Campamento Columbia, the army base outside Havana, a little coterie formed with a view to protecting their interests; Batista was their secretary. They plotted without arriving at any conclusions and sought support without much success, and that might have been the end of it if one of their group hadn't told a sympathetic officer of their schemes. Captain Torres Menier approached the NCOs and offered to mediate between them and the government. Batista abruptly declined and instructed the NCOs to relieve all the officers of their posts and take command. It was an audacious and bloodless coup; the ordinary soldiers, who thought the NCOs' regime would mean better footwear for them, went along with it. Batista thus made his entry onto the stage of Cuban politics.

In Havana Céspedes fell, student radicals elected Dr Grau San Martin president, and Batista, who had now elevated himself to colonel, threw in his lot with them. The new president took power on 10 September 1933 but would not swear an oath of office because that would have meant accepting the constitution of 1902, with its hugely unpopular Platt Amendment.

Plainly the US was not going to go for Dr Grau. The US ambassador, Sumner Welles, was living at the time in the Hotel Nacional, a glorious piece of architectural confection overlooking the Malecón. Only thirty of Cuba's thousand-odd officers had gone along with the sergeant's coup and there was a large number of these disaffected souls knocking around. Some 300 of them, alarmed at the prospect of a planned purge of Machadistas, took up residence in the Nacional. With Welles on hand, the hotel became a centre of counter-revolution. The officers had to go, and the man for the job was Batista.

The attack started at dawn on 2 October 1933. It was over by 4.45 in the afternoon. The officers were marched out. A crowd who had gathered urged their summary execution. Batista's troops fired over the crowd and into the officers, killing seven and wounding twenty-two.

If this was restrained, the response of Batista's forces to the attempted coup a month later by enlisted men and officers who hadn't been in the Hotel Nacional, was not. They were overwhelmed in the Atares fortress and as they marched out to surrender, they were mown down with machine-gun fire.

With this brutal suppression, Batista established himself as the power in the land. At Batista's insistence Grau now went and was replaced by Carlo Hevia, his compromise choice, on 16 January 1934. Then Hevia went and was replaced by Colonel Carlos Mendieta on 17 January 1934 (yes, one day later) who was Batista's real choice.

Batista now lost no time in making capital out of his position. In May 1934 he summoned Rafael Montalvo, the man who supplied the army with uniforms, and informed him that henceforth uniforms would cost fifteen cents apiece more, with the additional money going to himself. So he commenced using his political power to milk the system, a habit he was to continue.

1936 saw the resignation of a disappointed Colonel Mendieta, who had not been able to get Cuba's various political parties to agree on the date of the next election. The next election then took place (the presidents since Machado's fall having all been appointees) and Miguel Mariano Gómez became president in May 1936. He only lasted six months, the cause of his downfall being that he opposed Batista's policy of rural schools run and staffed by the military. Gómez was replaced by Vice-President Federico Laredo Bru, who was completely Batista's man and filled his cabinet with the colonel's cronies. In 1940, Batista's position was finally formalised: he was voted president in what was—it is important to stress this—a fair election. In his early days, Batista had some pretensions to be a democrat. But honesty was never his forte. It has been estimated that when he completed his term of office in 1944, he had accumulated some $20,000,000 by devious means in the preceding eleven years, the bulk of it during his presidency.

The administrations which followed, first of Dr Grau (1944–48), and then of Dr Carlos Prío (1947–52), were characterised by unbridled corruption on the part of the government, and overshadowed by escalating violence on the part of the security forces and political parties. Bombings and assassinations were frequent. Democratic politics had mutated into gangsterism. In 1952, with the presidential elections looming, and the likelihood of his electoral success flagging, Batista allowed himself to be persuaded by a group of young officers that he was the saviour of Cuba. On the night of 9/10 March he repeated his coup of 1933, effortlessly and bloodlessly again taking over the Campamento Columbia.

In his 1940–44 administration, Batista had overseen some good work; rents had been controlled and conditions and terms of labour much improved. He had moreover supported the constitution of 1940. He came to power in 1940 in a fair election and he lost power in 1944 in a fair election. But the Batista who seized power in 1952 was not the man he had been. He was lazier. He was a glutton. He now spent hours playing canasta with his military cronies or watching horror films, rather than attending to matters of state. He cultivated the Cuban *haute bourgeoisie* although they disapproved of him, whereas in the Thirties and early Forties, he had been a man of the people and contemptuous of them. More importantly, he was greedier and more given to overlooking the barbarities of his subordinates. Many of the insurgents who attacked the Moncada and Bayamo Barracks with Fidel Castro in 1953 (in the hope of starting a reaction which would topple Batista) were horribly tortured after their surrender (three men were dragged for miles behind a jeep, for instance) and then summarily executed, with the approval of Colonel de Rio Chaviano, the military commander. Everyone knew what had gone on but Batista was unresponsive to the popular feeling of revulsion. Chaviano was, after all, defending his, Batista's regime.

Turning the blind eye went hand in hand with a disregard for proper democratic procedure. Having seized power in 1952, Batista now sanctioned his position with a bogus election in November 1954 in which he was elected president without opposition and with only half the electorate voting (although voting was nominally compulsory). In the presidential elections of November 1958, Batista went one stage further; he had the election papers marked up in advance, thus ensuring the success of his candidate, Rivero Agüero.

With the naked pursuit of power naturally went corruption; but how exactly did it operate? Hugh Thomas in *Cuba* offers the best guide:

> Corruption, of course, is a complicated matter and is hardly explained by merely saying that the rulers could not restrain themselves from putting their hands in the till. What was the exact style of the corruption, who did precisely what? No less important, how did they get away with it, why did no vigilant member of the opposition, newspaper or legislator, make an effective protest? There is also the question, how did the corruption affect the life of the state in the long term?
>
> In general, these frauds had their origin in Spanish practice whereby civil servants and judges were paid so little, or had themselves paid so much for their jobs that corruption was the only effective method of recompense. There was also the lottery which, under Spain, had given many opportunities for enrichment. That had been further used under the Republic, by means of the collectorship system which, farmed out among senators and newspapermen, explains much of the second question under discussion: critics were in fact silenced by being allocated lottery collectorships. Others were threatened by physical reprisals, by the dismissal of their friends, or by visits of unmistakable menace by police officers or hired gunmen. There were few public men who did not themselves look forward to their period in power as a time when they too would be able to make their thousands of pesos through some agreement to provide food for the army, through control of customs houses or even through the establishment of a series of imaginary jobs in, for instance, the Bureau of Communications.
>
> How governments carried out corruption varied. There were the bogus jobs in government departments. Pardons could be bought. Buildings could be rented to the government (particularly as schools). Old government stores could be sold. Contracts for public works (as well as concessions for

development) were given to favoured builders or engineers without tenders being made. The money passed directly to the politician responsible. (This practice is no doubt the commonest form of graft in Latin American as in European and North American politics.) There were, finally, actual thefts or misappropriations of public funds.[1]

Material remuneration arose by virtue of one's position in society. In Batista's case the rewards were very high indeed because he was at the head of it all. The money came from everywhere. From legal sources, such as those wanting building licences, to illegal sources, such as those running protection rackets. Batista is known to have received $1,280,000 per month from this source alone, although he did have to share the money with others. By 1959, it has been estimated, he had $300,000,000 invested abroad, the fruits of his diligent abuse of the system. His corruption was echoed throughout the country. Nothing was possible without bribery.

Meanwhile, the security forces behaved monstrously in an effort to keep a lid on dissent, and did this with the tacit support of the government. In the village of Cojímar, close to where Ernest Hemingway lived, they tortured and executed, according to his count, twelve boys. This was just one of the thousands of incidents which, together, were eventually too much for the country. Popular support flowed to Castro and the revolutionary opposition. Batista's forces wore themselves out trying to contain what was uncontainable, and on 1 January 1959, at 3 in the morning, Batista fled with a group of followers, including the heir apparent, Agüero. He eventually settled in Spain where he lived in luxury until his death in 1973.

---

[1] *Cuba, or the Pursuit of Freedom*, Hugh Thomas, 738–739.

7

Five to One

The day after the beach we had lunch with Marge. She was a US citizen who'd lived in Cuba since the early Sixties. We were sitting in the Sierra Maestra, the restaurant at the top of what used to be called the Havana Hilton and is now called—a lovely little revolutionary sarcasm this—the Havana Libre. At the next table two newlyweds were eating baked Alaska.

We were talking about the Cuban economic system in comparison to that in the West.

'Under capitalism,' said Marge, 'the worker is insecure about his job but once he's earnt his money, he can buy whatever he wants, provided he's earnt enough. In Cuba it's the reverse. Everyone, more or less, has a job and everyone has some money. The worker's anxiety instead is channelled into consumption, into getting hold of scarce goods.'

One focus, perhaps *the* focus of Cuban consumer desire, is the Dollar and Tecno shops which are all over the country. There was a whole complex of them on the ground floor of the Havana Libre which we had already explored. In these air-conditioned emporia, in absolute contrast to the shops on the streets, there were Japanese refrigerators and fans and jewellery and cosmetics, US cigarettes and Coca-Cola and all sorts of other luxury goods. There was an abundance of them, they were reasonably priced and they were of high quality; and this was only a small selection, we gathered, compared to what some of the mammoth Tecno stores had on offer. But such shops were for foreigners only, tourists or technicians with hard currency.

Despite socialism, however, the Cuban people have remained the sons and daughters of Adam. Years of indoctrination have eliminated neither the desire for goods nor the willingness to resort to devious means to obtain them. There is an enormous currency black market in Cuba, far bigger than anything I'd experienced when I had travelled in Eastern Europe. At the time of our conversation with Marge, we'd already had in the previous two days some twenty approaches in the street to change money. It was obviously a world we were going to have to penetrate. It happened two days later, without its being planned.

It was late morning. We were under a covered walkway at the bottom of the Paseo de Martí, just on the edge of Old Havana and half a dozen blocks away from the Museum of the Revolution. We could dimly hear the amplified roll call that played there continuously over the public address system. There were shuttered shops and men leaning against dirty, ragged pillars, spitting, smoking, picking their teeth, a battered 1957 Buick Century Riviera parked by the kerb and a strong smell of cat. A youth stepped in front of us. He was thin and black with curly hair and couldn't have been more than eighteen years old.

'Five to one, five to one . . .' he sang, shifting nervously from one leg to the other and looking furtively around. We both made a pretence of thinking seriously about his offer while India skipped about on the pavement. We didn't want to get arrested and deported. In the event, there were no police to be seen, only the men we'd already passed under the arches. I agreed. We would change twenty dollars. He would give us one hundred pesos.

A second youth loomed up behind the other, undid the zip pocket of his parachute trousers and pulled out a dirty roll of Cuban pesos.

I started to count. They didn't look like the pre-revolutionary notes which we'd been warned against. I got as far as twenty-five and stopped. I realised I was frightened. I looked up and all the faces along the arcade seemed to be staring at us in an unfriendly way.

'Police,' hissed the first youth.

Sod it, I thought. The twenty-dollar bill vanished from my hand and they were gone. We hurried across the road away from the staring faces and counted properly. We'd been duped. We'd got two pesos to the dollar.

A few minutes later in a smaller side street, we fared better. A solitary youth, a mulatto with an unshaven face, came up and asked if we wanted to change. I remembered his face from the arcade and I realised they had probably all been money-changers and their looks had not been malevolent but envious.

We agreed. He went over to a man standing in a crumbling doorway. The man was middle-aged and wore a cream suit and a straw hat and had a straggly moustache. He gave the youth a roll of money for us inside a copy of the national newspaper, *Granma*. I counted the pesos while pretending to read an item, put the dollars in the paper, rolled it up and gave it back to the youth. He said goodbye. We went on our way.

What happened to our dollars, I imagine, was as follows. The man with the moustache used them to buy items from Tecno or Dollar shops. (How the Cubans, who were banned from such establishments, got in to make their purchases was another story.) These items were then sold on the black market at vastly inflated prices. The pesos so obtained were then used to buy further dollars at an extraordinary exchange rate of five, six, seven to one. Sales of items on the black market would also provide the money-changer with an income to live on.

★

Now we had pesos, we decided it was time to enter the Cuban mainstream. No more the Sierra Maestra at the top of the

Havana Libre. We were going to do as the Cubans.

We had noticed the Pizzeria Milan in Vedado. We retraced our steps there. Its entrance was obscured by an enormously long queue which was not for the pizzeria but for an ice-cream stall twenty-five yards down the street.

We went through the queue and into the Milan and found ourselves in a long, gloomy room. Stretching down the whole length was a counter which curved like a roller-coaster track with about fifty fixed stools in front of it. Every seat was occupied and there was someone waiting behind almost every one of them. Along the side wall, there was another queue of about 200 people for the take-away counter at the back. Add to these the queue of ice-cream *aficionados* we had had to get through in order to get inside, and the impression I had was that I was in the middle of a Babel of queues.

We each found a space behind a stool. I was behind a woman with curly hair. Her armpits were shaved so bare they seemed polished. The neon strips overhead, most of which were blown, began to swing gently in the faint breeze blowing from outside.

After perhaps half an hour (I don't know exactly how long, I was so bored I'd stopped looking at my watch), the customers at the little section of roller-coaster in front of us paid and left in unison, and we, along with the next wave, moved forward—about fifteen of us—to take their place.

The counterhand was middle-aged and portly. He cleared away, put a leaf of flimsy carbon between the first two leaves of a little book and started to take orders. Glancing over my shoulder, I saw that the next wave who would take our place were already waiting, and there was another wave waiting behind them again. It was lunchtime.

When he got to the third customer, the counterhand got his top copies and his duplicates out of order. He said, 'Tut-tut!' out loud and waggled his pencil in the air and shook his head as he leafed back to make the necessary alterations. The tut-tutting and the pencil wagging continued all the way along the line.

Finally, the counterhand got to us. To eat or drink there was either unlabelled Cuban beer called Claro, literally 'Clear', or

Refresco, a sweet sickly orange drink, which I suppose was Cuba's answer to Fanta. To eat there was a straight choice as well: pizza with tomato or spaghetti with tomato. Following the lead of other customers, we ordered our drinks in duplicate.

The spaghetti arrived in a soup plate, grey, thick and overcooked, with sweating beads of cheese and a tomato paste which tasted of vinegar. Five minutes later came the pizza. The dough was thick and had a sour taste, and the topping of cheese and tomato tasted the same as that on the spaghetti, only it was hot and melted, rather than cold and separated.

Both dishes were disgusting. Of the fifteen people on our section of counter, not one finished their meal. This was the first fruit of our black-market transactions. The rest of the journey saw many more little ironies like this one.

We paid, and moved off. Outside the Milan stood a bent old woman with a handbag, wearing a starched dress, her face covered with white pancake, as women wore their make-up in the 1930s. I looked at her carefully, wondering if she was a remnant of the vanished bourgeoisie.

Now we joined the line for ice-cream. Many of those ahead of us took their scoops away in empty Coca-Cola cans with the tops cut off. After half an hour it was finally our turn. The vendor, a lady in blue slacks, very fat, was amazed we only wanted one cornet.

We walked up N Street in the direction of the hotel. The wind was blowing furiously, and schoolgirls were holding their tiny mustard-coloured skirts against their thighs. A gigantic cardboard box rattled down from the direction of the Hotel Capri and across our path. Tiny pieces of grit lifted by the wind stung the face, and pedestrians had their eyes screwed up.

We reached the Colina just as it began to spot with rain. On our floor, we found all the shutters had been secured in anticipation of the coming storm. It came, and we lay on our beds looking through the window at the black sky and the silvery needles of rain sheeting down, and listening to the buses sloshing along the street below.

Suddenly, there was a tremendous explosion, so violent the

glass rattled in the panes, and then another, even louder. It was the electricity sub-station across the road blowing. Naturally all the lights in the bedroom, and all over the district, immediately went out.

We lay until night fell, when the janitor brought us candles. The wax was like poor-quality glass with bubbles in it and the wick was like poor-quality yarn. The flame was yellow and died with the slightest breeze. Lying on the damp pillow I remembered the narrator in *Inconsolable Memories* thinking the worst punishment he could be given would be to have to list everything, from combs to automobiles, from buttons to paint, which Cuba was going to have to buy from the Communist bloc because the US had slammed the door.

8

Maspoton

It was time to hire the car. We went to the garage. We could have it whenever we wanted, providing we paid in advance, in dollars. This was a government institution where they only took hard currency, as in the better hotels and restaurants. The official who was called Henry expressed no interest in our driving licences.

'What about insurance?' Tyga asked.

A sea of rusting battered Ladas stretched around us in every direction.

Henry made an ambiguous gesture encompassing them all, as if to say: What, insure one of these?

'There is no need,' he added, in case we had not understood.

This was Friday. We arranged that the car would be brought to the hotel on Monday.

The plan was that first of all we would go to Pinar del Rio province in the west. Then we would return to Havana and go east, visiting all the towns founded by Velázquez and whatever else we wanted to see, until we got to Baracoa at the other end of the island. Then we'd turn round, and come back and go home.

In England we'd come across an advertisement for a place called Maspoton. It was described as a new resort in the south of Pinar del Rio province which offered extensive hunting as well as all modern facilities. We then came across mention of Maspoton in a brochure. 'Cuba's premier hunting lodge', it said, and gave an Alabama, USA address for those who wished to book to go. A friend in the US checked the address and it was genuine. This was too good to be true. A Cuban hunting lodge for Alabama rednecks. I booked us in for a week of what I thought would be glorious copy. 'Klansmen in Cuba.' It sounded great.

There was, however, a problem. Maspoton was not on the map. Not on our atlas, nor on any of the appalling maps on sale in the Dollar shop in the Havana Libre or in the excruciating *Guide to Cuba* we had bought there. We enquired at the tourist office and could find out absolutely nothing about it. But Henry, who brought the car to the hotel, had heard of it. 'Maspoton is very good for hunting,' Henry said, 'bouff, bouff. . . .' He drew an 'X' in our atlas in the middle of an empty expanse somewhere to the east and south of the town of Pinar del Rio. He also tried to correct some of the barbarities of our Spanish and wrote down how to ask the way grammatically.

We drove away along the Malecón curving by the sea—actually the straits of Florida. Big, dusty buses thundered by, imitation squirrel tails tied to the wing mirrors flying in the wind. There were Soviet bicycles with passengers sitting on the handlebars. Old US cars, impressive, stately looking, the drivers dangling their arms out of the windows. Rusting Ladas, like ours, puttering along and looking as though they were about to fall to bits. Boys fishing from the sea-wall, wreaths of spray around them like a fine mist. There were petrol stations with wastepaper blowing across their forecourts; rotting apartment blocks with a sea view, built for the rich, long departed; and the Riviera Hotel which I believe had once been painted the colour of US dollar bills and boasted a heart-shaped bed in the honeymoon suite.

We drove down into the tunnel under the river Almendares

and emerged in the suburb of Miramar. There were large stone houses on either side of the road, with columns, balustrades and baroque coats of arms carved from stone over the doorways. A central reservation ran down the middle of the road planted with shrubs and dotted with stone benches. Traffic policemen sat in their wooden, gazebo-like huts, whilst the old sheltered under banyan trees, with their impenetrable canopy of greenery. The rich lived here in the Fifties, and when they died were buried in the Colon cemetery to the south-west, some in mausoleums fitted with lifts, air-conditioning and telephones. Now they have all mostly departed to Miami or Venezuela. Their homes are schools or have been divided into flats. The 'largest theatre in the world', Miramar's El Blanquita, has been rechristened the 'Karl Marx'. Yet the atmosphere of Miramar has not changed. It is still leafy, secluded, exclusive.

We drove out of town onto an almost empty highway. All the way round the green, rolling landscape was dotted with *bohíos*, or shacks, and royal palms pointing upwards like fingers at the sky.

After hours on this silent, empty road, traversing the silent empty landscape, the Sierra del Rosario appeared to the right, dark and green and mysterious.

We stopped to ask the way from a man whose '57 Chevrolet had broken down.

'Take the next turning for Los Palacios, and then it's straight on,' he said confidently.

We turned off the highway onto a narrow winding road. There were more wooden shacks with crooked doors and windows and children staring at us from under trees. At the first crossroads, where we stopped in an attempt to locate where we might be on the map, something caught my attention. Beside a *bohío* there was something under a tarpaulin that was long and finny, with chickens roosting on top. I was suddenly seized by the idea that if I didn't look, I'd be haunted for the rest of the journey by the certainty that there was a Brougham under there.

I got out of our Lada and went over to the woman sitting

outside the shack on a rocking chair. I asked her permission and she waved me on languidly. I came up to the side of the *bohío* waving my arms, and chickens jumped down clucking and squawking, feathers floating after them in the hot air. I got hold of the cover and began to lift, my heart beating. The first thing I saw was a chrome bumper, pitted with corrosion. If it was what I was looking for, I would know immediately, because above the radiator grill would be a chrome 'V' and the magic word Eldorado. But it wasn't an Eldo: it was a Sixty-two sedan de Ville. Close, it was a Cadillac, but not close enough. I got the tarpaulin off and had a good look. It was cream. It had probably been manufactured in 1956, when over 100,000 had been made.

Fifteen kilometres further on was Los Palacios, a miserable town of wooden shacks, a few stucco-clad buildings in the centre, and a rusting railway line running down the main street. We asked three pedestrians and they all gave us the same information: 'Maspoton, *recto*' ('Maspoton, straight on)'.

Straight on brought us, towards evening, into a land of mudflats which seemed to stretch for ever. It was totally and utterly flat and criss-crossed with tracks and canals. In the vast water meadows, thousands of scrawny cattle roamed across the scrawny grass. They were mostly young bulls, fawn or dove-coloured, flaps of skin hanging down from their chins which waved slowly as they moved, and humps like those of dromedaries. Behind every beast stalked a cattle egret, picking with its long yellow bill at the hind legs or the marshy ground. Turkey vultures lined the fence posts like omens of bad luck and sometimes as we passed would heave themselves into the air and sail away. The grey sky seemed to be only a couple of hundred feet above our heads and getting lower all the time as the day wore on.

It grew dark. We became completely lost on the flats which were without people, houses, signposts or any lights. Finally, hours later, fatigued and irritated, we saw figures standing in the darkness and tins of kerosene with orange flames leaping out of them scattered around the ground. Between two wooden posts a thick chain stretched across the mud track. At first I thought they might be waiting to catch stray cattle. Then I saw guns. These were militiamen, armed and waiting, ultimately for counter-revolutionaries. They were part of Cuba's elaborate civilian defence system. They were the first people we had seen all evening.

'Yes, that's the way to Maspoton,' they said, pointing back out into the darkness. We were going in absolutely the wrong direction. We tried to translate what they said into a map which we could use to find a way through the maze of tracks but this defeated us all. Finally, a mulatto with grey flecks in his hair called Mingo said he would guide us if we would bring him back.

We drove away, on and on for miles, until Mingo suddenly said 'Stop'. Behind a barbed-wire fence we could see a sign with a red arrow on it and a picture of a man with a gun, the first sign of the evening. We both climbed out and he showed me how the barbed-wire fence could be lifted aside. The way, it appeared, to what we were looking for, was straight ahead.

We returned Mingo to his party of militiamen and came back to the sign. The night was warm when I lifted the fence aside. I could see lights glimmering faintly in the distance.

According to the reading on the speedometer when we arrived, the Club de Caza, Maspoton, was five miles from the fence. We drove past a blazing neon sign—it was the size of a billboard—showing a man with a gun and into what seemed like a garrison town with rows of ugly cabins. They were all dark. Perhaps there was no one around? We pulled up outside a bar with a picture of a cocktail glass over the door. No chance of getting lost here. The door was locked. Two men in fatigues appeared from the darkness. 'We couldn't find our way,' was the first thing we both said. The men were extremely apologetic and ran off. Something clicked in the darkness somewhere and suddenly all the lights came on, dozens and dozens of them. Rusting tin mushrooms with bulbs under the canopies lined the pathways. Leaves floated in the enormous swimming pool. It was like a dismal holiday camp.

The men took us into a room smelling of soap with a huge

billiard table. There was a television flickering, playing at full volume. On the screen I could see Phil Collins. He was singing 'I Can Feel it Coming in the Air Tonight'. The solitary viewer was a dark Cuban man wearing a gaucho hat who turned to stare at us. Several more Cuban males appeared. All in fatigues and boots, and with knives dangling from their belts, they looked like the sort of men in the magazine *Handgun*.

We explained we'd come a long way and got hopelessly lost. It had become very important to us that they admitted the way wasn't properly signposted. The men, who had gathered round, all nodded sympathetically. 'Ah, but surely it was just *recto*. Out of Los Palacios and straight on,' the *jefe* Orlando shouted above the television. This was not what we wanted to hear.

I looked around the room. Beside the television there was a shelf covered with camouflage material on which sat three stuffed birds with glazed beaks and shiny webbed feet. On a low table four broken badminton rackets with loose gut were laid out in a decorative square, and there were blurred black-and-white photographs hanging on the walls, showing middle-aged men dressed in camouflage fatigues, crouched in undergrowth, guns at the ready, or posing by dead birds that hung by the neck from wooden bars. The birds killed seemed to amount to thousands. Here were my Alabama rednecks, I presumed. Ominously, there were no live birds in sight.

We were shown to a cabin with tiny windows covered with mosquito net. Moments later a man appeared with a crate of beer and bottles of rum which he put into the large, humming refrigerator. There was a rat hole in the bottom of the back door and we used the empty crate to block it up.

Orlando and four or five others drifted in. 'What time do you want to start shooting?' Orlando asked. 'How many cartridges?' The season was over, I gathered, and I was the only male guest. A pity I hadn't asked my friend in the US to ask about such details when he'd checked out the Alabama PO Box for me. I looked at the five expectant faces and knew both that I'd made a terrible mistake and that I wasn't going to be able to get out of this. 'Oh, yes, I've used a gun before,' I lied blithely. Everyone's face lit up. Stuck out on these mudflats in the middle of nowhere, any hunter was clearly more than a distraction. He was an experience. We made our arrangements and said goodnight.

'Have you ever used a gun?' Tyga asked when we were alone.

'Once I fired at a tree.'

★

It was dark when I got up just a few hours later. I ate breakfast in a room with green baize on the tables and chairs covered with animal hide. There was a khaki-coloured frog on the back of the door eyeing me carefully.

Outside, Orlando gave me a Browning shotgun and I clambered into the back of a huge Russian bus with plastic seats. Obviously it was used for moving dozens of hunters in season. The guide Pedro followed, carrying a sack. Then he called back loudly through the open door. His face was round and dark with almond-shaped eyes. His moustache was thin and wiry.

After a noisy argument Orlando returned with a Belgian shotgun which he exchanged for the Browning. We bumped off into the darkness smoking untipped Aroma cigarettes and spitting out the bits of tobacco that stuck to our lips and tongues.

We stopped and got out by a shelter of palm fronds. There were flat-bottomed fibreglass boats on the bank filled with rainwater. We baled one out and glided away in it across totally black water. I was in the front holding the guns and cartridges. Pedro behind me punted expertly. We turned into a narrow waterway with trees towering on either side, dark shapes I could only dimly discern. The cobwebs which stretched across continually caught in my hair or on my face. I could hear a persistent, low moaning and bellowing which I assumed to be the sound of cattle.

'*Toros? Vacas?*' I asked, imagining cattle drinking at the water's edge. I was thinking of my grandfather's cattle in Ireland who drank from the river in darkness.

'No,' said Pedro, '*ranas.*'

'Oh yes,' I said, as if I'd understood.

We pushed out of the end of the channel into a flat, still lagoon of black water. There were mangrove trees growing everywhere with the tops of their roots showing above the water like candles. Suddenly I realised what I was hearing. It was bullfrogs of course. I wouldn't have lasted five minutes in this landscape without a guide, I thought gloomily.

We got to a mangrove tree growing alone in the middle of the lagoon. Pedro emptied the sack, tumbling out our duck-like plastic decoys into the bottom of the boat. The anchor weights were rusting nuts attached with nylon wire. We threw the decoys onto the surface of the water and glided away to the base of the tree. A wooden ladder led up to the hide. There I broke open a packet of cartridges and loaded.

I stared out over the top of the leaves and down at the *decoys plasticos*. In the quarter light, their dark silhouettes looked totally real, at least to me. Mosquitoes buzzed around us. 'The ducks come in just like them,' said Pedro. 'Zzzzeee, zzzzeee,' and he laughed.

Pedro touched my arm and crouched down. Without my noticing, a blue-winged teal had come up and was about to land amongst our decoys. My shot missed by yards and it flew away. Pedro said I had to aim at the water in front of the bird, because squeezing the trigger pulled the gun upwards.

A second blue-winged teal flew in. Again I missed. It went on like this, firing and missing until suddenly I saw, after having blasted and sent water whooshing up, that there was a dark shape lying sideways in the middle of the ring of plastic decoys.

'*Muerto*,' said Pedro, with pleasure.

As I became more accustomed to what was happening, I began to notice a number of things. The perverse feeling of pleasure as the gun came up. The receding of all thoughts, great and small, as I looked down the barrel. The certainty, autonomous from any of the normal processes of decision-making, about the point when the moment to fire had arrived. The spurt of orange at the end of the gun, a long tapering flame that lasted only an instant. The extraordinary prescience, even before the truth was evident, as to whether I had a hit or not. And finally, the quite unsentimental matter-of-factness with which I noticed the lopsided shape in the dark water as the current carried the dead bird towards one of the distant banks.

By dawn, the fifty cartridges were gone. We climbed into the boat. Pedro pushed on the pole and we glided over to the carcass lying nearest in the water. It was a teal. I lifted it out of the water. The wet body was rigid. So was the second, a white-cheeked pintail. The third, however, another teal, was still alive.

Pedro took it from me. He pinched it behind the head between his finger and thumb. It stretched its wings out and flapped them frantically and scrabbled with its feet in the air. I was expecting him to twist its neck, but instead he plunged the teal into the water and began to agitate the body. After a few moments, he lifted it out. Its wings started to beat again and its feet began to scramble. He squeezed the neck and blood bubbled out of the mouth and dripped onto the dark surface of the water. The wings started to beat frantically and the legs raced in the air. It went on and on until the movements couldn't go any faster. They then began to slow down, with longer and longer intervals between them. It was as if the teal was a machine winding down. There was a last spasm, and movement finally stopped. Pedro passed the bird over. I put it in the front of the boat with the other carcasses. There were spots of blood on the wings.

We collected nine in all and went back to the camp. All the men came out to see the kill. As I was having myself photographed India came out of our cabin with her mother. She pointed her finger at me and said I was to kill no more birds. Not mummy birds or daddy birds.

We went to the dining room. All they had was *café con leche* made with boiled tinned milk and small stale rolls with faintly rancid, bright-yellow butter. We had to get out. We decided we'd go to the tourist office in Pinar del Rio, try to get our money back for the week in Maspoton we'd booked, and attempt to find somewhere else to stay. Still, we would have to return for one further night: the ducks still had to be eaten.

★

We were in a dirty, pot-holed street somewhere in the centre of Pinar del Rio. We were near a butcher's—two scrawny-looking carcasses of buff-coloured meat were offered for sale—and the metallic smell of blood wafted through the car window.

We parked, and were advised by a young man who had come out of the butcher's that our bumper was touching that of the army jeep behind. I rolled the car forward a couple of inches and the three of us climbed out and we locked everything. The young man was still there. A thin, adolescent growth of hair covered his chin and upper lip and his expression was sly. I asked him where the tourist office was. He told us to turn right and go up to Martí. He didn't ask for anything.

Martí was a wide street. Old neon signs stuck out from nineteenth-century buildings and there were crazy tangles of wires and power cables overhead. The road was crammed with buses, bicycles, lorries going up and down very fast.

About a hundred yards up was the Globo Hotel, its dark foyer lined with tiles. We ambled in. A moment later I felt a tap on my elbow. It was the young man. 'This is not the tourist office,' he said. 'You have to go much further up the street. I will show you the way.' It would have been easy to say no, but we didn't, I think because of lethargy combined with curiosity to see what he was going to try to wheedle out of us.

We went outside and walked very slowly. We were in an arcade with shops and department stores. Our self-appointed guide went ahead, carving his way through the crowds, stopping every now and again to shake hands with friends, and then pointing in our direction so they would know he was with us.

In one of the huge stores, three or four pairs of shoes were on display in an otherwise empty window. There was a little cardboard sign beside them (like a 'reserved' sign in a restaurant) which read '*Venta Libre*', 'Free Sale'. Anyone with pesos could have these shoes, they were not rationed like the cane-cutter's boots lying in splendid isolation in the next bay behind glass. These far more durable items could be yours only with the requisite coupon.

Two other curiosities struck the eye: one was the lower

section of a female mannequin which had been put upside down in a shop window and had a pair of tights stretched over the legs. These were so small the crotch ended halfway down (or up) the thigh. The other was the window of a hairdresser's, where a sign announced

Apoyando planteamientos de Fidel
Esperamos el 10 de Enero
Aniversario del Triunfo de la Revolución
('Supporting the planning of Fidel, we are waiting for the 10th of January, anniversary of the triumph of the revolution.')

Appreciation of the city's commercial life, and some note-taking, slowed us down. The young man in his red teeshirt got further and further away. I hoped we were going to lose him altogether, but he waited for us at the corner. We passed an art gallery filled with brightly coloured pictures which were all imitative of different twentieth-century styles. The centrepiece was a picture of the Viñales Valley, north of the city. Our guide blew kisses at the frame and began to eulogise about the beauty of Viñales. We walked on, but his skin was thick and he ran after us.

At the top of the road, by a building from which the sound of a girls' choir wafted, he pointed to a gloomy doorway. 'This is the tourist centre,' he said. 'I want a cigarette please.' He put two fingers to his lips in case I hadn't understood his Spanish. I said, 'No,' and shook my head.

He shrugged his shoulders and sauntered away. We climbed the steps and noticed another door. Perhaps this would lead to the singing? I was pushing it open when I again felt a tap on my arm. 'No, this is wrong,' he said. 'I just told you, the other door is the tourist office.' I wished I had given him the cigarette.

He brought us down a dingy corridor and into a room with posters on the walls. A large woman sitting behind the counter was shouting on the telephone. 'Cigarette,' he said again, putting his fingers to his lips. I gave him one this time.

I moved away and began to look at the pictures on the wall. There was a large colour poster advertising Leningrad ('City of

Contrasts') and another with dozens of different views of Cuba. The big woman was still arguing on the telephone. A second woman had appeared, a tiny creature with Indian features and lank black hair. Tyga started to explain our situation.

'I work here,' said the young man, puffing furiously at my side. 'Yes, in this office. That's how I knew how to bring you here. Yes, I work here, behind that desk. . . India is beautiful . . . Viñales is beautiful. . . I have two daughters, also very beautiful. . . Your wife is pregnant. . . Yes, I have noticed that. . . I am very observant. . . You have a daughter, so it is my opinion that the next one will certainly be a boy. A little *chico* for the *chica*. Ha, ha, ha. . .'

He brought in a man from the street to interpret who looked like a troll and whose English was worse than our Spanish. After half an hour the troll left, smiling, believing he'd achieved wonders, and we reverted to our appalling *castellano*. Finally, the lank-haired woman behind the desk went off to ring Havana to see if she could give us our money back and we could go to another hotel. The other woman by now was off the telephone.

'How do you know that man?' she asked.

'What man?'

'The one who brought you in here.'

'Oh, the one in the red teeshirt. . .'

I felt like saying, 'But he works here', when I looked around and saw he had gone.

'Does he work here?' I asked pointlessly.

The woman shook her head.

I went and sat under the poster of Leningrad on a greasy plastic sofa. Why, I wondered, had he praised Viñales? Well, now I would never know. The telephone call to Havana was another incomplete narrative. No one could say if we'd get our money back. We would have to try at the office where we made the booking. 'But that was in England.' 'Then you'll have to go back there,' said the lank-haired woman.

At least we made progress in another direction. We had a room for the following night in the valley which the charlatan guide so loved.

Outside the office, Martí was as frantic and crowded as we had left it. The arcades were filled with queues, the shoppers clutching their ration books. We'd decided earlier we would allow at least two hours of daylight for the drive back, and now it was gone six and there was less than an hour to go.

When we got back to the mudflats, we found it had been raining all day. The light was fading. I saw the track disappear in front of us into a long, glimmering, silvery sheet of water.

We rolled in. Water sloshed below. All seemed to be well. Just so long as progress was slow, steady and forward. No braking. No sudden acceleration. The three of us were shouting and urging the Lada on like an animal. I could see the start of dry land creeping closer and closer. I felt certain we would get to the end. I said: 'We're going to—' and at that second I realised it wasn't forward we were going but sideways. I panicked and pressed down the accelerator. The engine roared, the bonnet of the car visibly dipped; and we came to a complete standstill. I climbed out into the warm, red, sticky mud, and saw we were sunk up to our door sill.

The situation seemed worse than it was because it need not have happened. If I hadn't accelerated we'd probably have got out. I found a jute sack in a field and laid it under the wheels but it turned soggy and fragmented like damp tissue when we tried to use it to get out. The only piece of wood I could find wasn't long enough to be a lever, but how could I hope to find a piece long enough in this treeless desert? There was nothing else for it. We would have to walk.

At this point it wasn't the walk that worried me. Or that I didn't know the roads. Or the absence of a light, anywhere, at which we could point ourselves. Oh no, I was concerned that the car, abandoned in the middle of nowhere, at least twenty-five kilometres from the nearest village, would be broken into. All the dire warnings we'd received in Havana about the necessity of always locking up, and never leaving our belongings inside because the Cubans would steal absolutely anything—warnings which I'd continuously ignored—returned with a vengeance. I emptied everything out of the glove compartment: my cigarettes and Zippo lighter; sunglasses and Spanish dictionary; bottle opener and Ambre Solaire. After these were crammed into my pockets, I carefully locked all the car doors, feeling like Robinson Crusoe securing his cave whenever he left it.

I scrambled up the bank to the mother and child.

I was still furious. 'Right, let's get going,' I said.

We started to walk along the broad red track. It was perfectly straight with a fence on either side and a canal glimmering to the left. Somewhere to the right, I didn't know how far away, lay the turn-off to Maspoton marked by a small round rusting sign.

The last of the daylight disappeared and it became pitch. The track in front of us was like a black river disappearing into darkness. Fenceposts and the screw tops on the sluice gates of the canals were invisible until one got very close to them, at which point they loomed like monstrous shapes. Long buried memories of unpleasant childhood encounters with cows, bulls and bullocks were now surfacing. I found a bit of log lying by the trackside. It made me feel a little better to hold it, wet and muddy in my hands. The bullfrogs began to croak and a bird which we startled suddenly rose up, invisible to the eye, and flapped away. The fireflies came out and hurtled around like bits of debris from a firework. Hours and hours passed, as we crawled along, the pace being set by India who had no shoes and a small stride and kept sinking up to her waist. I didn't speak much and for the whole time my ears were straining for the sound of a hoof, my eyes for the outline of a flank, and my nose for the dusty smell of a beast. Then suddenly I thought I saw it. I ran up and by the flickering light of my cigarette lighter I saw the faded red arrow.

The new track was narrower and wetter. We had to keep crossing from side to side to avoid long sluices of water. All around the whispers and little movements in the grassy verges and along by the edges of the waterway seemed to increase. A few spots of warm rain fall.

It was an hour before we could see the yellow neon sign which stood at the entrance of the camp. Thunder rumbled and the rain started in earnest. In seconds the hair was stuck to our faces and our clothes to our bodies. We started to run and didn't stop until we got to the clubroom. Nothing had changed, not the stuffed birds, nor the camouflage drapes; even the man in the gaucho hat was again watching the television with the volume turned up to deafening level. Yet everything seemed almost welcoming.

We washed the mud off ourselves in the cabin. The freezing water tasted of brine. The men went out in the storm with the bus and a long length of rope to fetch the stranded Lada. With our mackintoshes thrown over our heads we ran to the dining room. Three places had been set at the head of a long banqueting table. We sat on the hide-covered chairs and the ducks appeared, quartered and covered with a brown sauce. I told India it was chicken and she tasted a small piece of the brown-coloured meat. 'It's chicken which has been taken from a duck,' she said, 'and I won't eat any of it.'

After supper many of the men came in: the man in the gaucho hat, who it transpired was the cook; the young curly-haired kennel boy; the pool maintenance man; Orlando; and four or five others. A cassette was put on—a medley of Mexican songs—played at a very loud volume on the public address system. The speakers shook and vibrated whilst India danced around the floor in her nightdress and everyone smiled and said, '*Musica, musica. . .*' At the end of the evening we showed India's diary which read, 'My daddy went bird hunting and he caught nine birds.' Underneath was a picture which showed Pedro and myself standing on the platform of the hide, holding the ducks and the gun. Everyone went to bed happy and I felt a little sorry we would be leaving.

9

Viñales

The next morning we made our way across the mud to Los Palacios, on to Pinar del Rio, and then north to the Viñales valley, rather inaptly named because in fact when we arrived what we saw was a plain stretching to distant mountains. The land was divided into squares of tobacco, malanga, citrus, or bare red earth and dotted with rocks the height of skyscrapers, standing completely alone. Called *mogotes,* they looked as if they'd been dropped out of the sky. They were so big, trees and greenery grew on top of them.

We pulled over and read our terrible guidebook with the engine running. During the Jurassic period, these *mogotes* had supported a plateau. This collapsed but they, the supports, we gathered, remained.

I climbed out to have a better look at the Viñales valley. All twinges of nostalgia for the mudflats had vanished. One grows attached to a place, even a horrible place, but as soon as its forcefield has been left behind, it exerts no hold at all.

Around the next corner we found the Hotel Los Jazmines. It was built on a little rise. There was a green 1951 Plymouth sedan from Cranbrook in the car park.

It was lunchtime and we went into the cafeteria on the ground floor. All places to eat in Cuba are graded, a fact that makes one feel that the real heart of Cuban socialism is a passion for order. This cafeteria was a category IV. There were battered turnstile stools along a switchback counter, like the Pizzeria Milan. We ordered yoghurt and cupcakes and sat down to wait in front of the menu board. This was shaped like a shield into which the day's items, hand-painted on wooden slats, could be inserted: *Refresco 10 cents, Café 30 ml. 10 cents,* and so on. There were flies everywhere, crawling over the counter, our hands, the slop pail beside the sink.

A party of adolescents entered, very excited, perhaps forty of them. They all wore boots and olive-coloured trousers. The military clothes emphasised the hourglass figures of the girls.

They sat down and were each served an identical meal: Refresco, a *bocadillo* or sandwich filled with corned beef and tiny bits of Polish gherkin, and a vanilla ice-cream. Not food for military training. As they ate they all stared at us, especially a young girl sitting close by.

She finished eating and came and stood behind us, pretending to look at the board. I could sense her edging closer. Suddenly, she reached forward and began to stroke India's hair, softly like a lover. It appeared to be an act of compulsion which she was unable to stop. I looked round and nodded.

'Are you Russian?' she asked and then, correcting herself said, 'Soviet?'

'No. English and Irish.'

'That is very interesting. Do you have a dictionary?'

Acting as if some invisible barrier had been dismantled, her friends clustered around.

'No. What's your name?'

'Mary—just the same as it is in England.'

She was about sixteen years old, wearing spectacles, and with acne scars on her cheeks.

'Why are you in a uniform?' I asked.

'It's because of military service,' she said and then she corrected herself and said, 'No, it's not military service. We're still at school but we're receiving military training.'

A man in his forties, a teacher I presumed, appeared at the side of the group. Everyone fell silent and stopped smiling.

'We must go,' he said, nodded politely but curtly to us and walked away.

Mary smiled behind her big spectacles, touched her red earrings and said goodbye.

★

We carried our bags up to the second floor and found ourselves in a long corridor with doors leading off. Our room was halfway along. It was large, with a huge humming refrigerator, empty except for a plastic bottle of water and a gigantic Soviet television set which gave me a mild electric shock when I touched the controls. At the back was a bathroom with an extraordinary 1950s medicine cabinet, with mirrored wings and neon strip lights. Clearly it came from a technology which valued bulk over economy, the same which produced the Cranbrook sedan.

We were at the front of the hotel with a view over the valley. There were french windows and a small balcony. India went out, and a couple of moments later I heard her talking her pidgin Spanish. I went out and found her speaking to the couple in the next room, on their balcony. He was Albert, a young man of about twenty-five, good-looking, and she was Leila, younger, curvaceous, with black hair dyed straw-blonde and a permanent smile on her broad face. She was leaning her elbows on the railing with her bottom sticking in the air, while Albert, with his immaculately polished left shoe on the railing, was pulling up his silk sock. He had been doing all the talking, as if India was a predator from whom his female had to be protected.

I said hello.

'Your daughter is very pretty,' said Albert.

After the usual pleasantries and questions about where we had come from and why we were in Cuba, Albert told me he was a tour guide, escorting a party of about thirty, all native Havanians, who were having a week's holiday.

'You probably saw our coach in the car park,' he added.

I hadn't. I'd only had eyes for the Cranbrook, with its beautiful curves and chrome trim. 'Oh yes,' I said.

'I invite you all to come as my guests tomorrow,' he said, 'to see the famous mural,' and then, like a bad politician, he leant across, tweaked India's cheek and said, '*Que linda*' ('How pretty').

★

The next morning we were woken by tremendous banging. I went to the door and found a workman in overalls holding a toolbox.

'Can I go into your bathroom?' he asked.

'Yes,' I said, assuming his visit was connected with the water. It had stopped the night before and it still wasn't running. A few seconds later I was surprised to hear splintering plaster. I went after him and found he was hacking the medicine cabinet from the wall, dislodging tiles and creating clouds of dust. The maid rushed in.

'How am I expected to clear this mess you're making,' she demanded.

'With a broom.'

At eleven we went out to the car park. The medicine cabinets had been ripped out of all the hotel's bathrooms and were being slung into the back of a lorry. Their replacements, from the People's Republic of China and wrapped in cheap porous cardboard, were piled in front of the *carpeta*, the desk.

We climbed aboard the tourist bus with all the holiday makers. There were a couple of battered fans on the dashboard and a variety of Mogurt—Hungarian Trading Company for Motor Vehicles—stickers decorating the windscreen. Assorted pennants from the same source hung from the ceiling. Whatever the politics, transport always gets decorated.

Albert sat in a dentist's chair beside the driver's seat. His looks were typical of a white Cuban. A smooth, sallow complexion, almond eyes with large brown pupils. He pulled a microphone on a lead out from the dashboard. After some seconds of violent feedback, we were introduced and everyone applauded.

It was only a short distance to our destination. This was the Dos Hermanas, or Two Sisters, one of the largest *mogotes* in the valley. It had a long, exposed cliff face on which an artist called Gómez had painted a mural illustrating the process of evolution from snail, through dinosaur, bear and platypus, to the Guanajays, the first Cuban family—an Indian man, his wife and their child. The whole work was about 200 feet high and 300 feet long.

The bus stopped by a thatched verandah where there was a long table. We all filed out. One or two of the party, who were middle-aged with few exceptions, took cursory photographs of the mural as soon as they were outside. 'Gómez painted it in 1961,' Albert told us, while Leila stood at his shoulder grinning and nodding, 'with the help of twenty-five *campesinos*. He stayed on the ground directing them through a megaphone, and they hung down the cliff face on ropes and cradles.'

The coach party, meanwhile, had gathered in the shade of the verandah and started to play charades, a pursuit they had followed at the hotel all the previous afternoon and evening and since breakfast that morning. They laughed and giggled as they played, and the sillier the charade, the louder they got.

At a distance the figures on the mural were pale in the sunlight. I wandered over and found the background against which they were set had been achieved by drawing quarter-inch-wide alternate lines of yellow and blue, tens of thousands of them. I sat on a rock and watched the charade-playing and the turkey vultures floating overhead, spiralling round and round with their long black wings outstretched.

At one o'clock everyone was summoned to sit down at the long table. The carcass of a pig roasted on a fire nearby. I was sitting opposite an old couple with leathery necks like tortoises and next to a big man who was a body builder. I had already seen him parading around the hotel swimming pool in tight black trunks.

We sat in silence. Nobody spoke. Cold beers were put on the table by an old waiter but nobody poured any out. A man in spectacles combed his luxuriant hair carefully and then shyly took a piece of bread from a basket in the middle. A faint wind rustled the palm fronds of the roof overhead and the vultures circled.

The waiter started to bring the plates two at a time, yams, rice and gigantic cuts of pork already heaped upon them. Two at a time the guests picked up their knives and forks like automatons and began to eat. There was the noise of chewing, munching and swallowing, but not a word of speech. The concentration was exclusively on getting the food in and down.

The sun was slowly dipping and a line of shadow crept across the cliff face. The pale figures of the mural became more visible now, and the story they told of man's progress from the slime more readable. The steady sound of eating continued all around. I was beginning to regret this.

Second servings of meat were handed round. Then the body builder asked for a third, and for the first time there was a human reaction, some laughing and polite table-banging. His girlfriend looked up and down the table, beaming with pleasure as the waiter hurried towards the couple with another plate of meat and an arch expression on his face. 'What an extraordinary man,' the girlfriend said, white teeth protruding, 'to have a third portion.'

I offered the tortoise couple on the other side of the table some pickled salad from the bowl in front and they jolted into life. 'No, no, after you,' the man said. 'The meat is very good,' said the old woman, to him rather than me, pulling a piece of fat from her mouth and adding it to the mound on the side of her plate. 'Yes, isn't it,' he agreed. 'Are you going to ask for some more?' she said. 'Everyone's onto their second and some are onto their third helpings.' 'No,' he said and touched his stomach. 'Yes,' she responded, 'you have some more. We have paid for it.' 'No, no,' he said again and shook his head. The man with the luxuriant black hair ran his comb across his head for the hundredth time.

The tortoises heaped salad onto their plates and began to chew, and I could hear their false teeth clicking.

When the cheese was served, Albert came and sat with us. There was a Montuno, a Cuban-assembled motor car which looked rather like a Mini-Moke parked beside the coach.

'What's it like?' I asked him.

'Shit,' he said quietly, 'but everything we make is shit. Our furniture is shit. Our jam is shit. Our roads are shit. Our shoes are shit . . .'

The meal was over, everyone fled the table to the shadow cast by the *mogote* and, with their backs to the illustration of man's evolution, they again started playing charades.

★

We left Viñales intending to take the coast road to Havana. It was a bright morning. In the distance there were mountains in every direction, but we were on a valley road which twisted and turned. We passed two or three curing platforms, hung with tobacco leaves, dry and curled like kippers, and several sheds with silvery corrugated roofs, which reflected the sun back at us. In one field, a tobacco farmer was being photographed by tourists.

We continued our journey north until we hit the edge of the coastal plain, where we turned east. The road became straighter and busier. We passed several *gauchos* trotting along on scrawny ponies, and carts pulled by donkeys or oxen, one with wheels which had been cannibalised from a Chevrolet. After the village of La Palma, there were valleys of evergreens, and the car was filled with the clean smell of pine and spruce. Finally, we left the valleys behind and came right out onto the coastal plain, flat, dusty and planted with green cane which swayed gently in the offshore breeze. In the distance was the smoking chimney of Central Manuel Sanguily where the cane was ground into sugar, and the sweet, cloying odour of molasses carried for miles across the countryside. There was also a glorious piece of roadside Americana: a sign advertising Pajarito Beach, with a picture of a girl in a Fifties bathing costume, wearing winged sunglasses and sitting on the sand beside a beachball. It was a rare survivor, for the roadside billboards which had once carried advertisements in the best traditions of America now carried moral and political exhortations. We had already passed several with texts such as, '*Ahora sí vamos a construir El Socialismo*' ('Now we are going to construct Socialism'), and now, outside the town of Las Pozas, we came across a billboard showing 'woman' studying, labouring and doing military training. The accompanying text read '*La Mujer Pinuereña Combatiente en Todos Los Frentes*' ('The Pinarian Woman [i.e. from Pinar del Rio province] Fighting on all Fronts'). In Las Pozas itself the streets were almost empty, except for a single female struggling in the heat, a yoke across her shoulders from which hung two buckets of water. If 'woman' was going to learn to use a microscope, as she was shown doing on the billboard, first she was going to have piped water.

We followed the road on. There was only cane growing as far as the eye could see: great, green swaying oceans of it, for mile after mile after mile. Nothing broke the monotony apart from the centrals, blue-black smoke billowing from their high chimney stacks, hoardings urging '*Con eficacia, más azúcar*' ('With efficiency, more sugar'), and long lines of oxen and carts waiting patiently in the sun for their loads of cane to be transferred to rusting rolling stock. The railway lines which carried these sugar trains ran across the road, ungated. Outside Cabanas, a man with a red flag motioned us to stop in front of one of them. We did, and turned off the engine. The rails started to sing, we heard a huffing, puffing noise that I hadn't heard since childhood, and over the top of the cane we saw curving towards us a plume of white smoke. It was a steam train destined for Central Abraham Lincoln, the linesman said, and it was pulling several dozen wagons with rusty wheels which sent up clouds of bright, yellow sparks. It took several minutes to pass and on the footplate of the last wagon, with their legs dangling down, were three men who shouted and waved a rum bottle at us.

Just outside Mariel, a town another thirty kilometres down the coast, there was a large Moorish-looking building on a hill surrounded by palms. With the blue sky behind and the burning sun above, it was like something out of *Beau Geste*. The town beyond was not. It was all docks and factories and dusty, thirty-foot-high pictures of Ché. If Mariel is known at all abroad, it is because in April 1980, during President Carter's administration, which had seen a tentative normalisation in relations between the US and Cuba, this was the site of the Mariel boatlift, when 120,000 Cubans were permitted to board small craft, and sail away to Florida. When the Cuban government put a stop to the operation—perhaps they hadn't expected such a large exodus?—there were still another quarter of a million Cubans who had registered their intention to leave. The boatlift was underpinned by the wish on the part of both governments to bring together divided families. But it has subsequently become another source of tension between the two countries, with the US accusing Cuba of having exploited it to send all her worst criminals to Florida.

With one exception the rest of the journey was boring. At El Salado, a resort twenty-five miles west of Havana, I spotted a 1957 Bel Air sports sedan V8. It had a green-and-white two-tone body, white upholstery and a white steering wheel. Its private Cuban owner (all the cars are privately owned) must have devoted all his spare time to keeping it immaculate; it could have come straight from the showroom.

After El Salado we met the very outer reaches of Havana's urban sprawl.

10

The POW

After we had checked into the Hotel Colina I went outside to walk around the block. As I stood on the pavement thinking about which direction I wanted to go in, a man came up to me. He was about sixty, and wore a Sam Browne belt and a baseball hat.

'You speak English?' he said. He had a pronounced Southern American accent. 'You staying in this hotel?'

'Yes.'

'Me too, and I wonder could you give me some advice about this black-market thing. I've got these kids over there and they say they want to give me five times the official rate for my dollars.'

About twenty yards away three youths stood in a cluster looking shifty and pathetic at the same time.

'I want to know if this is on the level,' said the man.

We started to stroll towards the university steps at the back of the hotel. He told me his name was Rod. I told him he was being offered the usual rate but sometimes it could go to seven to one. When I finished he said, 'Seven to one. You reckon I could stick them for that?'

We got back to our starting point outside the hotel doors. The youths were in the same place. Their faces lit up when they saw us.

'Seven pesos to the dollar,' he said, laughing to himself, 'here we come,' and hitching his belt, stalked forward.

At breakfast in the hotel dining room the next morning, Rod came up to our table.

'I did pretty good yesterday afternoon,' he said and winked. He asked if he could sit down.

Rod was a retired veterinarian and a resident of San Francisco, California. His home state was Texas.

'I've been in some pretty weird places in my time,' he said, unfurling his napkin. 'I like seeing cities from the back of a motorcycle but I guess that's not possible here in Old Havana.'

After we'd ordered I told him how good his Spanish was. It was.

'Oh yeah. I've got a pretty convincing accent owing to having spent the first five years of my life in Chile, I guess. That was before Texas. When it comes to speaking the language, I kinda got the advantage on you there,' he continued, and laughed. He laughed after everything he said.

We spoke about the US love affair with automobiles, and I asked Rod if he'd noticed all the old Fifties US cars in Havana?

'What are you talking about? I've only seen one old car,' he said, and laughed. 'But then you get three witnesses to a crime, they all swear they're telling the truth in court, and they all end up saying completely different things.'

He laughed again, long and hard. This was a really good joke. Tears came to his eyes. He wiped them away. 'Everybody sees things differently,' he said, and laughed yet again.

Rod had been a flyer in the war. His bomber was hit somewhere over Germany, and he was a bit hazy about that part of it. He jumped out of the aeroplane but he didn't pull his ripcord immediately. He knew parachutists high in the sky were often strafed by fighter planes. He waited. There were ten of them in his bomber and they all escaped safely, except for one who got a few puncture marks in his legs from a reception party of irate German farmers with pitchforks.

He was put in a camp with 10,000 men. It was in a place no one has ever heard of. Even Germans he'd subsequently met hadn't heard of it: 'And you wouldn't either,' he said to me. It was way out east somewhere, way out. As the Russians approached in 1945, all the POWs were marched out on a night when it was forty degrees below.

'That was a memorable night,' he commented, and laughed.

'How did you come to Cuba?' I asked.

'I just went to the little old Cuban embassy in Mexico City and got me a visa, hopped on a plane, and over I came. It was as simple as that.'

'Americans aren't meant to come here,' I said naively.

'No. No. Uncle Sam doesn't say you can't come here. Just you can't spend your dollars here. But they're crazy here for the dollars. So they don't stamp your passport.'

He laughed long and hard. It was the best joke of all.

*

In the middle of the afternoon, Henry came pushing into the foyer. He was wearing a tight cheesecloth shirt over his square chest, and now I was seeing him for the third time I saw his head was also square.

'Maspoton, very good for shooting, bouff, bouff,' said Henry amiably.

'Don't talk about it.'

'You didn't like it, Carlos?'

I led him outside.

The car hadn't worked properly since it had stuck in the mud. The brakes were spongy; the timing was out, and the linkage which connected the accelerator pedal to the carburettor had snapped and had been mended with a piece of wire. Henry took the car away, and left us with an identical Lada. The new one had fewer rust patches and a lower mileage on the clock. Great, I thought.

Tyga and India came down from the bedroom. We got into the car. I put the key into the ignition. Nothing. Not even the oil light came on.

We walked round to the garage in a fury. Henry was sitting on a deckchair, out of sight, with a girl on his lap. Her blouse was undone. He didn't seem very pleased to see us.

'The new car, it's not working,' I said.

'How? I drove it to you.'

'Flat battery. It won't start.'

'You should have kept the other car. This is what happens when you change cars.'

Henry drove us back at breakneck speed and got out.

'Open the door,' he said.

He was holding a large monkey wrench.

I unlocked the car. He climbed in and started to beat the steering wheel and the steering column with the wrench. Nothing happening, Henry got out of the car, sweat pouring from his brow, lifted the bonnet and started to beat the battery terminals. Miraculously the dashboard lights came on.

'Hey, Henry very clever,' he said in English. 'You have problem, you come Henry. . . .'

We said goodbye, got into the car and drove down La Rampa. At the bottom we had to stop for a red light. As Tyga pulled on the handbrake, the electrics cut out. I got out and lifted the bonnet. Havana's busiest street was choked with rush-hour traffic. The lights changed and suddenly a thousand horns started up and every driver had his head out of the window and was shouting at us to get the fuck out of it.

'Hey, *amigo*,' I heard behind me.

I turned round and saw a rather spindly black youth in a leopard-skin teeshirt and Stevie Wonder sunglasses.

'You want to change money?' he asked.

'No, thank you.'

'I like your sunglasses. Eighty pesos, *amigo*.'

'No.'

I took off my shoe and hit the positive terminal as hard as I could. The dashboard lights came on and Tyga turned the key. I jumped into the car and as we moved away I heard through the window, 'Hey *amigo*, a hundred pesos. . . .'

We got onto the Malecón and started to drive west. There were no traffic lights and as long as we kept going we could be certain we'd be all right. With all the toing and froing to the garage, it was almost evening and the buildings looking out to the ocean were glowing pink from the sun. It was a phenomenon I had read about and disbelieved at the time. The buildings actually looked as if they were giving out this pinkness from inside. Waves crashed against the sea wall sending spray flying. The sun was a red hemisphere sinking rapidly towards the blue horizon. Just as it was about to slip out of sight, we descended into the tunnel under the river Almendares. When we came out into Miramar on the other side, the sun was gone, literally having vanished while we were underground, and it was dusk. There were no more façades oozing pink, just ordinary houses, and an imminent sense of velvety darkness.

We had come to this suburb because I had a letter for Titon Alea, the director of *Inconsolable Memories,* the film I had seen at university. My plan was to give him this letter, and ask him to introduce me to Edmundo Desnoes.

We found Titon Alea's house easily. His wife answered the door, I handed over the letter and she asked us in. She brought us into the living room and we were given hot, sweet coffee in enamel cups which burnt our fingertips. There were bookshelves filled with books and pictures on the walls. I hadn't expected anything like this. Then my quarry appeared and he was equally unexpected: a thin, ethereal-looking man, when I'd expected someone solider and more bulky. He was wearing real jeans, and looked like a person who could survive quite happily at Cannes or the Los Angeles Film Festival. He sat down on the edge of a chair and started talking about an Indian film director who was in Havana and was giving a lecture that evening.

'Would you like to go?' I heard him asking.

I realised I should not have come. The reality of Cuba had superseded my memory of Desnoes' book, although I still thought it was a fine work. I was not interested in going to a lecture or being amongst those who talked about such things. That was too like the world I had come from.

'I don't think so,' I said, and invoked India's bedtime as the reason for being unable to go.

Then the unexpected happened. In the corner there was a woman asleep in a rocking chair. She had a blue pillow, which looked as though it had a medical purpose, under her neck, which Titon and his wife had been adjusting ever since we'd arrived. Now she woke up and, quite unprompted, started to talk about Edmundo Desnoes.

'An old, dear friend,' she said. 'He's left Cuba you know and gone to live in New York.'

We said our goodbyes and went outside. It was now pitch dark. I beat the battery terminals with a piece of two-by-four which I found lying in the gutter and the car came to life. We retraced our steps, passing under the Almendares river, and found our way to a restaurant in Vedado called El Cochinito.

There was a queue at the entrance. Several young men came up and asked us if we would like to change money. The other people standing in the queue didn't appear to be at all interested in these approaches. We said no, in any case. This was a dollar restaurant.

After forty minutes of waiting, Tyga went to look over the hedge into the open-air part of the restaurant. A third of the tables were empty. We slipped out of the queue, went through the hedge and took one of the empty tables. We were served immediately. The meal consisted of large, greasy pieces of pork and *moros y cristianos*—Moors and Christians, rice with black beans—the Cuban national dish. At the next table an old black man sat drinking by himself. He was a happy drunk, smiling and wrinkling his nose and shouting out words of encouragement to the three plump men serenading a distant table. When he finished his bottle of beer, he tried to whistle to the waiter for another but he couldn't purse his lips together properly. Then he saw we had noticed. Despite being intoxicated, he tore his placemat with '*Gracias por su visita*' written on it in half, and made two beautiful, paper boats. He lurched over with these, presented one to India and one to Tyga, and shook all our hands. This was authentic, I thought, in a way that the earlier part of the evening had not been. The real Cuba. It was of course no more the real Cuba than Henry with the girl on his lap, or the money-changer with the Stevie Wonder sunglasses. It was just an old drunk being agreeable to three tourists.

We asked for the bill and the waiter brought it on a saucer. I didn't ask what currency he wanted to be paid in. I assumed it would be dollars. We'd read about this place in our tourist guide. It had to be. I counted out several single-dollar bills, green and grubby and bearing the words, 'In God We Trust'. The waiter came back to pick up the saucer and winced. This was a restaurant with no *mecanismo* and we had no pesos.

We sent the waiter off and I went out onto La Rampa. Whenever I'd walked it, I'd been accosted and asked to change money every few minutes. Now of course there was nobody of the kind I wanted to meet. Only young lovers, strolling along with their arms over one another's shoulders, and knots of soldiers. Just when I was beginning to think I would either have to go back to the Colina or ask the waiter if we could wait until the next day to settle the bill, I heard a voice say, 'Hey buddy.' I turned round and saw it was Rod. He was with three white Cuban youths. We exchanged pleasantries and I explained our situation to him.

'I'll be darned,' he said, and laughed. 'Maybe I can help you out. You got any film? This kid wants me to get him some.' Rod jerked his thumb at a youth who was staring at us with his big, dark eyes. 'If you have, sell him.'

As it happened, we did. I got the roll of Kodachrome from Tyga's handbag and sold it for sufficient to pay for the meal and have enough left over to buy everyone a bottle of beer.

When we went back to the car later, the engine started straightaway, without the battery needing to be hit.

11

Friday the Thirteenth

I should have known from the date to have stayed indoors. We were in the car somewhere between Vedado and Miramar, lost in the one-way system. It started to rain, torrentially. Then the yellow light began to flash, warning that the tank was empty. The idea of running out of petrol in a Havana rainstorm was unthinkable. In the first petrol station we went to they only had diesel. In the second, a dwarf with a hoarse voice said they were out of everything. With the third we hit bingo but it was pandemonium.

A classic 1950 Raymond Loewy sedan and a 1951 Oldsmobile Super 88 faced one another at a pump, each trying to make the other go back. A motorcycle forced its way between their bumpers and got to the pump. We were behind a rare 1953 Chrysler New Yorker with a huge tank which took several minutes to fill. Finally, the cap went on.

'*Cuarenta litros por favor*,' I said, recalling Henry's assurance that our car took forty litres.

'*Momentito.*'

'*Cuarenta litros.*'

'*Si, si.*'

There was a long discussion between the attendant and the driver of the Chrysler. Finally they went into a huddle and large quantities of petrol coupons and money went back and forth.

'*Cuarenta litros por favor,*' I repeated.

'*Si, si.*'

The attendant wandered off, jingling his change.

'*Cuarenta. . .*'

'*Si, si, si. . .*'

He nonchalantly pulled a lever. The rain was pouring and on Linea the traffic was roaring through the wet. An open lorry passed with a dozen men in the back in sodden shirts and shapeless straw hats.

The tank took thirty-five litres but each pre-paid coupon was for twenty. I gave him two and asked for change for five back.

He shrugged.

'I'll come back tomorrow for the rest.'

He shook his head. No change.

We drove to the edge of Old Havana and parked in the Calle Neptune. Rain sheeted down from the sky and streams cascaded along the gutters. We found an open bar-cum-cafeteria but they had nothing for sale except boxes of matches. On the empty shelf behind the counter, a large handwritten sign prohibited gambling of all kinds.

We went back outside and stood in the entrance of the Roseland department store. Apart from a few saucepans and some dusty glasses, the enormous display windows were empty. I watched a few people running in the rain with newspapers or plastic bags over their heads, and filthy buses sloshing by, crowded with people, the windows covered with condensation. I thought about the trouble we'd had getting petrol, and not being able to get anything in the bar, and the empty shop windows, and suddenly everything combined

★

together to produce the single thought: this is a nightmare.

In the afternoon we were standing outside the hotel under the arches, sheltering from the same rainstorm. On the other side of the street there were giant bouquets of flowers eight feet high leaning against the wall, cordoned off with wooden fences. In the road alongside them a phalanx of soldiers marched on the spot, one shouting slogans, the others chanting back in unison. A large crowd had gathered to watch. This was an important day, the anniversary of the attack by students from the nearby Havana university on the life of Fulgencio Batista. This is what happened.

Castro sailed from Mexico to Cuba in the *Granma* in 1955 and afterwards set up, with great difficulty, a revolutionary army in the mountains to the south-east of the island. However, much of the sabotage and anti-Batista activity outside this area was not the work of his 26 July Movement but of other groups. There was a strong group in Havana who supported Prío, the president whom Batista had ousted in 1952. The leader was Carlos Gutiérrez Menoyo. But the most important and active elements in the non-Fidelista opposition were the Havana university students and the Directorio Revolucionario (with many members from the university). This last was democratic, middle-class, anti-communist and Catholic, despite what has been suggested about them. In 1957 these bodies and a few Auténtico party supporters threw in their lot for a direct attack on the Presidential Palace. The soldiers marching in the rain and the bouquets of flowers were part of the thirtieth-anniversary celebrations.

The plan was simple. It was to be a medieval-style coup. Corner Fulgencio Batista in his palace and murder him. It also offered the Directorio the opportunity to steal the initiative from the Fidelistas in their mountain stronghold in the Sierra Maestra. Fidel Castro had recently given a long interview to the US journalist Herbert Matthews, which on publication had made him something of an international figure.

On 9 March the conspirators began to gather in an apartment rented by Carlos Gutiérrez. The Soviet poet Yevtushenko, who heard of the gathering second-hand, described it in *A Precocious Autobiography*:

> Each had his favourite occupation—one was reading, another writing poetry, others were playing chess. Among the revolutionaries were two painters, a realist and an abstract artist. They painted, arguing furiously (though, in view of the special conditions, in whispers), and very nearly came to blows. But when the final instructions arrived, both the realist and the abstract painters went to fight for the future of their country and were killed together.

They were Luis Gómez Wangüemert and José Briñas, and Yevtushenko got it wrong: the first survived.

There were seventy-eight attackers in all and naturally, with such numbers, Batista discovered what was afoot. His knowledge came from intercepted telephone calls. His response was to send a message through the secret police to Cándido Mora who sat in the House of Representatives. The message was for Cándido's brother Menelao, and Menelao's son Albert, who were among the conspirators. The rebels decided to strike immediately. On the day in question, unaware the attack would be in broad daylight, although he knew something was coming, Batista was reading *The Day Lincoln was Shot*.

The attack was to be in two waves. The first, numbering about fifty, drove to the palace in a variety of vehicles, including a van marked 'Fast Delivery'. The second wave was to number twenty-six. Meanwhile, Echevarría the Directorio's leader and accomplices were to take over Radio Reloj, literally Radio Clock. The usual minute-by-minute announcements of the time with the news and advertisements in between would cease and in their place would come a dramatic announcement of the dictator's demise.

The first wave shot their way into the palace and up to the presidential offices. Not finding Batista at his desk, they realised he had gone up to the 'presidential suite' on the next floor. Unfortunately, even though they'd got from Prío plans of the palace layout, the staircase proved impossible to find. There was a very good reason for this. There wasn't one.

The attackers then realised Batista had concentrated his defences on the top floor. The telephone rang and Gómez Wangüemert answered and declared enthusiastically, 'Yes it is true, the palace has fallen. Batista is dead. We are free.' The caller was a woman journalist in New York who'd been telephoned there with news of the attack. The second wave, meanwhile, had not even arrived. As soon as the firing had begun, the palace had been surrounded by policemen and soldiers who must have given the impression to those outside that they were the attackers. Over in Vedado, Echevarría had captured the radio station. He broadcast an excited message which included the remark, 'The presidential palace has been taken by our forces and the dictator had been executed in his den.' Listening to his wireless in the Sierra, Fidel Castro remarked, 'Something big is going on in Havana,' but it remains in dispute whether he really was ignorant of what was happening or whether he encouraged it.

After finishing his message, Echevarría blew up the central control panel. Attempting to escape, he was immediately shot dead by the police in the street outside. Back at the palace, the men on the second floor went on firing and throwing grenades and then retreated. Most died on the marble staircase. Only three of the men who got as far as the presidential office came out of the palace alive. Firing continued through the afternoon, with the soldiers around the palace shooting indiscriminately. They wounded several bystanders. There was a lot of blood in the little park near the palace at the end of the day—the very spot where the *Granma* now stands—and many of the nearby buildings were chipped with bullets.

The death toll was thirty-five members of the palace guard and one US tourist who came out onto his hotel balcony to see what was happening. In the aftermath an unknown number of students, suspects and known members of the opposition were rounded up, using the attack as a pretext, and shot—many, as usual, after being horribly tortured. The most sensational retributory murder was that of ex-Senator Pelayo Cuervo, nominal president of the Orthodoxo Party. The next morning he was found dead by the lake in the exclusive Havana Country Club. Papers apparently found by the police on Echevarría's body had implied he was to become the next provisional president if the attack was successful.

All these deaths, sadly, were the result of a scheme which could not work. The third floor of the palace was only approachable by lift, and the attackers could never have got up there once the lift was blocked at the top. The lift was a modification installed by Batista since Prío's incumbency, and proves the point that old intelligence is never to be relied upon. The attackers made no provision for the retaliation they got, nor did they arrange any hiding places. It was the 26 July Movement who helped with the wounded. They also took into protective custody a lorryload of the Directorio's arms which had not been used and these soon found their way to the Sierra and the Fidelistas. One ex-Directorio member subsequently maintained they were stolen. But whatever went on, the anniversary of the attack became one of the most important dates in the revolutionary calendar.

An old newspaper seller was pushing his way through the crowds sheltering, like ourselves, from the rain.

'*Granma, Granma* . . .' he shouted desultorily.

He was competing with the soldiers, now being led by a woman.

Buses stopped and people alighted and the crowd around us swelled. A damp couple leant against a column embracing, her lipstick on his chin. The old *Granma* seller in his green-tinted spectacles with condensation behind the lenses sat down on the hotel steps and lit a cigar. In little toy police cars parked by the kerb there were police, and outside there were more police in wet oilskins.

We had been invited out to dinner and went upstairs to get ready, leaving the gathering crowds and the rain falling on the street.

It was a long evening and we came back to the hotel very late. I sat down in the lobby to make some notes and was writing when Rod the ex-POW came in.

'I don't know what I was saying about there being no American cars the other morning,' he said. 'I've been seeing them everywhere since we had our talk,' he continued and chuckled.

Then he said, 'Guess you saw Castro earlier?'

'. . . ?'

'Oh,' he said and laughed. 'You saw all those people and the flowers and the soldiers . . .'

'We went out to dinner,' I interrupted.

He laughed again. ''Bout nine o'clock, old Fidel moseyed along, spoke from the university steps just around the corner. I'm Room 402, I know you're 302. I had a fantastic view, and so would you if you'd been in. I guess it ain't much good now crying over what's gone, but I wouldn't have missed it for the world. Fantastic. Can that Fidel speak. He must have been going for two hours without notes. Can you imagine Ronnie doing that? He couldn't last two minutes . . .'

'Well, I've got to get my beauty sleep, so I'll just be saying goodnight.'

That was our Friday the Thirteenth.

12

America

That Saturday night we found her road in the southern suburb of Havana, just as she said, by the old Fifties neon sign that read 'Superlunch'.

We climbed out of the car. She emerged from the low Florida-style house. She'd been watching, waiting for us to arrive. She began to undo the string which held the gate shut.

America was a small, old woman, with bow legs and a brooch at the neck of her paisley blouse. Her hair was short and black, her arms firm and unwrinkled. She was over eighty. Tyga and her grandson, Alex, had grown up together in the Middle East. This was why we had come.

She had brought us past the wrought-iron front door and sat us down in the vestibule, just inside. There was a huge, swaying, dusty chandelier. The other part of the room, where the dining table stood, was screened off with a sideboard piled with books. That area was for the family. It was an intimate place. Where we sat was not.

America spoke English slowly and precisely, with a strong American accent. She had neat, quite even teeth that met exactly.

'Are you well?'

'Yes, I'm very well.'

'You look well.'

'Yes, I am very well.'

'How come you look so well?'

'I don't look that well, do I?'

'You do.'

'Do I?'

'I promise.'

'You promise.'

She shrugged and wiped her hand over her face. I changed the subject to her family.

'I have three children. Christina lives here in Cuba. Anita and Raoul live in the United States.'

'Oh yes.'

'Anita has a son called Alex. Well, you know, Tyga. Until he was six years old, Alex lived right here in this house with me. This was after the revolution. Then his mother came and took him away to *Egipto*.'

'Egypt.'

'Yes, and that boy was out of Cuba until he was seventeen. Then he came back. He came here. He said, 'I want to live with you, granny,' and the Cuban government said he had to stay ten years without seeing his mother who was in the US by then. What boy can go ten years without seeing his mother? He went back to the US.'

She rubbed her eyes with her wrists.

'Now he's the *jefe* in a company. They make computers out in Oakland, in California. He's so important he wears this box on his belt. . . .'

She described it with a beautiful movement of her hands.

'. . . And when it flashes, he has to go wherever it says. Yes, it sounds amazing. It's a box, this size, on his belt, and it tells him where to go.'

She sat straight in her chair, her feet flat and tidy on the floor.

'I was married when I was nineteen,' said America, unprompted. 'We went to Pittsburgh in the United States straight away. That was 1923. My husband had a barbering business and that's where the children were born and went to school. We stayed twenty-five years and when we came home we had $50,000. We bought a real nice house with it, in Miramar. It had three rooms downstairs and a kitchen and a water closet, and four rooms upstairs and a bathroom and a water closet. A room for each of the children. But they wanted to go back to the US, that's what they knew, and Raoul and Anita went there and Christina left home too. Then it was just the two of us.

'Now my husband never believed in automobiles. "They're too much trouble," he always said. "They need gasoline. They need oil. The tyres need to be pumped up once a week." We had no car. But the buses from Miramar were terrible. Long queues whenever I wanted to take one downtown. So we sold the house in Miramar and bought this one here in Casino Deportivo, on the way to the airport.'

She paused and then she said, 'Fifty-seven years we were married.'

She savoured the figure and looked across at us.

'He always went to the store for me,' she said. 'He always did the buying. Come.'

We followed her from the lobby past the sideboard piled with books to the pale green dining table hemmed in by the huge Soviet refrigerator.

She produced a big jam jar in which she had mixed *mojitos*, a cocktail made with rum and lemon juice. She poured the drink into glasses with leaves of mint. They were small and leathery and dotted with black spots. We started to drink.

'I have been to Vienna, twice. . . .'

She held up two crooked fingers.

'. . . To stay with my daughter Anita when she was out there working. Come. . .'

I followed her tiny figure across the room to one of the sideboards. She bent slowly from the middle and pulled open one of the doors. Inside, the shelves were crammed with yoghurt containers. She picked one out and showed it to me.

'Every day I'd go to the park with my daughter and we'd have our yoghurt. And every day we'd just throw away the pots and one day I thought, "This isn't right," and I said, "I'm taking them home with me." Anita said, "What, you're taking them back to Cuba?" She thought I was mad.'

America drew herself up.

'After that I collected them every day.'

She waved the pot she'd been showing me.

'My daughter never thought I would, but I did.'

The pot went back in the sideboard and the door was shut.

She sat down at the table.

'When I came back from Vienna that time, I had $3,000. At Havana airport there was a Dollar shop. I bought a colour TV for my granddaughter Denise. A refrigerator. Fans. Many things. I had $1,000 left over. A customs official found the money in my handbag and made me go to the bank and change the dollars. I only got 800 pesos. What can you buy with that? In the stores, a Soviet fridge is 3000 pesos but in the Dollar shops a fridge is only a few hundred dollars.'

She shook her head.

'When I bought this fridge. . . .' She pointed at the Soviet refrigerator behind us. '. . . Did I sell the old one over there?'

She waved at the US fridge in the kitchen.

'No, I've kept everything. I've never sold anything I've bought in my life,' she said emphatically.

The inference was clear. She was not a black marketeer.

America put a bottle of *vino quinado*, a sweet Cuban wine, on the table. She poured herself a tumbler and drank it in one. After a couple more glasses she leant over and stared at me.

'Why are you in Cuba?' she asked.

'To write.'

'You won't write anything bad, will you, not about Fidelito?'

She went over to the huge photograph of the leader on the sideboard, patted the glass and chuckled.

'I never saw a door when I was a child. We were so poor we didn't have one. Never went to school. The first time I wore lipstick and powder was when I married. In Pittsburgh, girls who worked downtown would come to the house in the morning. "Make me a dress like this," they'd say and they'd have a picture from a magazine. I'd make it for them in a day and they'd wear it in the evening.

'After the revolution, everything happened just as Fidel said. You didn't need dollars any more if you were sick. Everyone got to go to school and learned to read and write. Cuba is a better place than it ever was.'

She picked up the frame with the photograph and kissed the glass.

'Ah, my Fidelito.'

I was both convinced and suspicious. Cuba was a better place and her confidence was real. Yet it was alarming that her views and the state's should be so convergent. This suspicion was confirmed at the end of the evening when she leant forward and suddenly, in Spanish, said:

'Anita sent me five dollars before I took the aeroplane to Vienna the last time. The inflight film cost five dollars. But at José Martí I was searched. They found the money and took it away. I never saw the movie.'

The state which provided and the state which penalised were two different entities and America made no connection between the two; a symptom of indoctrination, I thought. Fidel was flawless, it was just his crazy officials who made the citizen's life difficult; the same schizophrenia that afflicted medieval rebellion. Uprisings were never against the king but always against his corrupt courtiers. What Fidelito did had nothing to do with the regulation that if Alex was to stay in Cuba it had to be for ten years or with having to change $1,000 into 800 useless pesos, or with having the money for the inflight film taken away. Fidelito was God.

We said goodbye. The gate was untied. We drove off. On the way back we passed factories and gas stations and the empty Plaza de la Revolución, the centre of government, where the creator of America's world, her beloved Fidelito, I imagined, was sleeping soundly in his apartment.

13

Varadero

We left Havana on Monday. We drove along the Malecón, took the tunnel under the harbour, and emerged on the eastern side. Our destination was Varadero, a resort about sixty miles further along the northern coast.

A friend had given us advice. On the far side of the tunnel, we would find ourselves on a six-lane highway. We would see a small turning off it, marked Playa del Este. Strange as it might seem, that was the road we were to take for Varadero. If we stayed on the highway, it would take us in the opposite direction, doubling back under the city and ending in Mariano on the other side.

But when we got to the turning marked Playa del Este it looked so small, and there was no mention of Varadero, and the road we were on was a huge six-lane carriageway. Surely there was a mistake? Carry on, I thought.

An hour later we indeed found ourselves in the western suburb of Mariano.

We turned the car on a bridge over a muddy brook where boys were fishing with rods of bamboo.

When we finally got onto the right road, the way east took us past one of the ubiquitous shooting ranges. From the frequency of these I had begun to imagine Cuba as a militarised society. This range had metal cut-outs of tanks, helicopters and infantrymen in US army metal hats, but the complete picture undercut the first impression because, among the targets, which were painted white, there was a herd of defecating cows, unconcernedly loosing off their stools all over the range. Beyond here the landscape was rolling. There were quarries for red stone, slogans on the old advertising hoardings about Fidel and the party marching towards the year 2000—the same as on the matches—and parked outside a café called the Cafeteria Americas, a 1955 New Yorker sedan, which was a Chrysler car, with a pillar-box-red body and a cream roof.

Somewhere near Santa Cruz del Norte, a girl was standing by the side of the road trying to thumb a ride. We pulled up in a cloud of dust and she climbed in. She was small and carried an Aeroflot bag.

Her name was Maria, and soon she was telling us about herself and giving us her opinions. There was no order to what she said; everything just tumbled out. The Cuban people were lazy because once they had a job it was forever and there was no incentive to work. She only had the clothes she was wearing, because the night before someone had broken into the room in Havana where she'd been sleeping, and taken her suitcase with everything in it. She was nearly thirty and had studied philology in Czechoslovakia for five years. Now she had returned, she could not find a job in her field, and was working as a translator for Czech geologists. Whatever the government said, there was serious unemployment in Cuba and we weren't to believe otherwise. She was on her way to her parents in Santa Clara for a few days. She had intended to take the bus, but in the Havana bus depot the queues were so long she'd decided to hitch to Varadero and try to pick up a bus there. Her economic situation was terrible. She was paid 190 pesos a month. After contributions to the Federación de Mujeres Cubanas (the Federation of Cuban Women), the CDR (the Committee for the Defence of the

Revolution), the Territoriales (the militia), and the Sindicato (the trade union in the workplace), she was left with 176 pesos a month. Food and rent in Havana took 120 pesos a month, which left her with just over 50 pesos a month to go to the cinema, buy cigarettes, and buy clothes. With a pair of jeans costing 150 pesos it was not enough. Life was very hard for the Cuban people and there was much discontent.

'To make ends meet, many Cubans turn to the black market, buying and selling dollars,' she said, and leant forward into the front of the car holding one wrist over the other.

'One year for each dollar they are caught with,' she added dramatically.

I had no idea what to make of her long, breathless diatribe. I was in the front passenger seat and I looked out of the front window. We were coming into the town of Matanzas (the Spanish word for 'slaughter'). Just in front of us was a policeman on his Italian motorcycle, spurs flashing on his heels, rocking backwards and forwards like a metronome as the road curved. There were people beside the road and I thought we'd stumbled into a political parade. Then I realised the crowd was a queue, a long, long queue. Maria saw them too and, catching my attention by squeezing my elbow, archly raised her eyebrows when I turned round to her.

She pulled an airmail letter out of her Aeroflot bag.

'I am learning Italian,' she said. 'Last year at Varadero I met an Italian couple. They were like you, husband and wife.'

She repeated this.

'We became very good friends. This is where they live.'

She pointed at the address on the back of the envelope.

'Do you know La Spezia in Italy?'

I said I thought La Spezia was a town where Byron had stayed.

'They invited me to Italy for a holiday,' Maria continued. 'They sent me money for the ticket. I went to immigration with the money and they said I couldn't go. They said Italy was a capitalist country.'

Her brown eyes filled with tears.

We were on a plateau of volcanic rock beside the sea, with oil derricks see-sawing on either side of the road, and pipes flaming in the distance. This was where all of Cuba's indigenous oil was produced.

A few miles later we came to the town of Varadero. The resort lies at the base of a long finger of sand which stretches twenty miles out into the Atlantic, a town of palm trees and big old hotels. A few US cars and a number of holiday-makers on Soviet bicycles cruised along the wide streets. In the 1930s the US industrialist, Irénée Dupont, bought many properties in Varadero and built an estate on the peninsula beyond the town. In the 1950s came the hotels, many US-financed, including the Varadero International, a close relation of Miami's Fontainebleau. After the revolution the speculative hotel-building stopped, and after President Kennedy's 'quarantine' in 1961, so did the US tourists.

We went through the town and passed out the other side. Before we dropped Maria at the bus station or found our house, we were going to visit the old Dupont mansion. Maria pointed out Fidel's Varadero house, a guard at the gate and aerials sticking out of its roof, and a moment later we passed through the gateway into the old Dupont estate and started to cruise along a straight road which rose and fell like a roller coaster. There were immaculate, undulating golf links on one side and the blue sea on the other.

A Chevrolet, a red 1952 DeLuxe Styleline sports coupé, rumbled past. The shadows of the palm trees lay across the cropped grass as if they'd been painted there. There was a distant view of two men swinging their golf clubs. It was like stumbling into a rich Miami suburb in the 1950s.

We neared the Dupont house. It was an elegant, white mansion. It overlooked a beach lined with palm trees. The sun was sinking and the crests of the waves were points of silver. All this had once belonged to one family of North Americans. After the revolution the house had been nationalised by the state and turned into an extremely grand restaurant, with the dining room on the first floor in the old library.

'That's where the servants lived,' said Maria, pointing to

dreary outbuildings which looked like a cross between stables and an almshouse. Of course, I thought, the servants of the Duponts would have lived worse than their masters and every post-revolutionary Cuban would be brought up to know that. But Maria's tone was utterly mechanical and quite unlike the way she'd been talking all afternoon. I sensed she was going through the motions out of habit.

At the top of the entrance steps, there was a flunkey in a Louis Quinze chair whose job it was to keep Cubans out. We spoke English very loudly and brought Maria in. We went to the bar in what had once been the wine cellar. The walls and the niches where the bottles had been stored were covered with new cement, and the customers' voices echoed off these surfaces. There were two or three South American women in flounced gypsy dresses with tight bodices which showed off their bosoms. Their escorts were neat men with impenetrable expressions. They were to go skiing at Easter but the ladies were tired of Bariloche in Argentina. Dupont has gone, only to be replaced with more of the same.

★

We had arranged to rent a room in a house in Varadero. We dropped Maria off and found it a couple of blocks away from the bus depot, at the end of a short street which ran down to the beach.

Casa C—— was made of yellow stone, two storeys high. Upstairs there were bedrooms with sloping roofs and tiny windows, and bathrooms filled with English sanitary ware, old, heavy and fed by lead pipes which chattered and rumbled when the taps were run. The atmosphere was similar to a run-down country house in Ireland. Downstairs was different. In the kitchen there was a gigantic US refrigerator, its door corroded by rust but still functioning within; a dilapidated stove missing its bakelite knobs—the gas controls were turned up and down with a knife; and an extraordinary freezer, circa 1950, which had long since been turned off because it gave terrible electric shocks to anyone who went near it. Piled in the cupboard and scattered on the worktops was an amazing array of culinary Americana. Aluminium saucepans, pressure cookers, whisks, ladles, ice-cream scoops, egg slicers, meat hammers, early electric mixers, omelette pans and plastic beakers, along with a great deal else which I didn't recognise. But whilst as a museum it was interesting, as a place to cook the kitchen was infuriating—only one sharp knife and no vegetable peeler.

The rest of the ground floor was taken up by a huge living room. There were two refectory dining tables with a wooden candelabrum hanging above, bookcases, and immense leather sofas hollowed with use and age. At the end of the room there were buckled french windows. They opened onto the garden with its dribbling shower, washing line, and rickety wooden sun-seats. A low wall split by cracks boxed in Casa C——, and beyond it lay the gentle incline of the beach and finally, a dozen paces away, the sea. The other guests were Raoul, a young Cuban, and Kate his girlfriend, and her two children. Kate was English and worked for the Cuban press agency, Prensa Latina.

The first morning I woke up and saw a sloping roof above, and heard the murmur of the sea. A few minutes later I found Raoul lying on the sand, below the garden wall, reading a book. We walked out into the water together and at waist depth slid down and started to float on our backs. Raoul was talking about the Cuban press. 'It tolerates no dissent,' he said. I noticed how warm the water was and how silky it felt on the skin, it was like no water I had swum in before.

When I came out I found Maria on the beach. She was a tiny figure, sitting on her haunches, her Aeroflot bag beside her, staring out to sea. Uncharitably, I found myself wondering if she had lingered in Varadero in order to attach herself to us. None the less, I asked her to come inside. When she said she wouldn't I sensed she knew what I'd just been thinking. Finally, I insisted she came in out of the sun, and sitting inside at one of the enormous dining tables, she told me there had been no room on the evening bus. She had had to stay overnight in a hotel. 'It was horrible,' she added, 'I had an argument with a policeman.' She wouldn't tell me what the argument was about, only that all policemen were awful. It was a verbal giveaway, the tip of an iceberg, there was a huge bulk of story beneath the surface. I kept questioning but I got no further, and I only found out about it all much later.

Towards midday Maria left, having extracted a promise to visit her.

★

Every morning in Varadero, at around ten o'clock, I would go with Tyga and India to the little *bodega* or grocery store on the corner of the bus-depot building. Here we would buy bread, butter, milk and eggs, which were all freely available, unrationed. This was what we lived off, along with what Kate gave us.

The woman behind the counter in the shop had a moustache and the curious habit of always serving two or three customers simultaneously. Sometimes we would see her with poor customers, men in filthy, frayed trousers and greasy hats, opening a packet of Popular cigarettes and counting them out ten, five or even two, and then giving them a few matches to take away.

On the third or fourth morning she gave India four *galletas*, the ubiquitous sweet biscuits sold loose, and then advised us to buy some.

'If you don't, you'll regret it,' she said, 'we'll soon be out of them again.'

As they were being weighed up and bagged, I looked at the shelves. There were gigantic jars of tomato paste, available only on the ration and essential for eating pasta, bottles of banana liquor, and bags of sugar, vanilla and macaroni. That was about all. The display under the glass-topped counter consisted solely of Sputnik razors and razor blades.

Our bill was written out on the corner of a coarse brown paper bag and added up twice. We paid[1] and went next door to the *puesto*. It was a tiny, dark, windowless room which sold fresh produce. As usual there were only potatoes and cabbages.[2] Because these were white they glowed faintly in the near darkness.

The proprietor was a black man in a straw hat with a gold front tooth. Hearing our appalling Spanish as we ordered, he lifted up a box hidden under the counter. It was filled with green peppers. He didn't need to tell us to buy because soon he'd be out of them. We ordered as many kilos as we thought we decently could without seeming to be greedy.

Outside again we blinked in the sun. We were now in the parking lot of the bus depot. Between two battered coaches, an old green 1953 Cambridge club sedan out of the Plymouth corporation, with the flow-through bumper lines and the one-piece windshield, stood with its bonnet up. Steam poured out of the engine and water cascaded from the radiator onto the tarmac. 'Cardenas', the name of the nearest town to Varadero, was painted on the roof above the windscreen, for this was a *maquina*, one of the inter-city taxis. The owner stood nearby with a baseball hat pushed well back on his head, staring in disbelief and pain and shouting, 'Why? Why? . . .' It was like an illustration from a Norman Rockwell cartoon.

A few steps further on brought us to the entrance to the ticket hall. Inside, passengers milled around the counters. A youth showed a friend the numbered ticket he'd been given, and they calculated how many buses before he'd get a seat.

They came down the steps past us and set off towards the *maquinas* standing in a row on the other side of the lot. They approached a bulbous 1950 Lincoln sports sedan distinguished by its sunken headlamps. It had 'Matanzas' written on it. We

---

[1] We had bought two litres of milk, seventy-five cents each; six eggs, twenty-five cents each; two loaves, eighty cents each; one packet of butter, eighty cents; and a kilo of *galletas*, eighty cents: total, six pesos twenty cents.

[2] They were in season and cheap. At other times of the year, they might have been expensive, scarce and/or rationed. During the journey I heard numerous complaints that Cuba's *puestos* offered appalling quality produce and little or no choice.

watched as they entered negotiations with the driver. He wouldn't leave until he had six passengers, he said—this was quite normal—and the youths turned away.

When we got home, I found Kate in the kitchen making Russian tea in an extraordinary strainer shaped like an auto-da-fé hat.

'We've got some peppers.'

'Whoopee,' she said. 'We'll have those tonight, we're going to have some of my meat ration.'

★

Cuba's rationing system can be interpreted—depending on the ideological view of the interpreter—as proof that the government is economically inept, or as proof that Cuba is a just society.

Cuba's per capita income in the 1950s—about $500 per person[1]—was higher than any other Latin American country except Venezuela (which had oil) and Argentina (which was relatively industrialised). There was plenty of food, and in terms of meat availability—*the* benchmark of prosperity in food terms among developed nations—the island could boast of seventy pounds per person annually, twice Peru's figure.

But for the poor, the landless and the marginal, perhaps two and a half or three million out of a population of seven million, life was economically harsh. Whilst seventy pounds of meat were theoretically available, in fact only four percent of the families of farmworkers ate meat regularly according to the Catholic University Association survey of 1956–57. Only two percent of such families consumed eggs on a regular basis (they had to sell their eggs instead), only eleven percent drank milk on a regular basis, and so on.

In pre-revolutionary Cuba, if you were wealthy you ate well,

---

[1] All statistics, unless otherwise stated, are taken from *No Free Lunch: Food and Revolution in Cuba Today*, Medea Benjamin, Joseph Collins and Michael Scott.

and if you were not you ate poorly. There are no official figures, but opinions incline to the view that the bottom twenty percent of Cuban society received about six percent of the national income, while the top twenty percent had about fifty percent of it.

The reason for these inequalities of income was the concentration of land, factories and so on in the hands of a small proportion of the population. In the 1950s this is how Cuban society was organised. First, the countryside. At the top were the owners of the sugar plantations and the cattle ranches. About nine percent of the farm owners possessed about sixty percent of the land. At the opposite end of the ownership scale, a good sixty percent owned seven percent of the land. Next down the ladder were about a hundred thousand tenants who owned no land at all but rented, often for exorbitant amounts. Finally, at the very bottom, there were nearly half a million farmworkers. They, along with their families, comprised about a third of the population.

Only about ten percent of these farmworkers were permanently employed. The rest were only certain of work during the cane harvest from January to May and were usually unemployed for the rest of the year.

In the cities there was a similar unemployed under-class (estimates of their numbers vary) who survived by washing cars, selling lottery tickets, stealing and begging. Above these were about a quarter of a million Cubans who lived off the tourist trade, as shoeshine boys, street vendors, prostitutes, pimps, pedlars and entertainers. Above them were the urban workers, about 400,000 of them and enjoying good incomes, on average about $1,600 a year, a high sum by Latin American standards. Next, there were those who worked in local or national government, about ten percent of all those employed. In 1950 an extraordinary eighty percent of the national budget was spent on their salaries. This type of work provided—besides a wage—numerous opportunities for personal enrichment. Finally, at the very top were the tiny majority who enjoyed the lion's share of the national income. Hugh Thomas, in his history, *Cuba*, estimates there were more Cuban millionaires—dollar millionaires—than anywhere else in the Americas south of Dallas.

In terms of housing, health care, education and literacy, the pattern in Cuba in the 1950s was exactly what one would expect with the distribution of wealth as it was. There was little food to eat if you were poor. There was nothing of anything else.

In the countryside, two-thirds of the houses were palm-thatched—which was probably not such a hardship considering the semi-tropical climate—and without toilets, which certainly was. Less than three percent of all rural houses had running water, and only one in fourteen families enjoyed electricity.

In the cities, the poor lived as squatters in makeshift shacks, or in cramped tenements. A fifth of Cuba's urban dwellers—and the average family size was five—lived in one room.

Education was dire. According to the World Bank, about 180,000 children started first grade but only about 5,000 entered eighth grade. By 1958 over half of Cuban children of primary-school age (six to fourteen) were not attending school at all. (The Latin American average was about thirty-six percent.) One in four Cubans over the age of ten could not read or write.

Onto this situation, one then has to graft Cuba's particular underdevelopment. Sugar is Cuba's principal industry, principal export, principal employer. Sugar was and is both Cuba's curse and her greatest asset. Cane thrives in Cuba's soil and climate like nowhere else in the world. It grew, and grows still, prolifically and effortlessly. It was a generator of sometimes fabulous wealth. For instance in 1920, the greatest year in the whole history of Cuban sugar production, the world price of sugar rose from nine and one-eighth cents a pound on 18 February, the first day of the harvest, to twenty-two and a half cents a pound on 19 May, the end of the harvest. It made plantation owners and investors rich. For the agricultural workforce on the other hand, it was a capricious provider. During the harvest it offered back-breaking round-the-clock employment, cutting or milling, but the rest of the year was a dead season with almost no work except for a little re-planting. *Sopa de gallo* (rooster soup) formed an important part of the rural diet during the idle months. It was a mixture of water and brown sugar.

At the turn of the century, Cuba was the largest producer and exporter of sugar in the world. By the 1950s she had slipped to seventeenth amongst the world's eighteen top sugar-producing nations. None the less, manufacturing sugar from cane remained the country's largest industry, and the entire economy was inextricably linked to it. For instance, the sugar estates and the mills were the principal customers of the railways. Half of all bank loans went to the sugar industry. Raw sugar and its by-products, alcohol and molasses and so on, accounted for eighty percent of the country's exports. When the world price of sugar fell, the country's economy went into spasm.

In 1955 US interests owned nine of the ten largest sugar mills, produced forty percent of the island's sugar and controlled fifty-four percent of the total grinding capacity. Standard Oil, Shell, Texaco, Procter and Gamble, Colgate-Palmolive, Firestone, Goodrich, Goodyear, Coca-Cola, Pepsi-Cola, Canada Dry and Orange Crush all had subsidiaries in Cuba. US firms directly employed 160,000 workers in the country itself. Overall, the US had a billion dollars invested in Cuba—an eighth of the total US investment in Latin America—and Cuba as a recipient of investment was second only to Venezuela. This is not taking into account the considerable *mafioso* involvement in Cuba which is impossible to estimate.

But more important than what the US owned (which in percentage terms had anyway been declining since the nineteenth century) was the fact that each year the US Congress made the single most important decision in relation to the Cuban economy. As they had since 1934, they set the quota of Cuban sugar that could be imported into the US market at the relatively high prices of the US domestic producers. Over the twenty-five years to 1959, Cuba exported about sixty percent of her sugar to the US. The economy was thus not only dependent on a single crop, but on a single customer.

The US quota did not come for nothing. In return for preferential entry into the US for some of its sugar (along with some of its rum and leaf tobacco which was tied to the same agreement), import duties on a large variety of US goods were cut; Cuba agreed not to increase existing duties on a number of other products; Cuban internal taxes on US goods were cut or reduced; and there was free conversion of pesos into dollars, which allowed capital to be moved easily out of the country.

In consequence of the quota agreement, Cuba lost the opportunity to compete with the US home industry on an economic basis. The agreement also bound Cuba to the US, and to the use of US goods. About eighty percent of Cuba's imports were coming from the US by the 1950s, everything 'from corn flakes to tomato paste; from nails and tacks to tractors, trucks, and automobiles; from thread to all types of clothing; from goods from Sears and other department stores to accessories for the home, fertilisers and insecticides for agriculture, and materials for industry and construction',[1] as Edward Boorstein, the US economist, put it. This in turn discouraged the development of a home manufacturing base.

Dependency on the US gave rise to a number of ironies. Cuba was an exporter of raw sugar yet imported confectionery. She exported tomatoes yet imported most of the tomato paste she needed. She exported fresh fruit and re-imported it in cans. Cuba produced vast amounts of tobacco and imported US cigarettes. Even Havana cigars were increasingly manufactured in the US in the Fifties. Cuba exported the leaf to Florida for US companies who had shifted there to avoid the high US tariffs on Cuban-produced cigars.

Cuba in the 1950s was a classic underdeveloped nation, and one of the severest symptoms of the malaise was the widespread hunger in the country. When the World Bank sent a study group to Cuba in 1950, Cuban doctors reported that forty percent of urban dwellers and sixty percent of those in the countryside were undernourished. Those who suffered in this way—or a great many of them—supported the Fidelistas because they thought

---

[1] *The Economic Transformation of Cuba*, Edward Boorstein.

this was a way they would get to eat properly. Those who weren't hungry and supported the Fidelistas did so because they wanted to see an end to the injustice of hunger. The revolution of the Fidelistas achieved fully what was expected of it on the issue of hunger, although no one before the revolution could have foreseen how radical that revolution was going to be in other ways.

★

The owner of the house in Varadero where we were staying was a tiny, dark woman. She stayed in the small extension at the back, facing away from the sea, while we, her paying guests, had the run of the place. At first the situation struck me as a basis for a West End play: bourgeois type stranded by the revolution, lives on, renting out her once-grand house by the sea while she survives in an outbuilding. This ridiculous fabrication died when I saw her one morning under her porch, curled up on the settee, a novel (I think it was by John Updike) propped open in front of her, and drinking her morning coffee from an exquisite porcelain cup.

Another morning she put her head round the door which connected her section with ours and I offered her some coffee.

'Oh yes,' she said, and we sat down at one of the long mahogany dining tables.

Her broad forehead tapered to a pointed chin. She was about fifty or fifty-five years old. She wore cerise-coloured lipstick.

'Oh, I see you have . . .' she said, and pointed to the novel *Infante's Inferno* by Guillermo Cabrera Infante which I was reading. The author was a Cuban and, after the revolution, was briefly head of the National Council for Culture and an executive of the Instituto del Cine, then, after 1966, settled in London an exile .

She continued:

'I can't understand the people who leave. How can they just turn their backs on their country and go? They don't like the system? Well, they should have stayed behind and tried to change it.'

'Maybe they didn't think they could change it.'

'But just to turn one's back. It's never made any sense to me. One has to be positive.'

'The reason most people left Cuba,' she continued, 'was not because of what they did before the revolution. It was because they didn't want to adapt to a new economic situation. It was very simple.'

'And your own family?' I asked.

She gave a marvellous shrug which said: Why ask? You know the answer.

'They didn't want to adapt,' she said.

'And you?'

Another shrug.

'When I told my family I wanted to stay they said, "What! You're crazy. You're a communist." But do I look like a communist? No, of course I'm not.'

She didn't. She was the owner of two houses. She was also sufficiently wealthy never to have to buy her food at subsidised rates on the ration, and she always shopped on the free or parallel market which was more expensive.

'My family said, "The communists will take everything you have away." Well . . .'

She pointed around the room, her room.

'They never took anything away which I used.'

This had the ring of the Cuban state, with its sincere, avuncular style.

'We had three places,' she said. 'The house in Havana, here and the farm. They said, "You can't keep all three places." I thought, "Well, the beach is better than the country. I get more out of it." So the farm went and here I am.'

'For those who left,' she continued, 'it has been hard. When the revolution came they thought it would be over in six months. They'd go to Miami, they thought. The children would learn a little English. Then the Americans would come back to Cuba and the country would go back to what it had been. Only the Americans never came back.

'Every ten years I meet my family in Costa Rica. My daughter too, she is in the States as well. When we meet up we have an unspoken agreement that we don't talk about Cuba. It would upset them too much.'

She looked at me with her large brown eyes.

'It is hard for them but there are difficulties for me here as well and they are not what you think.'

I wanted to ask her about them but at precisely that moment she looked at the wristwatch on her fine, brown wrist.

'My bus,' she said, 'it is leaving in five minutes,' and with that she vanished back to Havana.

Beyond the buckled french windows and the crumbling garden wall lay the sea, smooth and blue. I sat at the table thinking about B—— with her expensive foreign clothes, curled up with her painted toenails showing under the verandah, looking like an affluent member of 'the community', as the Cubans in exile are called. I would never know the nature of her struggle. Did she now regret not having left, or was her difficulty the disappointment that life had not turned out as she had expected? She was an optimistic woman who believed that change was possible and any system was malleable, and yet the Cuban one appeared to be immovable.

There was a bookcase in the corner. I went over and, from beside a Spanish edition of John Reed's *Ten Days That Shook the World*, I idly picked out a copy of the autobiography of Stefan Zweig, *The World of Yesterday*. Zweig, a Jew, an Austrian by birth, was a poet, essayist, playwright, novelist, and for a while librettist to Richard Strauss after Hofmannsthal's death. He was one of the best known German-speaking literary figures between the wars. He fled from Austria in 1933 and committed suicide in Petropolis, Brazil, in 1942 along with his second wife. There was a home-made dust-jacket on the book made of wrapping paper, which I later learnt had been put on the edition by B——'s mother.

The book fell open at a passage marked in pencil:

> I remembered a conversation with my publisher in Leningrad on my short trip to Russia. He had been telling me how rich he

> had once been, what beautiful paintings he had owned, and I asked him why he had not left Russia immediately on the outbreak of the revolution as so many others had done. 'Ah,' he answered, 'who would have believed that such a thing as a Workers' and Soldiers' Republic could last longer than a fortnight?' It was the self-deception that we practise because of reluctance to abandon our accustomed life.[1]

Here perhaps was a description of the difficulties B—— faced.

*

The new economic system to which neither B——'s family, nor tens of thousands of other Cubans, were willing to adjust was a socialist economy. It sought to increase the incomes of the poor, so they could buy more and eat better. The First Agrarian Reform law of 1959 was the first move in this direction. It granted some 100,000 tenant farmers, sharecroppers and squatters tracts of land for their own use, and it freed them from the obligation to pay rent to landlords. Simultaneously, it nationalised just over half of the privately owned land in the country to create state enterprises, and all-the-year-round jobs on these rose from 50,000 in 1959 to 150,000 in 1962. Sugar workers were also able to find work on the construction projects which the government was starting all over the country, during the dead season when the industry was at a standstill. A minimum wage in agriculture was also decreed. These and other measures gave farmworkers higher incomes than before the revolution. Only about a quarter of all rural workers earned more than seventy-five pesos a month in April 1958. By 1960 nearly sixty percent had achieved this.

In the cities, as opposed to the countryside, the government did not need to intervene, as wage increases were achieved by the unions. But, as in the countryside, there was a pattern of redistribution of wealth. By 1962 the lowest forty percent of

---

[1] *The World of Yesterday*, Stefan Zweig.

urban income-earners had enlarged their slice of the national income pie from six and a half percent (the 1959 figure) to seventeen percent.

Simultaneously there was legislation which enabled all households to have more of their income to spend on food and other essentials. The government made basic welfare free for everyone, that is schooling, medical care and social services. The government also made water, all sporting events, burials and even the public telephones free (for local calls).[1] Electricity, gas and public transport costs were lowered. The lottery and all other forms of gambling were outlawed. In 1960, under its Urban Reform Plan, the government decreed rent reductions of up to fifty percent. In 1962 it set the maximum rent that could be charged at ten percent of the income of the head of the household.

These measures, along with fuller employment, led to the transfer of fifteen percent of the national income from property-owners to wage earners in 1960 alone. A good many, but not all, of those who left Cuba in the early Sixties were on the wrong side of this equation.

With more money in more pockets there was a consequent rise in consumption, especially of food. Beef consumption alone went up fifty percent between 1959 and 1961. There were similar rises in the consumption of milk and pork.

The next stage, inevitably, was that supply failed to keep pace with growing demand. Agricultural production was handicapped by the departure to the US of those with administrative and technical skills who weren't prepared to adjust to Cuba's way of life. The newly created state farms and cooperatives produced less than they had done when they had been in private hands. In 1960 the US embargo on the export of most US goods to Cuba caused further widespread disruption to the island's agriculture, completely dependent on the US for machinery, pesticides, fertilisers, seeds and all sorts of other goods. To make the situation worse, there was also a fairly widespread pro-

---

[1] This did not last.

gramme of anti-Fidelista sabotage in the countryside. Fields of crops were burnt, cattle were slaughtered. Then came the invasion in April 1961 at the Bay of Pigs, diverting scarce resources into defence and lowering production even further.

The resultant shortages were felt particularly in the cities. Because there was less to buy after the embargo, small producers (tenants and sharecroppers) had less need for cash and so produced less for sale at the market. Meat began to disappear from city shops, and plantains (cooking bananas) were no longer sent every day from Oriente province to Havana.

Shortages fed further shortages, since the lack of one item led to an increase in demand for others. For instance, in 1961 when the root crop taro became scarce, there was a run on sweet potatoes.

The trade embargo—the single greatest contributing factor to the fall in production—also led directly to a fall in supply because Cuba had imported so much of her food from the US: seventy percent of her wheat, lard, rice, beans, poultry, eggs, onions and garlic. To find new sources for these products was extremely difficult. Consider pork lard, essential in the cooking of Cuba's national dish of pork, rice and beans. At the time of the embargo Cuba was importing eighty-five percent of her pork lard from the US, and when the government went to find alternative suppliers they found to their dismay that no one could supply as much pork lard and as cheaply. Cuba's food importation was also affected badly by the simple fact that with her principal trading partner, the US, being so close, the Cuban dock facilities were designed to handle short-haul craft which had come from New Orleans or Miami and were not geared up to receive ocean trade. During the early years the arrival of long-distance shipments of food often foundered because there was no warehouse big enough to put them in: the food either rotted or had to be given away. Finally, even when there was food available, its processing, packaging and distribution was often made impossible because the embargo ensured there were none of the machines, materials or trucks needed for the job:

> For the past few weeks there hasn't been a soft drink to be had anywhere. I never thought that the manufacture of soft drinks could be paralyzed just because there was no cork for the caps. That's what they say. That shitty cork I used to scrape off when I was a boy and then I'd flatten out the tin with a hammer, open two holes with a nail, and with a piece of thread make myself a disk that would spin and spin and was quite sharp. Once I almost lost a finger playing with it. Never, not then or ever after, could I have imagined how many insignificant things are necessary to keep a country running smoothly. Now you can see everything inside out, all the hidden entrails of the system. We're living suspended over an abyss; there are an almost infinite number of details that have to be controlled so that everything can flow naturally; it's overwhelming.[1]

In a free market the shortages would have led to higher prices. If this had happened in Cuba, the gains in living standards which urban and rural workers had achieved would have been lost, and there would have been a return to the situation as it had existed before. Those with high incomes would have eaten well, those without would not. Instead the government tried price controls. In March 1959 there were official prices set for milk, rice, bread and beef. In May, cheese, potatoes, pork, butter and some other items like soap were added to the list. Simultaneously, profit margins of ten percent and twenty percent respectively were set on wholesalers and retailers. In the following months, all remaining staples were added to the list of price-controlled foods.

It didn't work. Hoarding and profiteering became widespread. The government's next move, intended to stop speculation, was to nationalise the wholesale food business and many retail outlets. By 1961, 8,000 of these had been taken over. At the same time the government set up *tiendas del pueblo*, people's stores, in the countryside, to supply basic goods at official prices.

---

[1] *Inconsolable Memories*, Edmundo Desnoes.

There were 2,000 of these by 1961.

Having started to intervene directly in the economy, the government found itself, rather like the sorcerer's apprentice, with more and more demons to control than it knew how to cope with. The retail nationalisation programme and the *tiendas del pueblo* failed to curtail the black market (if anything, they increased it), and as supply problems multiplied, speculation increased. At this stage the government could have opted to make basic staples available to the poor at low prices. But the consequence of this would have been a dietary 'two nations', so instead they plumped for a rationing system for all Cubans.

In mid-1961 lard was the very first product to be rationed, when the government specified that the ration would be one pound per person per week. In March 1962, cooking oil, rice and beans were also rationed on a nationwide basis; toothpaste, soap and detergent in the twenty-six principal cities; and fish, eggs, chicken, beef, sweet potatoes, milk and root crops in Havana only. All these items were eventually rationed throughout the whole country, along with sugar, bread, salt, tobacco goods, cloth, clothing, shoes and most household items.

When rationing was introduced the government promised it would be short-lived. Officials were optimistic about increases in yield and production in agriculture. Some foreign experts supported them. It was widely believed rationing was an interim measure. It was not to be. Rationing remained (although bread, butter, eggs and milk did become freely available on the parallel market) and food remained scarce, just like the peppers withdrawn from their secret hiding place under the counter in the *puesto*, and carried home by us in triumph.

★

Every evening in Varadero, I used to go for a walk.

Towards six o'clock that day, I walked up to the avenue at the top of the road, crossed over to the bus station, and disappeared into the strange, suburban backwater of Varadero, the back part of the town along the fringes of the *autopista* which ran on to the end of the peninsula.

The bungalows here—all the dwellings were bungalows—were smaller than near the seafront. A woman was shouting angrily over a fence at two silent men in paint-spattered trousers, whilst her daughter played around a wooden kennel with a fluffy alsatian puppy. Chickens pecked around crazy-paving pathways. Old couples sat silently side by side on rocking chairs under porches or else the chairs were stood back to front on the porches, tilted against the wall so that any rainwater would drain away. This was one of Cuba's commonest sights. Two neighbours, male, were leaning on their respective gates, admiring a US car parked by the kerb.

Drawing closer, my heart started to race. There were the same fins, pronounced but not outrageous, the same chrome lengths of trim running above the rear wheels and cutting off a third of the way along the flank (a wonderful conceit of the design), and the same rear windscreen which curved on into the body of the roof. Could it be an Eldorado Brougham? I walked quickly up to it, only to find that my powers of distance identification were still hopelessly inaccurate: it was a 1958 Oldsmobile Dynamic 88 Holiday four-door hardtop, from General Motors. Nearly 150,000 of these were made and they had sold for $2,971. The car was red and had the word 'Mustang' painted on the door in the sort of script I associate with ghost trains at funfairs.

A young man in a garden, apparently showing a young girl of about fifteen a judo throw, was holding her closely and catching her as she fell, laughing, her skirt riding up her brown thighs. An alsatian watched them. There seemed to be dogs in every other garden, and flapping lines of washing wherever I looked. Youths around the entrance of a *microbrigada*-built block of flats (blocks built by volunteers under expert supervision) looked curiously at me as I passed but went on talking. A line of men were unloading tiles from an articulated lorry, passing the tiles along a human chain with much laughter, while the driver sat in the cab listening to the radio. A boy of perhaps three asked me to take his photograph. He posed, pointing the plastic gun he was holding at the camera. As soon as I had taken the photograph, he demanded to see it and took the camera from me and stared into the lens, believing he would be able to see it inside the body. His mother took him away shyly, almost apologetically. There was another US car at the side of the house under a canopy to protect it from the sun, but as I'd already had one disappointment I went past. In the Los Pioneros, the 'Pioneers' playground, there was a US pop song playing over the PA. An attempt was being made to get the children around the flagpole where someone was holding a blue-and-white Cuban flag. The children on the swings all shouted out for Chiclets and made the gesture of pulling imaginary gum from their mouths. The Pioneers all wore blue-and-white scarves over their school uniforms. The movement is not unlike the Boy Scouts or the Girl Guides. It provides primary-school children with recreational opportunities, in this case a playground. It also 'introduces Marxist-Leninist theory', and membership is compulsory. 'Chiclets, Chiclets . . .' sounding in my ears, I carried on.

Two fishermen, with enamel buckets filled with silvery fish, were smoking on the kerb outside the house when I got back. The sky above the sea was streaked with purple clouds and red shafts of light from the sun which had just disappeared over the horizon. The sea was silver again, like a vast piece of crumpled silver foil. The mosquitoes were out, large and black and clustered in great swarms, and I had to run through the door so as not to let too many in. In the kitchen I found Raoul pounding the steak with white garlic powder. The green peppers we ate that night, the first we had had for a month, tasted incomparable.

14

The Bay of Crabs

The following day was Sunday, and we left Varadero. The plan was to drive to the Bay of Pigs to see the museum there which told the story of the US-backed invasion in 1961, and then to go on to the city of Cienfuegos.

We drove from the peninsula back to the mainland and turned east, following the road along the Bay of Cardenas. It was a desolate landscape covered with maribu scrub; stunted trees with red, shiny barks; dilapidated shacks; and scrawny ponies.

In the town of Cardenas there were crowds milling around the bus station as there were in every town. They were waiting to start the long journey back to the city of Havana, although it was still early morning. A man on a bicycle with a box of live chickens on his pannier pedalled past. There were no signs for the next town, Coliseo, and all the verbal instructions we were given were contradictory. Finally, we found a schoolteacher who put us on the right road and sent us on our way with a 'Have a nice day' delivered in a terrible US accent.

Beyond Cardenas, due south, the land was flat and lush and we were back in cane country. Mechanised cane harvesters spewed stalks into the air and white cattle egrets trod behind them in the stubble. The chimneys of the Victoria de Yaguajay and Granma *centrales* smoked in the distance and the smell of burnt molasses hung in the air.

In Coliseo all traffic was stopped by a jeep in the main street into which four or five large ladies were attempting to squeeze. Further on, cane leaves blew across the road, wriggling like serpents. Jovellanos was a dusty, sleepy town where nothing moved except for a tiny black girl in a tattered white dress, who was just large enough to reach up to the handlebars of the enormous bicycle she was pushing along.

At Perico we turned off onto a tiny road, heading for the Caribbean coast. The landscape became more ragged. A white horse was stained red from rolling on the earth. A man necked with a woman in the cab of his tractor. In the village of Agramonte, old shoes were piled in the street waiting to be polished by the bootblacks.

A long way further south, we entered Cienaga de Zapata, a forsaken area of swamp and forest, now a national park. A huge billboard showing the Bay of Pigs invaders bore the legend '*mercenarios*'. We were getting close to the invasion site. Crabs in small, and then greater and greater, numbers came out from the dense, semi-tropical vegetation and scuttled across our path. I got out of the car with India to photograph one. Our subject had lost one of its claws. It was a big crab with a dark red body patched with black, about four inches across; from leg-tip to leg-tip it must have measured twelve inches.

We each returned to the car and drove on. Still green ponds lay to the side. Then we drove around a corner and suddenly the road ahead as far as we could see was strewn with the remains of crabs crushed flat onto the tarmac, thousands of them, a carpet of them, with hundreds of live ones crawling on top of the dead. The smell was half fish factory, half rotting carpet. It was disgusting and our interest in wildlife turned to revulsion.

We crawled forward at five miles an hour. I steered carefully from side to side to try to avoid the crabs. Through the open windows we heard the clacking of their claws on the tarmac as they ran across our path. Then came a noise like a Big Mac styrofoam container exploding, and with horror we realised this was our first casualty. I drove even more slowly, but the numbers of crabs running about increased until it was impossible to avoid them. They covered the road, and from under the tyres came an almost continuous sound of their bodies exploding. I put my foot down. Swollen-bodied turkey vultures, feeding from the road, waited until the last moment before heaving their swollen bodies out of the way of our bumper, and flapped away with pieces of crab meat dribbling from their beaks. The smell grew more palpable. It could be tasted in the mouth. We wound up the windows but the smell persisted. Dragonflies streamed towards us, crashed into the windscreen, and dissolved into what looked like pools of discoloured phlegm. The sky above was blue and cloudless and the sea glimmered turquoise beyond the trees.

★

Half an hour later we arrived. We went through the door of the museum and found ourselves in a chamber with the word 'GIRÓN' in huge letters in front of us. Although the Bay of Pigs is the name of the waterway along which the invaders approached, the invasion is known in Cuba by the beach, Playa Girón, which was one of the two places where the invaders landed. The word 'Girón' was covered with a collage of pictures torn from newspapers of the early 1960s. Here were some of the main protagonists in the drama: Fidel in spectacles, looking a little winsome; John F. Kennedy, his jaw jutting out aggressively; and ordinary Cubans waving placards condemning US imperialism and looking happy about it. The exhibition began by describing life in the Cienaga de Zapata—this swampy region—before the revolution. Peasant men, women and children with undernourished faces and big eyes stared down from the photographs on the walls. The accompanying text told of poverty; appalling housing; exploitation; no medicine; no communications between this inhospitable area and the rest of Cuba; and its total dependency on charcoal. Then came the revolution and, soon after, nationalisation; the First Agrarian Reform Law giving land titles throughout Cuba to 100,000 peasants; the literary campaign by the *brigadistas alfabetizadores*; counter-revolutionary sabotage, including the blowing up of the *Coubre*—a ship delivering Czechoslovakian arms—in Havana harbour and the burning-down of Havana's most famous department store, El Encanto. Finally there was the climax of the counter-revolutionary process, and the act to which the museum was devoted. After a bombing run by US B–26s, disguised in Cuban military colours, on Cuba's four principal airfields, the invasion took place on 15 April 1961 by 1,297[1] CIA-backed and CIA-trained Cubans. The Cuban military, especially the Revolutionary Guard, counterattacked. Fidel personally attended the operation. Four days later, in the early hours of 19 April, the invading forces, exhausted and overwhelmed by the defenders' superior numbers, destroyed their heavy equipment and attempted to disperse. The invasion had collapsed.

The whole story was told, predictably enough, with big maps showing the changing position of the forces, photographs, and numerous examples of the weaponry captured from the invaders. Following the events as told, it struck me that there was a tension between the desire to show the invaders as a truly serious threat—who but for the mobilisation of massive support behind the government from the Cuban people, et cetera, would have destroyed the country—and the desire to show that a Cuban triumph had never been in doubt, because their ideology was right and that of the US was wrong.

Had the invaders had success within their grasp or hadn't they? I wondered. Judging from what I saw in the museum, I felt the invasion had been doomed to failure from the start. To devote a whole exhibition to the state's engagement with, and victory over 1,297 men suggested an alarming inflatus. Later,

---

[1] The number that actually landed. The invading force was supported by US ships and warplanes crewed by US naval and air personnel.

however, when I learnt how President Kennedy's refusal to allow a second bombing run immediately prior to the landing, or subsequently, had sealed the invaders' failure, I revised my opinion. It was a pity there was no mention of this tactical error by the US in the museum. It would have helped the Cuban case.

The invasion was a military disaster which failed to achieve its original intention, to eliminate the Fidelistas and their ideology. Did it strengthen them? Well, since the invasion, opinion has been divided as to whether the Fidelistas were socialist from the start, or became socialist because of US mischief-making. There is also the view that the US, wanting to believe that the Fidelistas were (dangerous) socialists, generated the circumstances which led to their prophecy coming true. Hence the invasion, that time-honoured method of uniting your enemy. This debate will probably never be settled, but two facts remain incontestable. Just before the invasion, Fidel addressed a large crowd at the funeral of the seven victims of the B–26 bombing attack and, for the first time ever, he referred publicly to the Cuban revolution as a socialist revolution:

> Comrades, workers and peasants,
> This is the Socialist and Democratic Revolution of the humble, with the humble, for the humble. . . . The attack of yesterday was the prelude to aggression by the mercenaries. All units must now go to their battalions. . . . Let us form battalions and dispose ourselves to sally out facing the enemy, with the National Anthem . . . with the cry of 'To the fight' ['*Al combate*'], with the conviction that to die for our country is to live and that to live in chains is to live under the yoke of infamy and insult. . . . *Patria o Muerte, venceremos.*[1]

The second fact is that on 1 May 1961, Workers' Day, about a fortnight after the invasion, Fidel repeated his claim that Cuba was now a socialist state, and added that henceforth there would

---

[1] From *Cuba, or the Pursuit of Freedom*, Hugh Thomas. The penultimate sentence is a quotation from the Cuban national anthem.

be no more elections. This was because, as he explained to the crowds gathered in the Plaza de la Revolución, the revolution was the direct expression of the will of the people, and there was an election in Cuba every day rather than every four years. He ruled out the possibility once and for all of any return to the constitution of 1940, or democracy. The revolution had given to every citizen not the vote, but a rifle, he argued. He announced that only those who were not counter-revolutionary would be allowed to remain in Cuba. Finally, he singled out Spanish priests in Cuba for vilification; anti-Catholicism was to remain an obsession until a change of heart was forced on him in the Eighties.

The defeat of the invasion was an immediate personal triumph for Fidel. It also had immense long-term significance. It gave the state a central event for its socialist calendar, an event that became as important to Cubans as Easter is to Christians: the '*quince días de* Playa Girón', the fortnight of Playa Girón. It provided the regime with a concrete and irrefutable example of US imperialism in a raw and naked form which they have exploited ever since. Finally, it gave the Fidelistas a picture of their place in the world as they wanted to see themselves.

This self-image was most apparent from a frieze on the wall. It was an enlarged version of a list compiled under Fidel's instructions. It stated that the 1,297 men who had invaded had once owned in Cuba 1,000,000 acres of land, 10,000 houses, seventy factories, ten sugar mills, five mines, two banks, and so on: they were all rich reactionaries whose aim had been to take back what the poor had gained. After Playa Girón, Cuba's destiny lay with the defenders, the humble proletariat.

Socialism and capitalism were slogging it out in the Caribbean (as good and evil had slogged it out in the past), and Cuba was at the cutting edge.

The climax of the exhibition had a quality of human feeling and detail which was missing in Fidel's list and elsewhere. This was the section devoted to the 'martyrs', i.e. those defenders who had died in the fighting. On the walls there were photographs of them, young and innocent-looking, and below were displayed some of their personal effects. These included a broken comb; a toothbrush and toothpaste; one-peso notes (printed by the American Bank Note Company and bearing the company's logo); and an enamel, ornamental spoon from Brussels. That a man had gone to war with this in his pocket was a piece of real information for me.

*

We came out of the Playa Girón museum. It was about two o'clock. We were looking forward to the drive to Cienfuegos, about sixty miles further east along the coast.

We walked towards the car, and I could feel the sun on the top of my head. Tyga, six months pregnant, moved slowly on the roasted tarmac. Playa Girón was a small *pueblo* of about 300 people. Besides the museum, there was a motel, a beach, houses and a small workshop with antiquated and rusting steam laundry presses piled on the porch, and women inside who stared at us, the whites of their eyes shining in the gloom. 'Why walk your woman in the sun when she's pregnant?' one of them shouted, waving at Tyga. The other women laughed and the wag went on, 'It'll be a black one,' and the women laughed again.

I unlocked the car and wound down the windows. India complained about the heat inside. The steering wheel was like the handle of a saucepan that had boiled dry. The only way to cool the car down was to drive.

I put the key into the ignition. A man on a bicycle sailed behind. He whistled and shouted down at us. I turned round and saw him frantically waving an arm and then pointing to the ground. I got out. On the offside of the Lada, hidden from sight as we'd come from the museum, both tyres were flat. As tragedies go it did not amount to much, but it made us feel despondent.

Fifty yards away a petrol station shimmered in the heat. We started to motor slowly towards it. The wheel rims cut into the melting tarmacadam. The deflated tyres puckered and twisted horribly, and looked as though they were going to shred.

We reached the forecourt. The airline was beside the pump. I set the bell and started to inflate one of the tyres. Behind me, the bell slurred and finally stopped and I knew the prescribed pressure had been reached. I stood up. Within seconds the rim was on the road again. I tried the other tyre. It was the same story.

The pump attendant had been scrutinising us from her office. I went in to see her. She was a whale of a woman with greeny-blue eyes sitting at a rickety table. She spoke a rapid Spanish and would not slow down. I gathered that Valentín, the puncture-repair man, did not work on Sundays, but seven o'clock Monday morning he'd be at the garage. As a concession to my foreignness she held up seven fingers.

'Why don't you put on the spare?' she asked.

'We have two punctures.'

'*Dos*. . .' She widened her eyes. This was different. This she had to see. We trooped together across the forecourt and up to the car. She stared at the two flat tyres.

'*Cangrejos*,' she said, adding something rude about them, and imitating the scuttling of the crabs with a fat hand. Then she peremptorily stopped a youth passing on his bicycle and sent him off in search of Valentín.

It was about half past two now. Whatever was going to happen was going to take a long time. We decided to stay overnight. Tyga and India stopped a tractor, and the driver agreed to take them to the Playa Girón motel. They drove away standing in the cab.

I went and sat on the spare chair in the office. It was a dining-room chair, very simple. The attendant was behind her desk. She was making imitation flowers out of twists of copper wire and scraps of old stocking. Her fingers, though fat, were amazingly dexterous. On the table beside her work lay a book by Fidel with something about 'the march of history' in the title. The silver thread of the mercury in the thermometer on the wall stretched up to 102° Fahrenheit. I became extremely uncomfortable and I went and sat on the step.

'No, no, no, *compañero*, you can't sit there,' the woman called. 'You'll put dirt on those good clean trousers. Sit back on the chair.'

After an hour and a half a huge man, weighing at least twenty stone, appeared. I assumed this was Valentín. He was black and had a half-smoked cigar in his mouth, the wet end darker than the rest. He talked about the crabs. It was their mating season and so they left the sea, crossed the coast roads and went into the swamps to do whatever it was they did—he thought this was laying eggs. He disliked the crabs and the havoc they caused.

He took the wheels off the car and pulled out great shards of carapace from the tread to prove his point. I entirely agreed with him. It was very irritating of the crabs. He put the tyres in the back of his van and went away.

I returned to the chair. The afternoon wore on and shadows crept across the filthy floor sprinkled with oil and sand. The tap in the corner hissed and dripped.

A mud-splattered lorry, the first custom of the afternoon, rattled in and filled up. The attendant took the driver's money and went to the cash till. The name of the till's US manufacturer was on the side. I expected her to touch the old ivory keys, but instead she hit a mysterious spot at the back and the drawer sprung open.

The lorry went off. I smoked a cigarette. I stared at the safety equipment, a spade and a pickaxe and a rusting canister containing a fire blanket, all attached to the wall behind the attendant. I imagined the blanket inside the canister eaten away by moths. I studied the maxims of the regime pinned around the walls, especially their slogan for youth—'*Estudio, Trabajo, Fusil*' ('Study, Work, the Rifle'). I watched the attendant lower a huge, notched stick like a vaulting pole into the tank under the forecourt to measure how much petrol was left. I listened to the shouts coming from a baseball game on a playing field I could just see.

Finally, the point was passed beyond which I couldn't put up with the boredom any more. It was six o'clock. Nothing was going to happen to the car. They would find me in the motel bar.

I got up to leave. At that precise moment, a very small man appeared on a bicycle. The attendant introduced him as Valentín. This Valentín was a midget with an etiolated neck which suggested a lifetime's striving to be taller. He arranged to meet me in the garage at seven and got back on his bicycle. I presumed he was going off to find the cigar-smoker. I was then even more surprised than I had been by his arrival at the sight of the cigar smoker's van at some distance down the road, hurtling towards us and flashing its lights as if there were some emergency. The van screeched into the forecourt and stopped. I saw our tyres were in the front of the cab. They had been repaired and they were rock hard.

As the sun sank lower, Valentín put the wheels back on whilst the cigar-smoker delivered a diatribe against the crabs. Roadside tanks of acid, into which they would plop and fizzle into nothingness, were his solution. The word 'green' had no figurative meaning for him, ecology was not in my dictionary, so that was the end of the conversation. Towards half-past six, about four hours after the trouble had started, the job was finished. All the cigar-smoker would accept in payment was a bottle of beer. Valentín would take nothing, and after saying goodbye, he pedalled away.

Our luggage was in the garage office. I went to pick it up. The attendant was talking to the second customer of the afternoon: a Cuban family who were driving an old Model T Ford with yellow doors. When my back was turned and she thought I couldn't hear, I heard her saying:

'He sat here all afternoon, you know, and he even said thank you for the chair.'

*

The accommodation in the Playa Girón motel was in *cabanas*, cabins. The clientèle were mostly French-Canadians in their late thirties, oldish, fattish and vulgar. In the centre were the facilities. There was a swimming pool, a bar, a barbecue griddle, a ping-pong table, a hoop-la game, a bandstand and a vast notice-board. I learnt from this that the holidaymakers had crowned their King and Queen the night before in the Dancing Lights discothèque, and I was sorry in a grim sort of way that I'd missed it.

There was also a beach, and it would have been a lovely beach except that a hundred feet from the shore there was a concrete barrier which completely enclosed it. This was to stop swimmers going out; it was explained to us that there were no lifeguards.

US West Coast disco and French sentimental slush boomed continuously from the speakers, while Tourist Police with shining guns lounged by the poolside. Every now and then there were jolly announcements in English and French over the PA: 'Hoop-la competition tonight, show us your hidden talents and don't be shy. . . . Are you having a *good* time? . . . Check out our activities schedule with our play leader, Isabelle. . . . Happy Hour. . .'

The concrete barrier, which looked as though it belonged in the Thames estuary, the furtive expressions of the police trying not to look at young breasts and thighs, the French-Canadians roaring drunk under the Havana Club umbrellas and shouting at the harassed barmen in French, and everything else about the place, made it seem suddenly untenable as a place to stay.

'Right,' I said, looking at my watch, 'half past seven, we're going. We'll be in Cienfuegos in two hours.'

I stood up.

'But we've only just checked in,' protested Tyga.

I strode over to the *carpeta*, the reception.

'But you can't leave,' said the girl sitting behind the desk, '*los cangrejos*. . .'

'Oh yes we can,' I said.

I loaded the bags into the car and returned the room key. Just as dusk was falling we set off.

Half a mile on, we turned a corner and came to a halt. The road which stretched ahead of us—different to the one we'd arrived by, it led south and east towards Cienfuegos—was seething with crabs. Between the live and the dead ones it wasn't possible to see the tarmac underneath.

Fifteen minutes later and we were back at the *carpeta*. The girl gave us the key to our old cabin.

'Tomorrow,' she said with a smile, 'everything will be all right.'

★

As well as being a world crab centre, Playa Girón was host to a very large, black-bodied, fast-moving mosquito, whose preferred parts of the anatomy were the eyelid, the soft flesh between the fingers and anywhere on the ankle.

After each of us had been bitten several times as we sat drinking by the pool, surrounded by the appalling French-Canadians whom, needless to add, the mosquitoes were avoiding, we decided it was time to do something.

We went to the Dollar shop. There was a large and extremely impressive shelf of insect repellents. We stood for some minutes trying to decide which was best by the time-honoured method of shaking the bottles and listening to the gnomic pronouncements of the liquid slurping inside.

'I think you'll find the one you're holding is best,' I heard from behind.

I turned round and saw a small, slim man with a younger woman beside him.

'The mosquitoes have eaten me alive,' he said and scratched his arm. 'Are you from London or somewhere like that?'

He was about fifty-five years old and his accent was unmistakably Glaswegian.

After dinner we sat out by the pool under a Havana Club umbrella. Jim was with Maureen. She was his second wife. Jim had been born in the Gorbals, Glasgow.

'I left school at fourteen and went into the Royal Navy,' he said. 'I started out as a gunnery seaman but I soon changed that. I saw there was no future there. I needed a trade. So I became an electrician and then a chief electrician.

'An idealistic young sub-lieutenant thought I might be officer material. He started what they used to call my "white paper". This was to become an officer. Then he left and was replaced by a gunnery officer who'd risen from the ranks, and he called me in and said, "Darrock, with your background you haven't a snowball's chance in hell of being an officer." I listened and I said, "All right."

'After that, the next officer I served under was Potter. He was the stupidist, nastiest officer I ever met. We were anchored somewhere, and there seemed to be something moving past the ship. He thought it was a buoy; he said so. But I looked down and saw the mackerel markings on the water which could only mean one thing. The buoy wasn't passing us. We were passing it. "The anchor's slipped," I said, and there was another officer present when I said it and Potter never forgave me for that.

'We went out to the Mediterranean on a troop carrier. I was in the sea one day taking a swim and he was in the sea too. He was trying to get up the ladder. He had this big pot belly. He just wasn't able to do it. So I reached out like this . . .'

Jim extended his large, strong hand.

'. . . and as I was helping him out, I saw all the other men were looking down at us over the rails. And as I took my hand away from behind him, Potter gave me a look as if to say, "Don't ever touch me again, sonny . . ."

'We had one interest in common. We were both very interested in classical music. I'll give Potter that, he knew his music. One day, he came up to me and said, "The 'Antarctic Symphony' by Vaughan Williams is on the Third Programme tonight." "Yes sir," I said, "I know." "Would you like to come and listen to it with me in the wardroom this evening?" he said. "It'll be quieter than on the mess deck." I thought: Fantastic. Eight o'clock I turn up. I knock on the wardroom door. "Come in," said Potter. I'm standing there; he's sitting; radio on the table. "Listen, Darrock," he says, "there's not really room in here," and he asks me if I wouldn't mind going into the scullery next door and listening through the serving hatch. We were the same up here . . .'

Jim touched his forehead.

'. . . But when it came to the crunch, he was an officer and I was not, and he could not conceive of sitting in a room with a different being like me . . .

'Potter was the last officer I sailed under. Up until then all my service records had been signed "Excellent" or "Very good" but this bastard wrote down "Moderate" after my last voyage, which I didn't deserve. Now he knew that after I finished with him, I only had eight weeks to go on shore, for which I wasn't going to get any more added to my service record, and then I was out; and with a record that ended on a downer. Now I didn't use it to get a job when I got out, I didn't need to as it happened, but imagine if I had, what that comment might have meant?'

Jim's first civilian job was as a salesman selling Weetabix. 'But what did the hard-headed Scots want with that rubbish?' He had left England in the Fifties, 'because in those days you needed the right accent to get on and I didn't like that', emigrating to Canada. He trained as a speech and drama teacher, eventually becoming head of department in a Montreal high school.

It got later and later as we talked. All the other guests left and only our table was occupied. He had a bottle of Black Label Johnnie Walker.

'It cost eight dollars,' he said, 'and that's a price you can't knock.'

We filled our glasses under the table so the barman wouldn't see.

'I still remain friends with a lot of my pupils,' he said.

'Oh yes,' agreed Maureen, 'he hitches to Vancouver to have his teeth fixed by one of them.'

'I remember seeing Moscow Dynamo playing in Glasgow,' he said, 'when they came over just after the war. They drew 2-all with Rangers at Ibrox Park. They drew with Chelsea at Stamford Bridge. They beat Arsenal 4–3 at White Hart Lane and they slaughtered Cardiff 10–1.'

'How do you remember?' said Maureen.

'It taught me a lesson. The Russians never do anything unless they think they're going to win, or at least draw. Now the very first time their hockey team came to Canada, which was in 1971,

I remembered this. I took bets in the staff room. All the Canadians rushed in. They thought their team was the best in the world, invincible and so on. They lost 18–3. I made a fortune.'

He poured more whisky.

'Ibrox Park, November 1945. Willie Waddell, outside right, he missed a penalty. Torry Gillick, inside right. Charlie Johnstone, outside left. George Young, right full back.'

'How do you remember?' repeated Maureen.

'And I'll tell you the name of the Russian goalkeeper who saved that penalty. It was Tiger Khomich.'

Later that night, as I drifted towards sleep, I thought about what had happened. In the day there had been the schematic and banal picture of the struggle between the classes, as depicted in the museum. Then in the evening there had been Jim with his vivid and irrefutable portrait of the class system. In the context of what he described, revolutions were completely explicable. I felt generously disposed to the world, and even to the crabs, for without them it would not have turned out as it had, and we would have been in Cienfuegos.

15

Hotel Pasacaballos

We left Playa Girón the next morning. The clouds in the sky were the colour of lead. We passed the Dancing Lights disco and got onto the road that ran south and east, parallel to the coast, towards Cienfuegos. It was a straight road with swampy forest on either side and occasional glimpses of the sea. The girl at the *carpeta* had been right. There were no crabs.

The forest gave way to open terrain. It was ploughed with cane. Rain began to fall, a thin, fine rain which formed a thin, fine mist. Cane stubble had been set on fire in the fields, and what with the grey-blue smoke and the mist and the clouds overhead which seemed to be getting lower, and the lines of orange and red flames on the horizon, and the souls of the damned crouched in ditches, covering themselves with newspapers and fertiliser bags. It was as if we'd entered a grey purgatory with the fringes of hell in the distance. Later—when we really arrived in a sort of hell—it was an entirely logical scene.

In Yaguaramas there was a goat grazing on the railway line beside a cowboy on horseback. Fuchsia grew along the roadside and red blossoms were strewn on the muddy streets. Outside the village there was one of the ubiquitous shooting ranges, filled with iron cutouts of parachutists and tanks. We picked up a hitch-hiker. He was an old man in his eighties wearing purple-tinted spectacles and carrying two cardboard boxes. These were filled with old magazines from East Germany and Poland, and he showed them to India, pointing at the coloured pictures of footballers scoring goals and young women modelling evening gowns. She was not impressed and fell asleep.

In Rodas there was a handwritten sign tacked to the side of a shack which read '*Nicaragua–Libre*'. We passed over a dirty river and got stuck behind a lorry with a roadside-shelter—all-in-one moulded plastic—bolted to the back to protect its passengers. The road curved and it was impossible to overtake.

Later—I don't know how much later because progress was slow and I was bored—we arrived in Cienfuegos. The outskirts of the city were all built post-1959: massive six-lane carriage-ways, empty except for crowded buses and cyclists, and on either side of the roads great, gaunt, grey hospitals, technical colleges, dormitories for students, all named after a revolutionary leader—Frank País this, or Camilo Cienfuegos that, or Ché Guevara the other—and the monotony of the system stilled one's interest. I no longer paid any attention to what anything was called. Further on there were huge estates of *microbrigada*-built blocks surrounded by parched lawns.

The middle ring of the city comprised showrooms, petrol stations, small factories, warehouses, schools and the usual Florida-style bungalows. These were the fruits of Cuba's development in the Forties and Fifties. Finally, at the centre, was the old Spanish or colonial hub of the city. Pan-tiled houses with huge wooden doors and ironwork in front of the windows encircled an inner core of institutional buildings and wide commercial streets with elegant colonnades. It was little changed since the nineteenth century, except for the addition of modernish shopfronts and neon signs.

What had changed, of course—what has done more to alter the look of cities than the rest of the twentieth century put together—was the traffic. If it had still been horsedrawn, 1987 would have been quite like 1887 in Cienfuegos. But it was not:

the traffic was horseless, and there was a great deal of it. The roads were choked with motorcycles, lorries and cars, all going as fast as they could and without any apparent sense that they were sharing the roads with any other users. It made driving in Cienfuegos a much more disorienting and frightening experience than driving in Havana. In the capital city, every driver on the road had a shared sense as to how far they could go *too* far, and no further than that did they go. In Cienfuegos it was quite the contrary. The further the better seemed to be the motto, and if anyone, driver or pedestrian, got maimed or killed in the process, too bad. I felt pleased and relieved, as I slowly negotiated our Lada through the one-way system, hugging the right-hand kerb while constantly being overtaken by furious drivers whose hands appeared to be permanently on their horns, that we had booked ourselves into a hotel twenty-two kilometres from the city.

We found the road we were looking for on the outskirts. The first twenty yards were 'up', and to warn motorists the road-works had been ringed with kerosene cans which smoked and burned although it was the middle of the day. We drove south, following the east side of the landlocked Cienfuegos bay. It was a landscape of rounded hills and views of distant water. There were few signs of human habitation, but for a solitary petrol station, visible at a great distance because it was painted blue and white in the middle of a green landscape.

We turned in and stopped on the forecourt behind a 1953 Ford Customline Six sedan. It was a big, off-white car with a trunk and hood which appeared to be the same length and a cab on top in the middle. There were no fins and its only frills were thin chrome flashes on its flanks which I thought were ugly. In its time it had been the spearhead of the 'Ford blitz', the campaign in the 1950s by which the company sought to increase its share of the market. That perhaps explains its aesthetics.

Turkey vultures hung in the grey sky above, or were sitting on fence-posts in the empty landscape, staring at us. The Customline drove off. The attendant brought his face to the window. He was white-skinned with yellow eyes and yellowed teeth. He told us it was just a few kilometres to the hotel and that it was '*muy lindo*', 'very pretty'.

The guide which we had bought (it was so bad it was becoming compulsive) was equally fulsome. 'The hotel Pasacaballos is the most beautiful hotel built since the revolution and is probably the best hotel in all of Cuba.' From the start, however, all the signs indicated the reverse. From a distance it looked like an enormous concrete block. The only good point was its location. This was at the top of the canal by which the landlocked bay of Cienfuegos was approached. The old village of Jagua was directly opposite on the other side of the water.

We parked and went towards the entrance. There was a tourist taxi abandoned outside, like some we had seen in Havana. It was a brand new Fiat Uno, for which Cuba had paid with extremely hard-earned foreign currency. It stood on blocks, without wheels, its axle ends flaking with rust. It was a bad omen.

Two armed policemen slouched beside the door and watched us without moving as we went through. Inside we found ourselves in what looked like an air terminal, with flying staircases of black marble, television bays cordoned off with beds of dusty stones, and a booming public address system to summon guests to the telephone.

Whilst we waited to register, I explored. Outside the lobby bar the different kinds of cocktails which were available were on display. The garish-coloured concoctions were crawling with small, black flies. Two identical twins sat on a sofa. They were French-Canadian by the look of them, and wore matching stockings and black starched dresses. Their hair, tightly coiled, was contained within matching hairnets.

El bellboy, as he was called, was another grotesque. He had the long back of a man who was six foot two and the short bandy legs of a ten year old. He swept up our luggage with his octopus-like arms and we trekked across the lobby to the annex from where the lifts departed. We squeezed into one and the lift (made by Hitachi, with a piped pop version of *Eine Kleine Nachtmusik* coming from the ceiling) whisked us all to the fifth floor. We got out and found ourselves on a walkway that ran down the side of the hotel. To the left there was a view across the water to Jagua, the fishing village with its sixteenth-century Spanish fort. It was, however, only to be enjoyed by guests *en passant*, because the architects had placed our bedroom (like the others) facing away from this and towards a modest hill with telegraph poles running across the top of it. The room itself was shaped like a railway carriage, long and narrow with a window at one end. The ceiling was painted olive-green and the furnishings, to match the door, were orange. *El bellboy* turned on the bedside light and the bulb went with a crack. He laughed.

El bellboy left and I went out to the walkway. On one side were the orange-painted bedroom doors and on the other a high parapet to stop people falling (or jumping) to their deaths. The wind whistled, blowing an empty Havana Club bottle along the marble floor. I looked up from the bottle and saw something I'd missed before. Painted on a wall on the far side of the water in huge black letters so guests could read them, '*Bienvenida a Cuba Socialista.*'

I bought a bottle of Nicaraguan Flor de Cana rum and spent the rest of the evening, while Tyga and India slept, trying to telephone Maria, our hitch-hiker friend from Varadero. Her city, Santa Clara, was not far from where we were. Four successful connections to her number over several hours all elicited the same, mysterious reply: '*No la conozco, campañero,*' 'I don't know her, comrade.'

The next morning I tried the number again. It was answered immediately.

'Hello, yes, speak.'

'Is that you, Maria?'

'Yes, how are you? I thought you were going to ring.'

'Is the telephone in your house?'

'No, no. A neighbour's. I'm there.'

'Last night I rang and they said, "Maria, don't know her."'

'No, they only know my mother's name. Are you coming over?' she asked.

'Yes,' I said.

'Come now then. We'll be waiting. Find the hospital. We're in the street behind. Kiss your little girl for me. Goodbye.'

We couldn't check out. We'd booked for five days and paid in advance, the usual Cuban practice. We just left, knowing we would have to come back.

16

Three Parties are Better than One

We took the right fork at the garage where the attendant had yellow eyes and headed north for Maria's home town, more or less dead centre on the map of Cuba.

At first the road wound through high bare hills. The turkey vultures still hung above, dark spots in the hot, blue sky. There were numerous rivers spanned by old cantilever bridges floored with railway sleepers which groaned under our wheels. The river waters far below us were brown and muddy.

After the small village of San Anton, the lower slopes became forested. A huge Soviet lorry, travelling in the opposite direction, flashed its lights as it passed. I slowed down, and sure enough, round the next bend, there he was waiting under a carob tree: a traffic cop with sunglasses glinting, clipboard at the ready, whistle poised. We smiled as we passed, and as soon as we were out of sight, I flashed our lights at every driver we passed for a couple of kilometres, so they would know to slow down. I enjoyed a small feeling of integration into the life of the country.

Two hours later we reached Santa Clara. We found the hospital easily. The enormous estate lay behind. There were twenty-six blocks, each with fifty flats. The once bright blue or pink painted walls were peeling, the concrete paths were cracked. We heard a voice and, looking up, saw it was Maria watching from the balcony outside her flat.

'I thought you weren't coming,' she shouted and ran down and embraced us.

We followed her to the second floor. She introduced us to her parents. Gabriel was a stocky man with a beard, about fifty years old. Miranda, his wife, was slightly younger, with blue eyes. She wore a print dress.

In the living room there were aluminium garden chairs to sit on and glass shelves decorated with empty Ballantine's whisky bottles.

We accepted a beer and sat down.

'This was our Christmas,' Maria said, taking photographs from an envelope and handing them to us. From the pictures the family stared back at us, their eyes glowing red from the flash: Gabriel, Miranda, Maria, her brother Ricardo, her sisters, nephews and nieces, and a man who was not identified. In the background stood a Christmas tree, in a pot with silver paper wrapped around it.

'It's a real one,' Maria said, 'we cut it ourselves in the forest.'

'So what do you do?' Gabriel asked.

'I'm a writer.'

'So you're an intellectual, or anyway, in Cuba you'd be an intellectual.'

'I suppose.'

'You aren't very rich?'

'No, we're in the middle.'

'Then you're like us. We're in the middle to. We're all middle class.' He paused and then he added, 'So you live like us then?'

'More or less. We live in an apartment . . .' I pointed uselessly around the room. 'Like this.'

'That is good,' he said, and it was as if some invisible barrier had been passed. 'Let's have some more beer.'

'Do you find Cuba expensive ?' Gabriel asked a moment later.

We shrugged politely.

'It is, very expensive. Also, it is very hard. I have to work every hour of every day to feed my family. Do you know what the *libreta* is?'

'Vaguely.'

He got up from his garden chair and went across to the island separating the living room from the kitchen. He opened a drawer and came back with a small buff-coloured booklet. This was the family's *libreta* or ration book. There was a page for each month covered with cross hatching, where the shopkeeper indicated if goods had been taken and, if so, how much. The monthly ration per person was something like this: beef 1lb.4oz. or chicken 1lb.11oz.; rice 5lb.; beans 1lb.4oz.; oil 8oz.; lard 1lb.; sugar 4lb.; milk (fresh) 4qt.; milk (canned) 3qt.; coffee 4oz.; bread 15lb.; tomato sauce 8oz.; other items (mayonnaise, sweets, cooking wine, baby food, et cetera) various amounts; *viandas* (root crops such as cassava, taro and sweet potato and also cooking bananas), 6lb.; fruit (oranges for instance), 1lb.; vegetables (tomatoes), 3lb. As I thumbed through the book, Gabriel explained that many other items were also rationed, including shoes, clothing, bed linen, crockery, household goods and toys.

He put the book back in the drawer and returned.

'You can't live on the food you get on the ration,' he said. 'A few pounds of rice, a few pounds of beans, a chicken every fourteen days. Impossible.'

'How do you eat then?'

'We have to buy on the free market. It's three times as expensive, maybe more. I don't know. Miranda does the shopping. I just work every hour God gives me.'

He was a geologist working in a mine.

Towards six I went out and stood with Gabriel on the front balcony. There were workers hurrying home along the paths below with bunches of onions and loaves of bread. It began to grow dark and in the vegetable shop on the corner, where wives and mothers were waiting, neon strips started to glow behind the mesh-covered windows. Gabriel touched me on the elbow and said, 'The women of Cuba, are not the women of Cuba beautiful?'

The mosquitoes came out and we went back inside. Below the living-room window was the hospital laundry, and the end of the shift was sounded with a steam whistle.

When it was over Gabriel asked, 'When a man goes to the doctor in England, does he have to pay?'

'No. Doctors are free. Hospitals are free. All you pay for are the medicines you get in the chemist.'

'Is that really true? It is exactly the same as Cuba.'

I told him all I knew. It was another barrier passed.

There was a knock at the door and a man came in carrying a kerosene tin with an improvised wire handle. 'The pig man,' said Gabriel, and explained that he took away scraps to feed the pigs he kept illegally. In return the family was supplied with a bit of extra meat.

'What about Mrs Thatcher?' Gabriel asked, 'do you like her?'

'No,' I said, and started trying to explain, over-elaborately, the British electoral system.

After a few moments Gabriel interrupted and said politely: 'There are three parties. Conservative, socialist, liberal. That's how it was in Cuba before the revolution. Now, there is just one party.'

I didn't have to ask the next question.

'Three parties are better than one,' he said and added, 'I would like to see a parliamentary democracy in Cuba.'

A huge woman came in. Her spectacles rested on top of her black curly hair. She was a child psychologist. She sat down in the corner and looked around and immediately said India's knees had something wrong with them and nodded sagely to herself.

We sat at the oilcloth-covered table to begin an enormous meal. It was the traditional fried pork and *moros y cristianos*. Below the window I could see the laundry smoking and steaming. The child psychologist was offered food. She blew out her cheeks and lifted her arms in mock despair. 'More means fatter and that's unthinkable,' she said.

The radio was tuned to Radio Martí, the Cuban-American radio station broadcasting from Florida. For many Cubans it was a cultural habit (Martí broadcasts a hugely popular soap opera), but for Gabriel there was another reason. His sister had been serving a six-month prison sentence in 1980 for hitting a policeman on the head with her stiletto—I never discovered what had provoked her—and had been one of the many prisoners in Cuban jails who had been shipped out during the boatlift from Mariel. Sometimes she broadcast on Radio Martí, and this was why the family listened in the evenings.

After we'd finished eating, Gabriel repeated everything I'd said about the health service. The child psychologist didn't believe a word of it. 'It's not possible,' she said. There was no free health care in the United States because the US was a capitalist country. There was only free health care in socialist countries. Britain was a capitalist country like the United States. Therefore, her argument now closing the circle, there was no free health care in Britain.

'No, no, no,' said Gabriel, and he repeated accurately everything I'd said about hospitals, doctors and prescriptions. But the huge woman, who as someone who worked within the Cuban health service should, one would think, have known better, remained disbelieving. Eventually Gabriel simply overruled her. 'He comes from the country,' he said, pointing at me, 'he knows what he's talking about.' Shortly after this, she left.

At half past seven the television went on for the regular evening slot of *Aventura*, the most popular programme on Cuban television. The current series concerned the struggle against Batista and this episode centred on a shopkeeper. He helps the rebels and a police agent subsequently comes to the shop. There is an argument and the agent shoots the shopkeeper dead. The deed done, he strolls behind the counter and fires gratuitously at the corpse. (The actor playing the now-dead shopkeeper registers the bullet, slightly in anticipation of the pulling of the trigger, with a theatrical spasm.) The agent helps himself to a packet of cigarettes and viciously tosses a coin onto the chest of his victim. . .

We went off for the evening to see Maria's sister, Luisa, and Luisa's husband, Filipo. They were building their own house in a distant suburb and, so far, had two breeze block built rooms, electricity and a sink. Currently a shortage of cement in the city was holding up work and they complained about this as we sat in their unfinished kitchen.

We came back to the apartment with Maria about eleven. She got out a red armband marked CDR and strapped it to her arm. It was duty night.

CDRs—Committees for the Defence of the Revolution—exist throughout all of Cuba, organised on a block-by-block basis. Membership is not compulsory but it is expected. The organisation was founded in the early Sixties to combat counter-revolutionary terrorism. Every night, CDR members patrol the streets of their area. Besides being a means for putting medical, educational and other campaigns across nationally, the CDRs are also, quite frankly, a means of spying on the population and getting information about them.

'When do you patrol, Gabriel?' I asked.

'Never.'

He pulled off a shoe and sock to reveal a bunion.

'How can I with this?' he said and laughed.

'And my heart is terrible,' Miranda said. 'A woman in my condition can't possibly do CDR duty.'

I followed Maria downstairs. She reported to a supervisor and was assigned an area to patrol. We walked round the estate to the polyclinic at the back, where we sat down on the steps underneath a huge portrait of Fidel.

'Do you see that man?' she said.

There was a figure looking at us from a ground-floor flat.

'Yes.'

'He's the CDR *jefe* here. While we were at my sister's, he came to the flat and asked my mother who you were and what you were doing here. She just told me.'

Maria stuck her tongue out at him although we were too far away and it was too dark for him to see what she was doing. The figure turned away.

She slipped a photograph out of her purse and handed it over shyly. 'This is my love,' she said.

He was a man in his late twenties, balding and with staring eyes. I recognised him as the stranger in the Christmas photograph. He was a Swiss laboratory technician. They had met in Bratislava and he had come to Cuba twice to visit her, the second time being the Christmas just gone. He wanted Maria to go to Switzerland but she couldn't. First she had to repay the Cuban government for her higher education. Once that had been done, she could then only go if $1,000 were paid for the exit visa. This would be valid for a year and if she then didn't return, she would lose her citizenship. Otto was working to raise the money. Every month, on the same day, she telephoned him and always put aside thirty pesos from her wages for the call. After Otto's last visit, she had had an abortion.

She touched the photograph. 'I love him very much, perhaps too much.' Then she said, 'Please,' and touched me on the elbow for a light.

We were given Maria's room for the night. There were pictures of her loved one around the mirror of the dressing table and a bottle of Gucci perfume on which had been written an address in Switzerland.

We spent the next day with Maria and her family and in the evening drove back to the Pasacaballos.

17

Cienfuegos

The next morning, in the hotel lobby, the display of cocktails was in its usual place by the bar, and the glasses and straws were thick with the same small, round-bodied flies that had been there at the start of the week. A few feet away was the principal dining room and the *mesa sueca*, a Swedish breakfast table. Among the foods laid out were segments of grapefruit, glazed brown and quite dry to touch on the outside, pieces of watermelon so shrunken with dehydration they resembled cotton-wool balls, and squares of ham, heavy, dark red and looking like off-cuts of a floor tile.

Everything about the hotel was so awful, it was becoming less depressing and more interesting. It was Thursday morning. Cienfuegos lay twenty-two kilometres away, waiting to be explored. It wasn't one of the original cities founded by Diego de Velázquez, but we'd come a long way to see it because we had been told it was big and important. We decided to take the bus in, which we thought would be more eventful. It seemed there was a fast and regular service every forty-five minutes.

At nine o'clock we were out by the stop in front of the hotel. It was a dry, hilly place with a single tree, its branches rubbed clean of bark by people who had sat on them waiting. Behind us lay Cienfuegos bay, a great expanse of landlocked water. According to a nineteenth-century traveller, it was a place where 'all the navies of the world could *rendezvous* and not crowd each other'. Shimmering in the haze at the other end of the bay lay the port of Cienfuegos itself.

By ten o'clock there were twenty of us waiting. A hot wind had started to blow, carrying grit which stung the face, and we all had our eyes screwed up. We could have gone and got our Lada, but wouldn't because it would have invalidated the time we'd spent hanging about. By eleven o'clock our numbers had swollen to forty. When the bus came at eleven-thirty, we were fifty.

It was a small Soviet vehicle, seating about twenty. It was empty because this was the first stop. We all squeezed on. Immediately, there was the overwhelming carbolic smell of Soviet soap. The driver engaged first gear. There was a horrible noise inside the engine of metal grinding with metal. Timidly, the driver crept the bus forward. We went over the brow of the hill and started to roll down, gathering speed. The window panes, the metal floor, the plastic seats, everything began to judder, whilst the passengers, crushed as they were against one another, began to sway in unison. We came to the bottom of the slope with a rush and hit the start of the next climb. A spasm ran through the bus as the inertia it had gathered dropped off and the engine became again the only power to drive it along. I could see the next incline beyond the heads of passengers and through the windscreen. It looked long and steep. I could not believe we'd get to the top and started to imagine that in a few minutes we'd be part of a scenario we'd seen all over Cuba, very, very often. The bus would be stranded by the roadside, bonnet up, and we, along with all the passengers, would be strung out along the road, desperately hitching. However, to my amazement, the bus began to climb, slowly and steadily, and continued, slowly and steadily. Finally it got to the top and started to roll down the hill on the other side, very fast. Then it came to another hill and up it started to crawl again. On and on this went, the pace the same as a roller coaster—slow, fast, slow—for an hour or so, until finally we arrived in Cienfuegos. The last stop was somewhere in the middle of a street somewhere in the middle of the city. After everyone had streamed out we asked the driver where the terminus was, where we had to go to get back, and he insisted, though it was out of his way, on driving us there in the bus.

We alighted and started to walk along Calle 56. Patient in the burning heat, a line of women waited their turn to enter a store which sold cosmetics and clothes. They all fanned themselves with their ration books. Calle 56 was the principal shopping street in the centre of the city.

Cienfuegos began, or could be said to have begun, when the Spanish began Jagua Castle, the fort opposite the hotel. Construction began in 1738 and was completed in 1745. At that time there had been no city to speak of. The fort had been built to protect inland areas and coastal villages from pirates. A sugar mill was constructed in 1751 near where the town stands. In 1796 the original town plan was drawn up. Eight years later the construction of the harbour was started.

What were needed, however, were people and in 1817, a French *émigré* from Louisiana came up with a settlement scheme. The scheme presented by Don Juan Luis Lorenzo d'Clouet to the Spanish captain-general, Don José Cienfuegos, called for the recruitment of white colonists in Europe, whose passage to Cuba and initial expenses would be met by the government. In addition, each white male, over the age of eighteen and willing to work, who shipped out was to receive a *caballería*, a unit of land containing thirty-three acres. The Spanish Cortes approved of the plan and by April 1819 137 *caballerías* of land had been turned over to d'Clouet's settlers. Not surprisingly, most of them came from France. With this new blood, Cienfuegos began to develop, starting as a village. A storm in 1825 destroyed everything, but by 1831 the inhabitants had rebuilt what they'd lost. By 1875 Cienfuegos was a city with all those indispensable adjuncts of civilisation: a cathedral in which to worship; water brought in by aqueduct; and a *plaza*. The wealth to do all this came from trading—fruit, tobacco and sugar—which in turn was made possible by the deep-water harbour. The dominant architectural influence was supposedly French.

To me, however, it looked just like any other Cuban colonial city, only there was a little more stucco work than usual. On the other hand, perhaps the French spirit of the place had eluded me, because to travel twenty-two kilometres had taken a morning and now it was lunchtime and we needed to eat.

In the first café we went into, they only had water and wafers with a synthetic cream filling. In the next we were luckier: salted fish and bananas. The cutlery with which to eat had to be wheedled from the lady cutlery guardian who sat at a special table by the door where she could watch everyone coming and going, though the knives were made of base metal and tasted of cod-liver oil and I couldn't imagine anyone stealing them. I supposed they must have, however, because they had to be returned to the guardian afterwards and not to the man who took away the plates.

Now we wanted a drink but they only had water that tasted of chlorine. We went out into the street and a few yards further on found the Naranjito, or Little Orange, a category IV cafeteria. The name seemed promising and we went in. Half of the counter was mysteriously closed, so we sat down at the other half. Everything was familiar: the worn counter stools; the two types of cigarettes for sale in their coarse paper packets, Popular and Aroma; the menu board shaped like a medieval shield in a school play; the day's fare, just eggs in this case, painted on the slats which had been slotted between rails; the cashier, immobile behind her till, sucking on her false teeth; the single waitress with dyed red hair, wearing the standard mini-skirt and white blouse, a genius at avoiding eye contact with the customers; and finally, the public, about twelve of us, waiting patiently and uncomplainingly. We had sat waiting in such places so many times before, I had grown inured to it. I smoked a cigarette and looked around. The people waiting were all middle-aged. Their hands were bony and hard-skinned. Everyone had done their best to make a good public impression. The men had shaved carefully, combed their hair and put on immaculately ironed shirts. The women had showered themselves, plucked their eyebrows and put on earrings and necklaces and what make-up they could lay their hands on. Even the customers' facial expressions looked as if they were the best they could manage. The Naranjito struck me as the quintessence of Cuba. If I had been a painter, it would have been a scene I would have wanted to paint. What I would have hoped to convey through my painting, besides their elegance, was the sense of certainty every Cuban exuded in these situations, the certainty that if one waited long enough, something would happen.

It happened for us after twenty minutes or half an hour. The waitress sauntered over and we each got a glass of heavily sugared fresh orange juice. A moment later the chef pushed a tray of *empanada de carne* through the serving hatch. These were flat pancakes, with a little morsel of meat in the middle, which had been cooked in boiling fat. In the same batch he had made two special sweet *empanadas* filled with sugar and a sticky orange substance, which the waitress presented to India. They were a special gift. The other customers smiled. It was the sort of moment which made one forgive the country everything.

There wasn't much of the afternoon left when we went outside. We wandered down to Parque Martí, a square with benches, trees, a gazebo bandstand and a statue commemorating the establishment of the Cuban Republic in 1902. There was a cathedral with its doors locked and weeds growing from the parapets. Close by, the old Primero Palacio, now the Poder Popular or local government headquarters, was very much open, with a television playing loudly in the lobby. In the last heat of the day, a tall black man was carefully carrying a two-foot-square iced cake past the cathedral.

We hung about until evening when we went to the Cienfuegos theatre. This impressive building overlooked the Parque Martí. Completed in 1895, it was called the Tomás Terry after one of the richest members of the Cuban sugar oligarchy. The proscenium was decorated with lyres, trumpets, laurel wreaths, and a bas-relief centrepiece of a bearded man who I think was Dionysus, while on the ceiling naked nymphs cavorted in a milky sky with fine pieces of strategically placed gauze. We sat in the stalls on old-fashioned, wooden fold-down seats, an audience of about forty in a theatre which sat over 900. The spectators were mostly French-Canadians with a sprinkling of townspeople. The show was a *spectacular*—a mixture of dance from the National Ballet Company and song recital from the Opera de Cuba. Among the composers listed in the programme were Tchaikovsky, Jorge Anckerman and Franz Lehár.

The evening opened with six dancers in spangled knickerbockers. The music to which they moved was taped and the piece had something to do—it was difficult to know what—with the battle of the sexes. The second item was Opera de Cuba, a lady singer in a shimmering white gown with shimmering paste earrings. As she started to trill, a swarm of bats flitted from the wings and began to tear about over the heads of the audience. Everyone shifted uneasily in their seats but the singer continued unmoved; obviously she was used to it. She was joined later by the tenor, a very tall bearded man who looked a little like James Mason and wore a heavy brown three-piece suit. He was sweating, it was so hot, and kept mopping his brow with a large white handkerchief.

In the intermission we went to the crush bar. They told us they had nothing; not even water, they said. Finally, we managed to persuade a young girl of about nine to find and open three bottles of Fresco.

The second half started with the first act of *Swan Lake*. The principal dancer wore a tartan skirt (his trunks underneath were brown) with white football socks held up with tartan gaiters. There was a plastic rock for him to sit on. Tchaikovsky seemed to bring the bats out more than ever. After *Swan Lake* the singers returned. They sang together, looking not unlike Dolly Parton and Kris Kristofferson. She was saucy, wringing her hands, playing with her cape, and wriggling. His style, on the contrary, was two-feet-firmly-on-the-ground-and-sock-it-to-them. Overhead swooped the bats. The audience fanned themselves. It was desperately hot. Children screeched in the street outside and the *spectacular* went on and on. . . .

Back in the railway-carriage bedroom in the Pasacaballos, there was a continuous drip onto the false wooden ceiling. Unlike my family, I could not sleep. Towards one o'clock, the door of the bedroom next door clattered open. A couple fell drunkenly in. I could hear laughing and slurring in German. 'Help me with my zip,' she said suddenly in Marlene Dietrich English and then in German, 'Shhh. My children are asleep.'

They tried to move the single beds together quietly but the legs screeched on the marble floor as they dragged them about. A moment later they were making love. He was reasonably quiet, but she made up for it by shouting. Their bed-head banged on the wall, synchronous with the action. I reached for my 'Blissful Quiet' earplugs, and found that in the heat they had half-melted.

18

Trinidad

The next day, a Saturday, we left Pasacaballos and drove eastwards, hugging the southern shore of the island, towards Trinidad. Rivers running down from the mountains had cut deep valleys through to the sea. At each bridge we crossed, we could see in the river estuaries below young brown boys floating on the glistening inner tubes of tyres.

Somewhere near Playa de Inglés hundreds of cattle were penned together in a corral, a tight, frightened mass. The air was filled with the smell of their droppings and their urine. Three or four gauchos sat on their horses, watching, doing nothing. One chopped at a fence post with his machete. Another asked us if we had any rum.

Further on the road was again layered with dead crabs and there was the familiar smell of rotting carpet and meat. In a village nothing moved except a cart made out of an old beer crate, a child with a whip in the back, and a goat between the staves pulling both along.

As we entered Trinidad, a veil of cloud floated across the sun. The car bumped on the cobblestone streets. One of the original seven cities founded by Diego de Velázquez, it has not been substantially altered for 200 years and some of it is very much older. The low, colonial houses are mostly red or yellow coloured, very faded like old clothes.

Late next morning I set out alone down the hill from the Motel Las Cuevas where we were staying. Below lay the city and its houses with their pan-tiled roofs, each a slightly different shade of terracotta. On the outskirts, a young child was bouncing a football off the bare, stuck-out bottom of another. Two toddlers with sickly-yellow dummies asked for Chiclets. On the pavement by the tumbledown Iglesia de Santa Ana, men sat playing dice, a puzzle because gambling is prohibited in Cuba.

I wandered on. The houses were small and low, with bars over the windows and the doors thrown wide open. Somewhere in the centre I found the Plaza Mayor, where several of the city's museums were located. The Museum of Natural Sciences, filled with stuffed birds and animals in glass booths, was like something from the nineteenth century. While examining a well-varnished Cuban crocodile, I met Señor Ribalta. He was an elderly mulatto guide with curly grey hair. He took me out to the steps.

'Cortés stayed over there,' he said.

He pointed across the Plaza Mayor, immaculately restored, with a little park in the middle, filled with green trees and gleaming metal benches.

'That was a hotel then. Cortés stayed there for twelve days. Then he went with his horses and his men the one and a half kilometres to the harbour at Casilda and sailed off to conquer Mexico.'

There was a familiarity to the rest of the story. Trinidad grew rich from smuggling slaves and sugar. Its closeness to the English colony of Jamaica gave it a unique advantage over other Cuban cities in this area. Trinidadian women went to Europe for rings and earrings of gold and silver. During the English occupation of 1762–3, Trinidad was a free port and business boomed. But the wars ended, and the king of Spain returned. For some years afterwards life was good, but Cienfuegos, a hundred kilometres away, gradually eclipsed Trinidad as a trading centre. The city became obscure, provincial, neglected, and stayed that way in the twentieth century. In the 1950s Batista declared the city a historic monument, but this only increased its stagnation because it obstructed all development. 'At the time of the revolution,' Señor Ribalta said, 'there were only 25,000 people in Trinidad. Now,' he concluded proudly, 'there are 48,000.'

The doors and shutters of the museum were being closed. We said goodbye, and I went on my way feeling ever so slightly puzzled by his friendliness.

I climbed through the back streets of Trinidad, the cobbles gleaming and shining in the sun. At the top of a steep hill was the Iglesia de la Popa, built in 1726. Three corroded bells hung above the door. The guidebook said it was used twice a year, but inside it was empty and strewn with newspaper; it smelt damp; and the holy water font was filled with the black and evil-looking droppings of bats. It hadn't been used in years.

I went outside. The old city lay spread out in front of me, miraculously unchanged. New green-coloured apartment blocks lay to the left. These must have been where Señor Ribalta's extra Trinidadians lived. Boys climbed past me with pitchers, mittens and baseball bats and started to practise in front of the miserable church.

I went back down into the hot city and found a tiny bar. Their only liquor was rum sweetened with bananas. There were also cakes in a glass cabinet. I bought one: dry and tasting of vanilla. An enormous black youth in silvery, flared trousers brought in a cage with a tiny bird and hung it over the doorway. He took a piece of cake, ate some, then spat it out, sending the crumbs and pieces spraying into the street.

I returned to the Plaza Mayor, immaculate, silent, depressing in the heat, its four museums shut. In nearby Calle Bolivar, a man sat on his handkerchief on a kerbstone, his companion on a newspaper. Beside them was a brown tin sign which read '*Los Dos Pilares de Nuestro Partido Su Unidad y Su Ideologia*' ('The two pillars of our party, its unity and its ideology'), with a crudely painted picture of the Granma underneath.

In the *guarapo* (cane juice) bar—famous because it was one of the last remaining in Cuba—there was a woman sleeping at a table behind the counter. She woke up and told me there was no cane from which to crush the sugary *guarapo* drink. 'Perhaps next week,' she added. The pastry cabinet was empty except for a few flies buzzing against the glass. The *galleta* tins were empty. There wasn't even any water to drink.

After much searching I finally found somewhere that was open and had something to sell: the Bar Juventud, category VII, the lowest. Its chief feature was a tin cover nailed to the counter, which buckled and rumbled every time anyone leant on it. This in turn jiggled the glasses lined along it. There was a Frigidaire refrigerator (*Producto de la General Motors*) and a till which rang up in dollars. I drank three-year-old Armenian brandy—all they had apart from a vile-looking green liqueur. Sitting on the window ledge was an old black man who talked to anyone who'd listen. Whenever he said something amusing, one of the men in the bar handed him a cigarette.

The sun was slanting over the roof of the houses and there was a faint breeze when I left. I started to retrace my steps back towards the motel. All afternoon all Trinidad had slept and now, as I could see through doors and windows on one flickering black-and-white television set after another, all Trinidad was watching the early evening baseball game. The commentator's voice seemed to follow me all the way out of town, past the remains of the Iglesia de Santa Ana, right to the gates of the motel.

When I went back into the city that evening, the streets were wet after a shower of rain. In the cigarette factory on Calle Cienfuegos, an old woman was sweeping up tobacco dust. I watched her find two cigarettes, look about herself—she couldn't see me watching from the street—and put them in her pocket.

At the cinema in Céspedes Park I bought a ticket. The auditorium was almost completely full; the feature was '*Un Detective Suelto en Hollywood*' (*Beverley Hills Cop*), starring

Eddie Murphy. The best moment in the evening, from the audience's point of view, was Murphy's impersonation of gay Ramon, hairdresser and sufferer from Herpes 10. It brought the house down, and the laughter was vicious and unfriendly.

The revolution has not been kind to homosexuals, and in its early years the kind of hostility evident in the cinema had an official expression, in the Units for Military Aid to Production (UMAP) camps. These were started in 1965. Their intended function was the rehabilitation of young men of military service age, whose 'ways' made them unsuitable for integration into the regular army. To these camps were sent malingerers, artists, supposed counter-revolutionaries (i.e. critics of the regime), clergymen[1] and those termed 'immoralists', a category which included homosexuals and transvestites.

Relegation to UMAP camps was arbitrary. Sometimes young men would be summarily picked up by the police and shipped there; others were simply told to report; others again were called in before their local Committee for the Defence of the Revolution, given a chance to defend themselves, and warned. The whole process was based on anonymous denunciation, either by the secret police or co-workers or co-students of the defendants, or more likely by the Committees for the Defence of the Revolution themselves.

As time wore on, the inevitable began to happen. Homosexuality was one of the biggest anxieties of Cuban revolutionary society; charges were fabricated against any suspected homosexual, however flimsy the suspicion, and homosexuals were instant scapegoats for any counter-revolutionary activities.

The camps themselves, whatever the original intentions, pretty quickly stopped being places of rehabilitation and became places of punishment. Graham Greene, visiting Cuba in the autumn of 1965, denounced them. In his view, the revolution could survive political or economic errors, but it could not survive moral errors. The UMAP camps were such an error.

---

[1] See p. 266 for current difficulties faced by priests.

In the autumn of 1966 Castro himself condemned the UMAP camps as concentration camps, and they were subsequently abolished. But attitudes seem to have remained.

As the credits on *Beverley Hills Cop* started to roll, an old woman with a pot-belly pushed open the fire doors, and the audience surged out into the dark, warm night.

I went to the Bar Juventud. The mad old black man who'd been on the window ledge in the afternoon was lying across the counter. He woke but was too drunk to stand and slid along the whole tin length, causing it to rumble faintly like stage thunder, before disappearing into the darkness. Then a dwarf came in. He ordered a large glass of green liqueur and began to smoke a huge cigar. He started a story. I heard him say, 'He took her hand and put it on his cock and he said, "It won't go to sleep."' The barman laughed so much he fell over. Making my way back to the motel, I caught the smell of tobacco from the cigarette factory, hanging like snuff in the air.

*

On Monday our daughter fell on the steps near the motel desk and cut an inch of her five-year-old head open just above the left eye. We drove off in a panic with her blood dripping through the coarse brown lavatory paper we'd taken to staunch the wound. Near the crumbling shell of the Iglesia de Santa Ana, a young boy agreed to show us the way. In the entrance of the Children's Hospital, parents and their children waited on a bench in a hallway. Some of these children were very sick but when we appeared, India's hair and teeshirt soaked with blood, we were told to go to the head of the queue and straight in to the doctor.

Through the door we went and we found ourselves in the emergency ward, a dark room with green walls. In one corner a young girl on an examination couch squirmed and retched as a nurse stuck a spatula into the back of her throat. In another corner there was a bathroom with an enamel basin standing under a leaking shower. The smell was antiseptic and pee and sick, all mixed up. The old backless radio, converted into a PA speaker, rasped and crackled on a table. Above the hospital duty roster, someone had put up a picture, cut from a magazine, of a pretty young girl with red lipstick.

They laid our child on a cold steel trolley covered with a piece of paper. The nurse, fat, middle-aged, with varnish flecks on her fingers, broke open a sealed brown-paper package and with a pair of forceps tugged out a piece of lint. When the antiseptic solution went onto the wound, India roared. The nurse told us to hold her still and we lay across the tiny, struggling body. She dabbed again at the wound, which we could now see running across the soft pocket of the eyelid. Out came a razor blade, and with a steady hand the nurse began to shave off the blonde eyebrow above, blowing away the little iron-filing pieces of hair before they could stick to the skin.

The bearded doctor arrived. He removed his large gold signet ring and unclipped his heavy wristwatch. He washed his hands and dried them on a grubby towel. The nurse opened a second brown-paper package. Inside were plastic gloves the colour of nicotine, which the doctor pulled on. From further packages of brown paper came scissors, thread and the stitching needle.

A sterile green cloth went over India's face. There was a hole in the cloth, an eye, and through this only the wound was visible. From under the cloth came her screams, 'Take it off, take it off,' and she tried with her arms to tear it away but her mother held her fast. A chorus of a good half-dozen women had gathered to watch, mothers from outside or the street who had heard the commotion. They watched the doctor with long sorrowful expressions, as he threaded the needle.

'It won't hurt, it won't hurt,' the chorus said in Spanish, stroking India's hot, sweating feet and hands.

I remembered those lies from my own childhood.

The doctor pinched the wound between his fingers. Some of the chorus looked away. He took the needle and forced it through the skin on one side and out the other. For a moment it was at rest, knitting the two sides together. I looked away and by the time I looked back, the needle was all the way through and two black strands of thread pointed into the air waiting for the nurse to cut them. Snip, she cut them, and they fell and the doctor caught them and tied the ends together.

'No more, no more,' India shouted from under the cloth.

The boat-shaped needle went into the flesh and out again, and the thread came pulling after it to be tied again.

'Do you think we need a third?' the doctor asked.

The chorus leaned forward a few inches and the nurse brought her face close to the slit with the small black knots.

The nurse nodded. The doctor pinched the skin.

'Let go of my hands,' India screamed from under the cloth.

'Only one more darling, then it'll be over,' her mother whispered.

The chorus crowded closer. The point went in and out.

'Stop it. It's the worst.'

The thread followed the needle through the hole in the side of the wound. The doctor knotted it. The cloth was pulled away and I saw a face wet with salt tears, the hair stuck to the red skin, the left eyebrow shaved away and, like a false eyebrow below, three small black spiders.

Outside in the hall we found the boy who had guided us there, waiting to know what had happened but also to be brought home. We all got into the car and I started to drive.

'The museums in my city are the most beautiful in the world,' he said, and blew a kiss from his lips. India wept in the back seat with her mother.

The rest of the day I could only think about a town in Mexico. It was 1982. I was there on holiday. Two *campesinos*, working on the rooftop of a friend's house, accidentally touched the metal ladder they were carrying against a high-voltage live wire. The metal of the ladder melted through their skins to the bone. They died after waiting sixteen hours outside the hospital. They were turned away because they could not pay. In Cuba the service is free for all and that included ourselves.

We made friends with the doctor, who was called Ronald. We went to his house several times, once for an enormous meal of *paella* made with lobster and we got very drunk together on Johnnie Walker whisky afterwards. He told me then—it was a boast delivered in the nicest possible way—'In Cuba the number-one killers are cancer and heart disease and automobile accidents,' and then he added, 'just like the USA.' Ronald was a Beatles fan and before we left I promised to send him a cassette of their hits. When the time came to leave he picked India up and looked at her face. The wound had healed, and he had taken the stitches out. 'You may forget me but you'll never forget Cuba,' he said.

19

Señor Ribalta

Trinidad's Museo Historico was housed in an old merchant's house, restored to its traditional glory. The grandest room was furnished with rocking chairs, alabaster amphorae and marble tables, as it would have been in the nineteenth century. In the succession of smaller rooms which followed, the visitor was taken through the history of the city, from the original settlements of the Indians onwards. There was the old bell from the ancient convent of San Francis of Assisi; the English coat of arms dating from 1762–3, when Trinidad had supplied Havana and the English with beef; a set of stocks used for holding slaves on boats from Africa (free introduction of slaves started in 1789; they were used in sugar factories); a water purifier from Manchester; and the dark, depressing nineteenth-century banknotes of the National Bank of Spain in the Island of Cuba, printed by the American Bank Note Co., NY.

The story continued with 'The Glorious Conflict' of 1868, which saw the defeat of the Cuban nationalists, and the 'Glorious Triumph' of 1895–8, when independence was finally wrested from Spain. To tell the narrative there were photographs of the nineteenth-century revolutionaries (who all looked extremely bourgeois, or did the old plate cameras make every subject look like this?) and their memorabilia: the revolver and bullets of the General of the Trinidad Brigade, Juan Bravo y Perez; the undershirt worn on the 1895 campaign by Carlos Perez Concio; the pocket corkscrew and the badge with the Cuban coat of arms, bought by José A. Garcia for ten dollars in 1895 in New York. Here was the same emphasis on having the original, the real, as once informed the early Christians with their saints' bones and fragments of the Shroud and the Cross.

Now the story rolled on to the Thirties, Forties and Fifties. There were membership cards of the Ortodoxo Party and Federación Nacional de Trabajadores Azucareros, (National Sugar Workers' Union), and black-and-white photographs of the celebrations held in Trinidad on the first anniversary of the revolution, and a beautiful scale model of the *Andrei Vishinsky*, the first Soviet ship to visit Cuba after the revolution. She entered Trinidad's port of Casilda on 17 April 1960. The bright pennants of the municipality, copies behind glass of Fidel's book, *Discursos de Fidel en Los Aniversarios de los CDR 1968–1972*, and photographs of those Trinidadian worthies who were Party members, brought the story of modern Cuba to its glorious climax.

Everything leads finally and inevitably to the present situation, said the exhibition; look what benefits you have reaped, said the photographs in the final room: a telephone exchange, a tobacco factory, a spotless maternity ward in a spotless hospital, a paper-pulping plant, even a municipal hearse.

Every museum in the world supports some ideology or status quo, but this was so brazenly propagandist, it was embarrassing.

I had been followed all the way through the museum by an official. I had been the only visitor. Now she followed me back to the entrance where she sat down behind her desk at the door.

'Please,' she said, handing me a pen.

I signed the Visitors' Book and left.

In the Plaza Mayor a few minutes later, Señor Ribalta hailed me outside the Archaeological Museum. It was our fourth or fifth encounter of the week.

'Let us talk,' he said and shepherded me into the centre of the square, with its white-painted iron benches. Because of the heat it was empty of people. Why has he brought me into the sun? I wondered. We talked about this and that and then it slipped out. He had ten dollars. Tips, he explained.

'Please, will you go to the Dollar shop in your hotel and buy something for me for my wife?' he said humbly. 'Tomorrow it's her birthday.'

'What would you like me to buy?'

'Ask for pullovers,' he said, 'and get me two. They're $4.90 each. Any colour. Small. No fancy collars. No slogans. And certainly nothing like "I love Cuba."'

He led the way to his house where the money was. We went through to the patio where he kept white rabbits in hutches.

'Yes, sometimes we do eat them,' he said, and made a chopping movement with his hand. There was also a cage of pigeons with rings around their legs. His wife and children were keen racers. Dozens of painted tins hung from the wall with cacti growing in them. His wife appeared, a tiny woman wearing spectacles. She carried a cactus with a single purple flower. She was greatly excited as it had opened only just a moment before in the sun.

We all went and sat in the living room. I was uncertain what would happen next. Then Señor Ribalta's wife suddenly left the room and he urgently beckoned me next door. I followed him into the dining room. From a trunk he pulled out the ten illicit, grubby dollars and pushed them furtively into my hand. One year in prison for every dollar, I remembered Maria saying. I couldn't imagine Señor Ribalta lasting ten years in prison. I couldn't imagine him lasting ten days.

In the evening I went back to Señor Ribalta's. He trembled as he took the gifts which, as he had advised, I had brought in an anonymous paper bag and not one of the Dollar shop's own bags. Then he ran into a bedroom where I saw him stuffing them under a mattress.

He invited me to sit, and drink some beer. After a couple of bottles Señor Ribalta began to tell me about his boy.

'My boy is twenty-five years old. He doesn't move,' he said, 'doesn't speak, just lies flat all day long. Something wrong in his head.'

He looked up at the ceiling. We could hear footsteps above.

'My wife is up there with him now. He is very sick.'

'Can't something be done?'

He shook his head and held his hand out flat.

'Nothing to be done,' he said, 'he's just like that.'

We sat in silence. Señor Ribalta's adolescent daughter came in and asked if I would like to hear some Cuban music? I said yes, and a moment later the room was filled with 'Guantanamera' played so loudly on the sound system, Señor Ribalta and I couldn't hear one another speak.

As I left, shortly afterwards, I turned back to look at the house and at the window of his boy's room I could see the cactus with the new purple flower.

20

The Prostitute

On Friday morning I was sitting on the balcony of our cabin at the Motel Las Cuevas. I heard someone shouting below, looked down and saw it was Maria coming up the road. She came round the side and appeared at the door a few minutes later. She was in a great state of excitement as she kissed the three of us in turn.

'I have something to show you,' she said, opening her handbag and pulling something out. It was a telegram from her love in Switzerland, and it contained a proposal of marriage. We opened a bottle of rum, and as she talked her brown eyes filled with tears.

The plan was to marry in the Swiss embassy in the summer and afterwards leave for Switzerland.

*

With Maria we drove out to La Varanca, a district on the outskirts of the city. It was an area of tiny, crooked houses and uneven streets of packed earth. We were searching for the *cabildo*, the church-cum-club where blacks had held their carnivals and practised Santería, an Afro-Caribbean religion which amalgamated African beliefs and Catholicism.

Slaves brought the African component; the Roman Catholic church was already established in Cuba; and from the start of the nineteenth century, the likes of St Barbara, St Joseph and Our Lady of Mercy began to be co-opted as supervisors of Changó, the god of war, Yoruba, the god of lightning and storms, and Obatalá who was the African La Mercé or Merced.

The religious practices of the Yoruba people (as distinct from the god of the same name), who came from what is Nigeria today, were the dominant African religious influence in Cuba. This was because, although the Yoruba were not numerically dominant, they simply got to Cuba first.

Also important were the Mayombé cult (via the Bantus from what is now Angola) and the Zarabanda, a mixture of the Congolese and Yoruba religions, Zarabanda being the Congolese equivalent of the Yoruba god of war, Changó. The Congolese also accepted the Yoruba vegetable deity, Osian, and it is reasonable to assume much other borrowing and cross-fertilisation between the sects.

'Santería' literally means 'the cult of the gods', or *orishas*. The central expression of Santería, whatever the racial lineage of its participants, was dance, principally to drum music, in which the participants mimed the gods and re-enacted their life stories. Particular drums had particular significance in the ceremonies, with names and magical properties.

On to this rich world was superimposed the Christian. The Spanish were adept at this sort of amalgamation wherever they went in the New World; in Cuba the process is associated with Pedro Augustín Morell de Santa Cruz, bishop of Cuba for fifteen years until his death in 1768. Having coped with a slave rebellion, Morell saw the wisdom of loosening strict Christian bonds, and under his authority, for instance, Epiphany became a time of indulgence and liberation for the slaves. They would select 'chiefs' from amongst themselves, dress them up and drink, dance and drum to celebrate the arrival of the kings.

The correspondence which developed between the two religions was a mix of the surprisingly direct and the idiosyncratic. Among the Yoruba descendants, Christ was Obatalá, charged with the interesting task of completing creation. His colour, perhaps unsurprisingly, was white. The wife of Christ was Odudúa, the goddess of the underworld where dead spirits went. As befitted such a gloomy occupation, she disapproved of alcohol. Odudúa was identified with Our Lady and even at times, the Holy Ghost. Obeisance was made to Odudúa by the monthly slaughter of white chickens. Another deity was Ogún, a drunkard curiously identified with St John the Baptist, and the patron saint of huntsmen, blacksmiths and soldiers. Sailors looked for protection to Yemayá. In her Christian incarnation she was Our Lady of Regla. She lived in the sea, her favourite colours were blue and white, and she was also the patron saint of fresh water. There was also Oshún, beautiful and sexy and known for her many affairs. Yellow was her colour and her Christian alter ego was the *Virgen de la Caridad de Cobre,* or Caridá or Cachita, the patron saint of Cuba: an association which has quite stunning implications.

Rituals in the *cabildos* varied. Each devotee had his or her individual patrons or *orishas*, regarded as family ancestors. And although worship was under the guidance of *Santeros,* priests, and to the uninitiated seemed almost Roman Catholic, with its Our Fathers, Hail Marys, Creeds, incense and candles, on other occasions there could be no doubt about the African origins, especially at fiestas when mass hysteria developed and worshippers were so overcome by the feeling of being possessed that they put on the clothes of their private *orishas*.

This century there have been two important developments. Firstly, the appearance of artists like Wilfredo Lam the painter and Alejo Carpentier the novelist, and of folklorists, most notably Fernando Ortiz, who mediated between the black and white worlds in Cuba, and awakened the white Cuban middle class to the beliefs, habits and myths of the Afro-Cuban life flourishing in their midst. It made them less fearful and less intolerant. The second development was that black Cubans increasingly came to regard Roman Catholicism as the Spanish version of Santería. The failure of the negro revolution of 1912 and the increasing assimilation of the black and mulatto middle class into white Cuban society are the two factors most usually invoked to explain this. Perhaps an equally likely explanation for the change is that white people began to attend the *cabildos*, even mayors and senators and other secular dignitaries. There was even a catch-phrase used by whites who attended: '*Yo no creo pero lo repeto*' ('I do not believe but I repeat the ritual'). By the 1950s one Cuban in four had attended a Santería festival at some time or other in their lives.

Our search for the Trinidad *cabildo* had another dimension besides simple interest to see what remained of Santería. It was that Batista, a mulatto with Chinese blood, had been a supporter if not a worshipper, who contributed to Santería and in particular Abakua.[1] In the summer of 1958, according to Hugh Thomas's *Cuba,* Batista had financed a reunion of all the prominent *Santeros* of Guanabacoa where many cocks and goats had been sacrificed. The Santería initiates in Cuba regarded him as one of their own, and nowhere was this more so than in the city of Trinidad. How could we resist going in search of Trinidad's principal *cabildo*?

We found the place at the end of a dismal lane. As we got out of the car, faces stared at us from doorways and windows. There was a small black child, naked except for a pair of white socks and shoes, playing with a piece of hosepipe in the gutter. The houses were made of mud, packed around a structure of sticks. There were horses tethered in front of most of the doorways.

The *cabildo* was a slightly better-looking long building about the size of a village hall. An old black man sat on the steps. He was thin and muscular, with very prominent purple gums.

'No service in this chapel,' he said straight away in Spanish, 'until the summer. But as you are tourists it is possible to arrange a special demonstration of Congo drumming.'

---

[1] A highly secret sect and, unlike Santería, which is found all over the Caribbean, is unique to Cuba. Sometimes known as *Náñgo*, the word used for its adepts.

'No, thank you,' one of us said. I felt like turning round and going, but the old man wanted to show us around.

We followed him up the steps. Whatever authentic expression of black African religious life had once occurred in this hall, the dead hand of officialdom had now fallen on it, for the first things I saw, the very first, were a framed picture of Fidel in his olive-green forage cap, and some sort of licence from the local Poder Popular. Beside these were the chapel's coat of arms in which the largest motif was two Union Jacks. It was explained that British ships had carried the slaves who had originally worshipped in this *cabildo* from the Congo, which was why the flags had such prominence.

On the walls there were also black-and-white photographs of a service; a man waved a banner; three men behind him beat their congas; a small number of communicants sat watching. It could have been a Caribbean night in a church in London's Notting Hill.

The old man led us outside to a stony backyard. There was an old kerosene can, a mongrel and the charred remains of a fire.

'This is where we pray,' he said and we stood in silence.

We left a few minutes later promising we would return in the summer, in July, at carnival, when the descendants of the slaves would be beating their sacred drums for visitors for a whole week.

Perhaps if I'd troubled to enquire, I might have found that the original spirit of Santería had survived; but I didn't. It has been brought into the light and anatomised quite sufficiently by historians and the state without my adding to the process.

After this failure we decided to do what people like us should have been doing: to go to the beach at Playa Ancon, a few miles from the city, and reputedly among Cuba's most beautiful.

We drove towards Casilda, the port, bumped across the railway line and struck out along the Ancon peninsula, which stretched south out into the Caribbean. Where the road met the coast stood a sparkling army barracks with the message across the front, '*Por Nuestra Frontera El Enemigo No Pasará!*' ('The enemy shall not pass our frontier'). In March 1961, when Kennedy had agreed to let the invasion by exiles go ahead,

Trinidad had been very strongly promoted by the CIA director of operations, Richard Bissel, as the best landing place. Kennedy rejected the idea, preferring a more low-key spot. He had already determined there would be no US military intervention, and in a sense was only going ahead because, having trained up the exiles to be landed in Cuba, what was there to do with them? As Allen Dulles, the CIA director, put it, if they didn't go there'd be a 'disposal problem'. They could only be returned to Miami where they would be resentful and complain loudly.

We stopped and found a place on the sand under a pine tree. In the water young boys played with a long spar of wood. We grew hungry. We had passed a hotel on the way down and I decided to go back to it, asking Maria to come with me. We drove there and as we turned into the car park she said, 'I was here with Otto, we came here for a holiday just after Christmas.'

I turned off the engine, but she did not get out.

'I don't want them to think I've another boyfriend who is *extranjero*,' she said.

I said I would pose as a university friend from Bratislava and she would only speak to me in Czech. We went up the steps and into the hotel and everyone remembered her, the policeman at the door, the girl behind the desk, the waiter in the bar, and I was Stefan when I shook hands with each of them in turn. I thought it was pure melodrama, but I didn't care until Maria asked what I wanted and mistook my guttural pseudo-Czech to mean ham when I meant cheese.

We got back to the shade on the beach and the four of us sat down to our lunch of sandwiches made with thick, white sliced bread, and beer and Fresco. Under the next tree, a few feet away, I noticed a man lying on the ground wearing a pair of old swimming trunks slightly frayed along the bottoms.

A busty woman, with her brassière strap showing and dyed blonde hair, was standing astride him with one foot on either side of his body.

'Darling Pipo,' she murmured.

He lay, unresponsive, staring in our direction with bloodshot eyes.

She knelt down and started to wipe away the sand stuck by sweat to the side of his face. Pipo closed his eyes and turned his head the other way.

Maria whispered, 'Prostitute'. Then she added, 'I have a story. I was on holiday with Otto in the hotel where we bought the lunch. This was three months ago, after Christmas. One day we were cycling to this beach, where we're sitting now. A police car went by and stopped. Inside was the Head of Security, the *jefe* for the Ministry of the Interior, for Trinidad, Casilda, the whole district. "Hey," he said, "leave that *extranjero* and come in the car with me." I didn't want to get in the *jefe*'s car. I said, "I'm with the *extranjero*. We're together. I stay with him." The *jefe* didn't like this.'

Under the next tree the blonde woman had squatted on the sand. She stroked Pipo's hair and whispered endearments in his ear.

'The next evening,' said Maria, 'we were in the dining room of the hotel, me and Otto. The *jefe* came in and said, "You're a *Cubana*. What are you doing with an *extranjero*? Come with me," he said. "No, no," Otto said, "not unless I come too." We all went to a room and the *jefe* said, "You're a prostitute, aren't you? That's why you're with this *extranjero*, isn't it?" Otto became furious. "Prostitute?" he shouted. "She is my fiancée, and once we have the proper papers, we're going to make our relationship legal." Then he said he was going to call the Swiss embassy in Havana. Of course when he heard this, the *jefe* began to get worried. "Of course if you're going to get married, that makes everything different," he said.

'We went back to the restaurant, the *jefe* behind. He ordered Cuba Libres. Huh! Rum and colas to make up for what he'd done. It was an insult. Otto went and bought a bottle of champagne to show the *jefe* what was required. And everyone was friends. Huh!

'A few days later I washed Otto's clothes and when I went out onto the balcony to hang them up, the *jefe* was there on the path. He helped me to put up a line. "Still going to get married?" he asked. Otto and I went back home to Santa Clara. The next day there were policemen in a car outside our block. They were watching us.

'The holiday finished. I went with Otto to Havana airport. We said goodbye. He went through. I went back outside and got into a taxi. The driver took me straight round the corner and there was a police car waiting there for me.

'I was taken to a police station and then it all started. "Why were you with the *extranjero*? You are a prostitute. How many dollars did he give you? Where are the drugs?" I said, "I'm marrying him. He's my fiancé. No dollars. No drugs." They didn't believe me. So they searched me. Here,' she said, pointing behind, 'and here.' She pointed at her sex.

'I started my night in the cell. At the airport, Otto's flight was postponed for twelve hours. He went to the house of my friend where we'd been staying. I wasn't there. "Juan," he said, "where is she?" Juan didn't know. They phoned the police and they said, "Yes. Maria Miguel, we have her."

'I got out the next morning, I saw Otto, I cried, and he flew off. I went back home, and then one day the *jefe* came. The one who'd bought the Cuba Libres. He'd come all the way from Trinidad to check everything I'd told him was correct: my name, my parents, my occupation. Then he said, "Still waiting for that *extranjero*? These foreigners, they just have sex, they go away. They never come back." I said, "He's coming back," and the *jefe* said, "No he won't," and I said, "Yes he will," and he said, "I want you to work for the police."'

Maria pointed to her eye and put her tongue out.

'I wasn't going to go running to them every time I saw something. I said, "No." He was furious. He said, "If I ever see you with another *extranjero*, you'll go to prison as a prostitute."'

Now I understood the charade at the hotel.

'Do you know what I'm going to do after the ceremony?' she said. 'I'll have a ring on my finger. I'll have a piece of paper. I'm coming back to this hotel here for the honeymoon. The *jefe* stays there sometimes. I'm going to find him. I'm going to show him the ring. I'm going to show him the paper. I'm going to say, "You thought I was a whore. But I was never a whore and now

I'm married." Then I'm going to say, "You sleep here at night. Your mother sleeps alone at home. Maybe she's the whore and you're the son of a whore."'

Beside us I heard the blonde woman coaxing, 'Let's go to your hotel. Screw me. Give me the money. I have two children. . .'

'Just before you picked me up when I was hitch-hiking,' said Maria, 'you remember what happened? I was sleeping at Juan's. Somebody broke in. They took my suitcase. Nothing else. I think that was the police.'

We were all silent. The blonde stood up, picked up her handbag and strode off in a huff. I remembered Maria telling me about the argument she'd had when she'd stayed overnight in Varadero. It had been with a policeman and the way she'd told me had made me think she had an aversion to policemen. Now I could understand why. The prostitute returned.

'Pipo, my darling . . .' she started again.

I went into the warm water and lay on my back. The prostitute was standing astride Pipo again. She was combing her hair with a red plastic comb.

I went back to our tree and lay down. Pleas, threats, declarations, every known way to make a man come to bed, drifted across. Pipo slid down the beach to catch the sun.

The sea was blue with dark patches further out where the seaweed grew. Some boys caught a silver fish which glistened like the wrapping from a chocolate bar.

The prostitute, left behind at the tree, shouted, 'If you don't come now we'll miss the bus.'

Pipo, near the seashore, waved her away in a desultory way.

She looked around.

'I'm telling you.'

She picked up Pipo's stack-heeled boots and all his clothes.

'I've got your things. You'd better come with me,' she shouted. She turned and started to walk towards the road, a hundred yards off.

'Hurry Pipo,' she shouted. Pipo drew himself onto his knees and in a leisurely fashion began to brush the sand off his body.

'Come on.'

Havana, San Lazaro, Chevrolet

Havana, San Miguel

Havana, Ford Custom-Line and Buick Sedanette

Havana, Malecón, baseball game

Havana, *'Parqueo'* sign

Car under sunshade

Viñales

Varadero, man on bicycle

Varadero, house

Varadero, soft drinks' trolley

Playa Girón, billboard

Santa Lucia, Chevrolet on beach

Camagüey, shop window

Cienfuegos, house

Cienfuegos, Buick Century

Cienfuegos, herding cattle

He walked a few paces and stopped to dust his knees.

'Pipo.'

He ambled across the car park to the road, where she was with half a dozen others waiting for the bus. She held out his trousers. He languidly took them and then with painstaking slowness began to pull them on. The other passengers looked at the prostitute and turned away, shaking their heads. He took his vest and shirt. She stared into the distance. The bus came. They got on.

The next day I saw Pipo and the woman once again. They were sitting in another bus in a Trinidad street. He'd taken off his shirt and vest, something I'd never seen anyone else do in Cuba on a bus, and she was staring ahead with her lips pressed tightly together. He smirked at me through the glass.

21

The Road to Camagüey

It was Saturday. We decided to leave Trinidad, and to skip Sancti Spíritus which was the next big city to the east. We dropped off Maria at the bus depot and headed for another city founded by Velázquez, what had been known in his day as Puerto Principe and was now known as Camagüey, along the *carretera central.* Though it is the main artery of Cuba, it is an ordinary two-lane highway with little concrete posts marking the verges, running through an unexceptional, flat green landscape. There was low cloud with the sun beating behind. The air was hot and sluggish, like that of a greenhouse. I was driving and I was bored and I took a couple of mouthfuls of rum from the bottle of Paticruzado which was in the glove compartment.

On Cuba's main roads there were numerous *puntos de control*, control points. Large signs warned of them in advance. When passing a *punto de control*, a driver was expected to slow down to forty-five kilometres an hour or less. The virtue of the system was that it forced Cuban drivers (as a rule, lunatics behind the wheel) to slow down regularly.

Somewhere near the town of Florida I did something very foolish. I saw the sign by the roadside warning of the *punto de control* ahead, but I paid no attention. Then I saw the *punto de control* itself, looking like an air-traffic-control lookout painted with white and yellow stripes, and again paid no attention. Then I saw a policeman standing by the roadside with a clipboard and still paid no attention. As the car flashed by I heard his whistle and I had to pay attention.

We pulled over, and he walked towards us. He was a traffic policeman wearing skin-tight trousers with a metal ring-pull on his zip which bobbed about, and spurs on his immaculately shiny leather boots which clinked as he walked. Spurs, on a motorcycle? I exhaled deeply to remove any smell of rum from my breath.

He put his serge-covered elbow on the window.

'Do you realise you were doing ninety in an area with a speed limit of forty-five?'

'Oh, I'm very sorry.'

At the sound of my accent, his face dropped. A man can't enjoy being angry with someone who can't properly speak his language.

'Driving licence,' he said abruptly.

At the bottom of Tyga's handbag, among a wet bathing costume, a piece of cake wrapped in a '*Gracias por su visita*' placemat, twigs, seashells and the bottle of Paticruzado, we found it.

He took it and started trying to puzzle out the English. His brow furrowed. He tried to copy down some details on the form attached to his clipboard. Useless. He returned the licence, squeezed my elbow hard and said, 'Go away.'

I drove off very slowly, and in the rearview mirror watched him stopping an enormous articulated lorry.

*

Roads developed late in Cuba. When the English occupied Havana and its environs in 1762 there were none. Communication was mostly by sea. There was one postal service from Havana to Santiago de Cuba, the second city of the island, once a month, which took the postman fourteen days, changing horses continuously. Road and rail communications really came with the development of the sugar industry in the nineteenth century, but the main highway from Havana to Santiago de Cuba—the *carretera central* on which we were now driving for the first time—didn't come until the twentieth. It was constructed during the dictatorship of Gerado Machado.

He was born in 1871 in Camajuani, a town in Las Villas province. Like all proper tyrants, Machado was disfigured: working in the family butcher shop, he lost two fingers from his left hand. During the second War of Independence, he worked as a cattle rustler with his father. In 1899 he became mayor of Santa Clara and the *audiencia* which contained all his criminal records burnt down almost immediately in mysterious circumstances.

The first years of the twentieth century saw Machado's conventional business life flourishing. He managed a small electric light company in Santa Clara and later a sugar mill. Later still he joined Cuban Electric—the Havana subsidiary of the enormous Electric Bond and Share Company—and became its vice-president. Starting in 1921, Cuban Electric started to buy up all the electricity supply companies in the city. By 1924 the company controlled most of the electric utilities in Havana.

Machado had ambitions to be president and in 1924 he decided to run. Electric Bond and its president, an American called Catlin, rewarded Machado for his services with a contribution of half a million dollars to his electoral expenses. At this time Machado was known in Cuba as a shark who did a passable imitation of a businessman, and as the owner of the Moulin Rouge theatre (via the agency of his barber) where risqué burlesques were performed. His allegiance was to the Liberal Party—he had served for a short while in President Gomez's Liberal cabinet before the First World War. The Liberal Party, however, had their choice in the person of Colonel Carlos Mendieta, a man who was regarded as decent and incorruptible. But Mendieta made a mistake. In the summer of 1924, during the run-up to the nomination, he rested, feeling assured of victory. Machado meanwhile was indefatigable. '*Chico*, come and see me,' was his catchphrase as he stamped up and down Havana. They did and he promised them if he was president the future would be golden. They believed him; he won the nomination, hired a 'victory train' and began to travel about Cuba promising roads, schools and water for everyone. The scheme worked wonderfully, proving once again that simple schemes work best. Machado defeated the Conservatives and became president-elect in May 1925.

Machado's programme, announced after his inauguration a month later, pleased everyone. Out was to go the Platt Amendment, which gave the US the right to intervene in Cuba's internal affairs; in was to come a new commercial treaty with America. Out was to go the Lottery—perhaps the single most corrupt institution in all of Cuba; in was to come autonomy for the university of Havana. Reforms of the judiciary and the educational system were promised, and finally there was to be no presidential re-election. Cubans began to form the impression that maybe Machado had been the man they were waiting for, after all.

Machado appointed his cabinet—a sort of balanced one. His Minister of Works (who was later to become important in the building of the highway we were on) was Carlos Miguel de Céspedes. During the early part of his term, Céspedes worked feverishly on the building of his luxury villa in Miramar and was often photographed on site surrounded by foremen, workers and so on. He was subsequently nicknamed by the press (whom he paid to put about this compliment) El Julio Verne Cubano or, more impressively, El Dinámico.

It soon became clear that Machado's package was not going to be forthcoming. Corruption persisted; there were labour troubles; and the world price of sugar fell. An unflattering comparison with Mussolini, made by opponents during the election campaign, suddenly began to look plausible. In 1925, the Havana newspaper of Armando André, a veteran of the War of Independence and a Conservative politician, enraged the president by hinting that his daughter was a lesbian. On 20 August André was shot while turning the front-door key of his house. The killers, evidence suggested, were acting on Machado's orders. André's fellow Conservative politicians, instead of speaking out against the deed, passed a bland resolution of regret. With hints of jobs for the boys, Machado had bought their silence.

The autumn and winter of 1925 saw more strikes; a worsening economic situation; and the wholesale deportation of anyone deemed to be dangerous, especially Spanish anarchists who had a high profile in the Cuban trades unions. Machado continued unchecked by his fellow politicians, protected by the magic circle of corruption. What senator could resist a lottery collectorship with the right to sell at between thirty and fifty percent above the marked price? Hugh Thomas estimates that the president and his cronies were now pocketing about $10,000,000 a year, about a fifth of the national product of the country.

Into this mess, the next ingredient added was an enormous programme of public works. In his inaugural plans of July 1925, Machado had promised such a scheme financed by extra taxes. Nothing more had been heard. Now a loan was needed. In September 1926 El Dinámico, Céspedes, announced the plan to build a first-class road, running east to west along the spine of the island, financed by the US Chase National Bank. Fourteen tenders were made for the project, but the tender went, because of lobbying by Machado's son-in-law, José Enrique Obregón (incidentally the manager of the Cuban branch of the Chase National Bank) and H. C. Catlin (Machado's old boss at Cuban Electric) to the little known Warren Bros which in turn handed over the construction rights in the provinces of Matanzas and Santa Clara to a company in which Machado had a strong interest.[1]

The inexhaustible Céspedes made the most of the photo-opportunity afforded by the project and was there at the start, turning the soil, dressed in an ancient Texan hat. Meanwhile, in America, the *International Labour News* reported that in 1927

---

[1] At the same time Warren Bros also obtained a $10,000,000 loan from Chase National.

Machado and his administration had killed at least 147 opponents. Despite these revelations the presidential term was now extended from four to six years; as senators and representatives were to enjoy the same extension, there was no opposition.

In October 1927 comparisons with Mussolini began to look even more appropriate. Four students, accused of being communists, i.e. critics of Machado, were dropped, with weights tied to their legs, out of the Morro castle into the sea where they were eaten by sharks. This signalled the start of outright confrontation: Machado, the police and the army on one side, the middle classes, their student children and trade unionists on the other.

In April 1928 Machado illegally extended his presidency again at a packed convention, to run until 1935. However, the extension backfired as it brought those who weren't automatically in opposition to Machado into open conflict. The rest of the year saw more murders and a failed army putsch.

In September 1929, rumbles came from the US Senate Foreign Relations Committee, which passed a resolution condemning Machado's corruption. US businessmen, and Warren Bros, already hard at work on the central highway, immediately began to lobby on Machado's behalf.

By 1930 the $60,000,000 Chase loan for the entire scheme was gone, and the central highway was nowhere near complete. In February, Chase came up with a further loan of $20,000,000. The rest of the year saw the development of a three-way contest. In the first corner there were Machado and his cronies who maintained a policy of assassination and indifference to Cuba's collapse. In the second corner was Colonel Mendieta and ex-President Menocal, who were privately requesting US intervention via the US ambassador, Henry Guggenheim. Finally, in the third corner there were the students who, because Machado had shut the university of Havana, now had the time and leisure to become full-time revolutionaries. It was their belief that they were the real heirs of Martí, struggling against those survivors of the wars of independence who had hijacked the revolutionary tradition and bent it to their own devious ends.

1931 came, and still the central highway was not finished. Chase National Bank sent one James Bruce to Havana who promised another $20,000,000 within ninety days. In his report on his return to New York, Bruce admitted there was no prospect of a personal loan of $130,000 to Machado ever being repaid, nor of various other loans which had been made to Machado's road-construction business. Bruce also described José Obregón, the president's son-in-law, as useless from the business point of view, but he couldn't recommend firing him because it would only mean that Machado would come out in his support.

Finally, at the end of 1931, the central highway was finished, and not a second too soon. If the next developments had occurred before its completion, I doubt it would ever have been finished, which would have deprived us of our route and this book of its structure.

Firstly, there was the invasion at Gibara by ex-war-of-independence types, an action which had the support of Mendieta and Menocal. The insurrection was ruthlessly suppressed by Machado's army. Many of the men were horribly tortured and shot, and innocent people in Gibara were also killed. The Gibara fiasco signalled the end of the old guard of the Nineties, and prepared the way for the second and much more important development: the formation of ABC. What the initials stood for was never clear, but what ABC was was never in doubt. A middle-class, underground organisation, with vaguely leftist and anti-US policies, it was committed to the downfall of Machado. Its chosen means was terror, particularly bombings, which were intended to provoke counter-terror from the state which would spark off open insurrection by the Cuban people who could no longer tolerate official excesses. Machado had come in by simple means, and now, by means of an equally simple formula, he was to go.

Buried in these confused times were pointers to the future. Anti-US sentiments had a pedigree which went back to Martí but it was not until the anti-Machado agitations that they became part of the common political vocabulary. In the hands of the

Fidelistas in the early Sixties, they would be used to devastating effect. The other development, which was not to bear fruit for twenty-five years, was the dawning recognition by some that the struggle was not just against Machado but against imperialism as well.

The US at the time was the dominant economic and political force: Cuba was in effect her client state. For the first thirty years of her independence from Spain, Cuba had been governed by men, or the sons of men, who had fought against Spain. The style of administration which these patriots offered was less than patriotic; the old Spanish habits of corruption and the desire for personal gain were far too ingrained. None the less, the US supported them. During the first quarter of the century US action, or the threat of action, had kept the Conservatives more or less in power, and the Liberals, under José Miguel Gómez —whose movement was genuinely popular—out of power. When the Liberals under Machado finally got their turn, there was an inbuilt system of rewards for whoever was in power which it seemed impossible for any man to resist. And these temptations were intimately connected with US business interests. It was only when Machado began to fall that it was perceived that the US did not want to work for a better Cuba, despite pious declarations to the contrary.

In 1959 this insight finally led Cuba into the Soviet camp, and in 1987 it was a perception that still dominated the Cuban view of her nearest and most powerful neighbour. Bizarrely, it was to those who were first propagating the anti-US view that Machado turned for help in the last desperate months of his reign: the communist-dominated Confederación Nacional Obrera Cubana (CNOC). They for their part had decided it was better to do business with the dictator than to allow the situation to deteriorate to the point where the US sent in the Marines. Early in 1933 the CNOC came to an agreement with Machado and, from April onwards, called for an end to the current strike whilst sending back their own workers and denouncing ABC as a fascist organisation. They later agreed to call off another strike in return for recognition. However, at this juncture the CNOC influence on the labour movement—currently all out on strike—was small. The strike continued, and Sumner Welles, the US ambassador in Havana, began to mediate between Machado and the opposition while simultaneously acting as midwife to the forces which finally pushed Machado out.

The dictator fled from Havana to Nassau on the night of 12 August 1933, taking with him five revolvers, five friends and seven bags of gold. His wife, daughters and sons-in-law (including the useless Obregón) were shipped out of Havana the day he left. Many of Machado's cronies did not get away as he did, and in the days immediately afterwards the public took their revenge. There was complete chaos. Many prominent policemen, along with Machado's gang of private killers (known as '*La Porra*', 'the Big Stick'), were hunted down and lynched, while the houses of many Liberal and Conservative politicians—the public were disgusted with them all—were ransacked and burnt, including that of Carlos Miguel de Céspedes, who had been responsible for the central highway.

★

The journey to Camagüey continued, uneventfully, with little to look at but the flat landscape and the billboards every few miles by the roadside. Along with the usual ones—exhortations to more efficiency, to produce more sugar—there was '*Vamos por el camino correcto*' ('Let's go the right way'), an appeal to drive more carefully, and runs of six, seven or eight billboards at a time extolling the virtues of named towns or factories; there were others with a new, ideological tone, which we hadn't noticed before: '*En esta provincia se respira aire de lucha, aire de historia, aire de leyenda*' ('In this province one breathes the air of struggle, the air of history, the air of legend'), and '*El pais esta enfrascado en un esfuerzo serio por la exigencia y la eficiencia—Fidel*' ('The country is involved in a serious effort for demand and efficiency—Fidel'), and finally '*Una vocación y una voluntad revolu-*

cionaria fueron son y seran siempre mil veces mas poderosas que el dinero' ('A revolutionary calling and will were, are and always will be a thousand times more powerful than money').

22

The Writer

On Sunday afternoon I was in a side street in the centre of Camagüey, alone. I was singing to myself when I heard someone saying in English behind me: 'You speak English.'

I turned round. There were two men standing in a doorway. One was short and fat, and wearing green-tinted spectacles which gave him a sinister appearance. The other was thin and etiolated; he wore a baseball cap and flared trousers which flapped around his narrow legs.

'I heard you singing in English,' said the thin one.

His big brown eyes and curiously sharp nose, with his thin body, gave him the appearance of a cartoon eagle. He was about fifty-five years old, and he told me he had learnt his English in the US where he had worked in the Fifties as an electrical engineer. He also spoke fluent French (his second language at school), German and Russian.

'I liked the US,' he said, 'the US was free.'

He was looking at me closely, and choosing his words carefully. The fat man was staring just as closely.

'You could buy what you wanted.' He went on in this vein, then he said: 'But there was too much liberty. Too many people taking drugs and thinking only of themselves.'

This was *Granma*-speak. In the national newspaper I had already come across a couple of articles which attempted to connect (in a US context): the taking of drugs; capitalism; and the illness of the bourgeois soul, selfishness.

'People in the United States are cold,' he continued, 'though if you have your own enterprise, if you have money, friends and a house, you have a wonderful lifestyle.'

His political position wasn't at all clear from what he said. The situation was reciprocal, and I could feel he was trying to gauge my views.

'I am a musician and music is one of my passions,' he continued. 'I have learnt many Irish songs when I was in the US. Do you know for example, yes, surely you must, you told me you were Irish, "When Irish Eyes are Smiling"?'

He fixed me with his big brown eyes and began to sing in a wavering voice:

'When Irish eyes are smiling,
It is like a morn in spring . . .'

There was an element of seduction here.

'And in the lilt of Irish laughter
You can hear the angels sing.'

'Is there a communist party in Ireland?' he asked.

'Yes.'

'Do they want to abolish all other parties?'

'No. If they participate in elections they have to accept democracy. That's the case with communist parties all over Western Europe.'

'But the communists,' he said, hatred suddenly showing through his inflection of the proper noun, 'always abolish all parties when they take power. They say: We don't need elections any more because now the people have the government they have always wanted. It is what happened here.'

The fat man, who'd been listening patiently, suddenly said, 'I'm afraid, gentlemen, I must ask you to excuse me.'

He looked at me closely through his green-tinted spectacles. 'I have to go to confession and I must go home and get ready. Are you a Catholic?'

'My family are.'

'But do you believe in God?' he retorted angrily.

My affirmative appeared to satisfy him. 'My name is Carlos,' he said, and he introduced the thin man as Manuel. We shook hands together and Carlos stalked off.

There was a pause. I had noticed that Manuel had abnormally long nails on his little fingers, and now I saw why, as he began to pick with them at the nicotine-stained stub of cotton wool in his cigarette-holder. Once out, it was dropped on the ground, a yellow and black periwinkle, and a fresh piece was inserted. With this makeshift he was hoping, if not to stop, at least to hinder cancer. He offered me a cigarette from a tortoiseshell case.

Manuel said, 'I am only a twenty percent Marxist. I approve of free schooling and free health. But for the rest, how can I support it?'

He shook his head.

'Fidel said: Those who are not with us are against us. I don't like that. It means war. If you don't agree, you have to leave, you're expelled.[1] Fidel said that too. They only give freedom to those who support the revolution, and nothing to those who oppose it.[2] This is Fidel's policy. I do not like it.' He shrugged his shoulders.

---

[1] Fidel Castro first gave notice of this direction in his speech of 1 May 1961 (just after the Bay of Pigs). Counter-revolutionaries, he said, were to be expelled. It was in this speech that he declared, for the first time, Cuba to be socialist.

[2] I think this may have been a re-working of President Dorticós' remark from 1964: 'Our principal aim has been full freedom for those who support the Revolution, nothing for those who are opposed.' Although Manuel wrongly attributed the remark, the spirit is probably supported by all members of the government.

'I am a writer,' he said. 'I am a musician too and I am an electrical engineer. I have three vocations, you could say. I became a writer by correspondence through the American Institute of Journalism. I have never practised the profession of writing, here in Cuba. There is no freedom here. All they publish is Communist Party dogma.'

There was a moment of silence and then he said, 'I would like to invite you to our house.'

Manuel lived in a suburban street of Florida-style dwellings. In the front room there were four old women in hairnets and heavy old dresses sitting on the chairs. I imagined we would sit with them, but as I moved towards a chair Manuel took me by the elbow and steered me to a door.

I found myself in a crowded bedroom. A young woman sat in a chair with toys piled beside her. This was Celia, his daughter. In the corner there was a cot where her boy Simón lay with black staring eyes. Celia gave me a square of cake and a glass of sweet wine. Manuel picked a nicotine-stained plug of cotton wool out of his cigarette-holder and pushed in a clean one. Simón began to cry.

'Did you notice that I'm repainting the outside of the house?'

'No,' I said.

'It's going to be, well, it's a sort of plum colour, unfortunately, not a pink, which I would have liked. I just couldn't buy it. This wall here,' he pointed behind him, 'is all done. I had to search everywhere in town, going from one hardware store to another, and finally this plum was all I could obtain. If only it was pink, but what can one do? Let me show you.'

He got up to open the window so I could see his work. The window was over the cot.

'What are you doing?' shouted Celia in Spanish.

'I'm opening the window so I can show my friend what I've done.'

'Do you want Simón to catch pneumonia?'

'It's only for a moment.'

'*No.*' She turned and smiled apologetically at me.

'As you insist, I won't open the window,' he said and sat down.

There was silence. The baby cried softly. To give us something to talk about, I asked Manuel what instrument he played.

'My instrument,' he said, 'was the piano. But I have not played the piano for eleven years. Eleven years.' There was truculence in his repetition.

'When my family left eleven years ago, the communists took it away with the cars, the house, even the air-conditioners.'

I was lost. What house was he talking about? What cars?

'I would like to recite one of my favourite songs,' I heard him saying. 'It's called "An Irish Lullaby."'

'Too-ra-loo-ra-loo-ral,
Too-ra-loo-ra-lai,
Too-ra-loo-ra-loo-ral,
That's an Irish lullaby.'

Simón stopped whining as his grandfather sang and stared without making a noise at the ceiling.

'Over in Killarney, many years ago,
My mother sang a song to me, in tones so sweet and low,
Just a simple little ditty, in her good old Irish way,
And I'd give the world if I could hear, that song of hers today.'

'That was sung by Bing Crosby,' he said when he was finished, and added, 'Come outside.'

We went round to the gable end of the house.

'I wish it could have been pink,' he said, 'that plum is too red. Shall we smoke?' he suggested.

'Why not?'

'I'm going to start practising my third profession,' he said, 'perhaps you can help me?'

'How?'

'I want to write the truth about life in Cuba. You are a writer.

You would agree, no writer should write anything but the truth.'

'No.'

'What I need is . . .'

He looked at the boys playing baseball in the road.

'. . . your advice about presentation.'

This was not what he had intended to ask me about when he'd started the question, I was sure of that. Halfway through the sentence his courage had deserted him. Or else he was still uncertain if I could be trusted.

'Of course,' I said, and we spent half an hour talking about spacing, paragraphing, punctuation and carbon copies.

'I am going to write the truth about this country,' he started again. 'We could write to one another, could we not? Perhaps you could write back to me with the address of a publisher to whom I might send my articles. I am going to write the truth, you understand. I'm going to say what Cuba is really like.'

'Yes.'

'The address must not be official. There must be no mention of newspapers or publishers. Or of any kind of organisation. It would be noticed.'

'I understand.'

He squeezed my shoulder with his long fingers. 'Just a private address. Completely anonymous. Otherwise . . .'

I nodded, and he smiled. We went back into the house. The old women had vanished from the front room but his daughter was there with Simón.

'Look at this,' he said. He took from the wall a small, framed colour photograph. 'My son is a *Marielito*,'[1] he said, 'he lives in Florida.' He pointed with his long little fingernail at the young man in his twenties on the left of the portrait. His son wore an 'I love Miami' teeshirt and was smiling.

'Pablo is finding it very difficult in the US. His English is poor. He has to pay for everything.'

He pointed to the small, elderly, bald man in the middle,

---

[1] See p. 188.

straight-backed and staring directly at the camera lens. The old man wore the pleated shirt common to Cuba, called a *guayabera*, and carried a cane with an ornate handle.

'This is my father,' he said. 'He is eighty. And this is Agatha, my aunt, and this is my niece.'

He tried to return the picture to the hook from which it hung by a tiny twist of string, but his hand was trembling and he was not able to do it.

'Would you please?' he asked, handing the picture to me.

As I put it back I wondered why he had stayed when his family had left. Perhaps he had not been allowed to leave because of his technical skills? Or perhaps he believed things were going to get better only to find out in time that they didn't, like Stefan Zweig's publisher?

We sat down at opposite ends of a glass-topped table.

'Look at that,' he exclaimed suddenly. 'That's terrible.'

I turned and saw over my shoulder that a huge swathe of wallpaper had come unstuck from the wall and was hanging down limply.

'The whole place is falling down,' he muttered, 'and now I'm going to have to find wallpaper paste. Where the hell am I going to find that?'

He took a ballpoint pen and a piece of paper.

'I'm going to write out my address for you.'

He wrote slowly. His calligraphy, for someone who was so punctilious in his speech, was surprisingly extravagant and large.

'Do you really want to go and live in the US?' I asked.

'We are friends,' he said, with a warmth that seemed false, 'and we can talk truthfully.'

I wasn't going to get an answer.

'I am a citizen not of any one country: I am a citizen of the world. Everywhere everyone can learn something from everyone else. What we need to make this world a happier place is more tolerance between people of different nations.'

To leave Cuba and go to the US is to betray Cuba: that is how those who leave are looked upon by the authorities. As I listened to Manuel's claptrap, I imagined it was what he had prepared for the unhappy time which lay ahead when he would be known as a *gusano*, literally a worm, as all those who emigrate are. It was a reply he had studied and pondered for so long that he was incapable of giving any other.

'Miami can be a very difficult place,' I said, hoping to start a conversation which would circumvent his prepared speech and get us on to something more interesting.

'I had many friends in the US who were policemen,' he replied. 'I always like policemen and they always liked me. They told me who was good and who was bad, what to do, what not to do.'

When he did get to Miami, he continued, he would make some new policemen friends. The US was full of crime because so many people were selfish and took drugs. The liberals wouldn't let the police get on with their job. Liberals shouted endlessly about civil liberties, yet they allowed thousands of babies to be murdered in their own country every year through abortion. His ideology chimed exactly with that of the right wing in the US.

When he had finished on law and order he said, 'Come out and see the well.' I thought, this is another gambit to get us alone. I followed him to the kitchen. There was a large General Electric refrigerator which he patted. 'Thirty-five years of service,' he said, 'they don't make them that way any more.'

In the corner of what he called his backyard, stood a hand-pump and a grey plastic water tank. The water, he explained, was thirty foot down. It was fresh and clean. The mains was only on in the evening, water being short in Cuba like everything else, so he pumped twenty or thirty gallons up each night which saw them through the day.

'If you say you want to leave this country, do you know what happens? The local CDR come round. They make a list of everything, right down to the last thumbtack. My father was a lawyer. He left in 1976 with my sisters and their children. The communists took everything. If I were to leave . . .'

If, I thought.

'. . . it would be the same.'

He waved towards the house. 'I've been here since 1957. Thirty years of my life are tied up with this house. I go, and I lose it and everything in it. I would arrive in the US like my family; just a suitcase of clothes and not a cent to my name.

'But what can I do? I can't just go for a holiday. If you're not a good communist, they won't let you. I have to go forever.'

It was getting dark. One of the old women I'd seen earlier muttered something angrily from the back door about Manuel's dinner. He waved her away and went on talking.

'I have to leave. I cannot stay here. Every three, six months the police and the local CDR, they come to search the house. The whole place is turned upside down. Then they always say to me, "We're watching you. We know about you." Those who do not want to become like the new man,[1] they must be expelled —remember, I told you that. They want me to go, that is why they search my house, yet they make it impossible for me to leave. In the end, I will, but what then of my Celia? She won't come. She's a communist. They've brainwashed her. I don't want to abandon her. You are a father, you know what a daughter is to a father. I cannot leave her. Or my lovely grandson. He looks like me. How can I leave him? Or the house? I'm just painting it. How can I leave them? I can't leave them. I must leave them.'

He was shaking with anger.

'I want to go to Florida. To help my son, to see my father before he dies. But I have to earn some money outside of Cuba before I go. That is why I want to write those articles I was telling you about.'

He saw me out to the car. I drove out of the space carefully. He

---

[1] After the takeover of many small businesses, shops and restaurants by the state without decree in the summer of 1962, and the nationalisation in December of most enterprises which used hired labour, the concept of the 'new man' began to emerge, presumably because this man was needed to run these acquisitions. The new man as envisaged was unalienated, lived to serve his community, was unsullied by the profit motive, and scorned the corrupt city, preferring a more virtuous and Spartan rural existence. One hears less of him than previously but he is still around.

stood in the middle of the road, waving behind me, a pale figure in the darkness.

'Don't forget that address,' was the last I heard.

★

The history of emigration from Cuba post-1955, in which Manuel's family were already a statistic and in which he was hoping himself to one day become a statistic, is long and unhappy; but at least there is a history of it, which is more than can be said for other regimes.

From the time of the takeover of power by the Fidelistas on 1 January 1959, and for several years afterwards, it was possible just to get on an aeroplane and leave. Even after the Bay of Pigs invasion, two aeroplanes filled with exiles flew out of Havana for Miami every day. Between 1959 and the middle of 1962, 200,000 Cubans left—about three percent of the population—mostly to the US but also to Spain, Mexico and the rest of South America.

It was one of the largest exoduses on record; and it had a catastrophic effect on the economy. To stop the haemorrhage the government introduced restrictive procedures, under which the position of a person wanting to leave became extremely unpleasant and involved loss of profession and possessions. Once notice was given, they were visited by representatives of the local Committee for the Defence of the Revolution. An inventory was made of their possessions, after which they were not allowed to sell or dispose of them. If the applicant had recently sold anything, he or she was required to make good the cost or retrieve it.

Thereafter, would-be émigrés were at the disposal of the government. They were given a place in the queue and they normally worked in the state farm system for a minimum wage. After two years, and sometimes longer, they received their permission to leave. However, males between the ages of fifteen and twenty-seven were banned from leaving altogether, as were certain technicians.

Initially, not many people were affected by these new

procedures because after the missile crisis Pan Am suspended flights between Havana and Miami. Then, in December 1965, an air service was re-established (called the Freedom Flights Programme) with airliners chartered by the US government. Each month thereafter, 3,000 to 4,000 Cubans, *gusanos*, were transported to Miami. During the five years the scheme was in existence, it flew about 200,000 people into exile in the US. When it stopped in 1971, however, there were still another 200,000 who wanted to leave.

The next mass exodus was in 1980. Somehow—reports vary—several thousand Cubans got into the Peruvian embassy in Havana and claimed political asylum, taking advantage of the tradition in South America whereby some embassies, Peru among them, have special sanctuary status. The government had to permit a temporary relaxation in its emigration procedures and, taking advantage of this, about 120,000 Cubans sailed in small crafts from the port of Mariel on the north coast of Cuba to the US, as illegal immigrants. But the Carter administration could not turn the *Marielitos* away so it granted them permission to stay temporarily in the US while they sought to make their status permanent.

Almost inevitably, the matter was not sorted out. After several years a Migratory Agreement was eventually signed in November 1987 between Cuba and the US. Under the terms of this the Cuban government has agreed to take back those *Marielitos*, about 2,500 of them, with histories of mental illness or criminal records, whom it had encouraged to leave during the Mariel boatlift. It was further agreed that perhaps in the future it would take back a further 3,600 Cubans who, having completed sentences for crimes committed since their arrival in the US, had not been released (because as *Marielitos* they were not *bona fide* immigrants). In return, the US agreed to accept about 3,000 former political prisoners and their families and a quota of 20,000 Cuban emigrants annually. What will happen to the Agreement after the 1987 summer riots by Cuban detainees in the US who fear deportation under its terms remains to be seen.

Until the Migratory Agreement is ratified, the position for

someone like Manuel will remain unchanged (and, who knows, it may be the same even after ratification). When he says he wants to go, it will cost him everything; although it will be possible for him to circumvent the two-year wait for an exit visa if his relatives abroad are prepared to pay large sums of foreign currency. (This seems unlikely.) If Manuel were a woman, marriage would be an easier way out. But it would be no less pricey. To marry Maria and take her from the country was going to cost Maria's fiancé Otto $2,000. Or, as many Cubans, impoverished, impatient or desperate, have done, he could resort to illegal emigration, by swimming through shark-infested waters to the US base at Guantánamo, floating on a makeshift raft to Florida, or stowing away on a ship or aircraft.

In the summer of 1987, two Cubans who stowed away on a ship, believing it was headed for the US, jumped overboard when it ended up in Antwerp harbour and drowned. They mistakenly thought Belgium was a member of the eastern bloc. Assuming he survived the journey, Manuel would not at least have made that mistake. One of the first things he'd said when we'd started talking in the street was that he had a pen friend in Brussels.

23

The North Americans

Manuel and his story cast a pall over Camagüey. We decided to give ourselves three days of luxury at a resort which principally catered to Canadians on the north coast of Cuba. It was a place which Manuel knew well. He had been one of those who had designed and installed its electrical system.

We drove out of Camagüey and on to Nuevitas where we turned north towards the sea. The countryside was flat and dry, with scorched trees and dove-grey cattle. There were occasional ponds of brackish water. A boy gaucho in a new straw hat rounded up knock-kneed young calves. At a crossroads with flat, shimmering emptiness all around, a few people sat in the bus shelter out of the burning sun, and a woman turned to stare at us from a dusty track as we roared past.

*

On our first evening at Santa Lucia I came out of the bedroom and walked along the corridor of our accommodation block.

'How you doin'?' a woman on the steps at the end of the corridor said to me. She invited me for a game of pool.

She led me to the centre of the resort where the desk, and the dining room, television room and other amenities were to be found. We went into the games room.

'How do you play this game?' she said to the attendant as we took our cues from the rack on the wall.

He spoke no English and stared at her, uncomprehending.

'I was lousy at this,' she said, bending towards the table. 'My brothers always licked me. Anyway, what is it?'

'American pool.'

'Have you got any chalk? You always have to have chalk.'

I handed her the blue, porous cube.

Half an hour later the game was over, 43–5 in her favour.

We went to the bar in the corner of the room. The attendant served us two beers.

'I don't mind this unlabelled Cuban stuff,' she said. 'It's not bad. Hey, you,' she called over to the attendant tidying her cue away. 'How about a glass? *Vaso*.'

She was Canadian with an English background. Her mother's family were from Manchester and her father was a Londoner. 'He always described himself as a Londoner with a Swiss movement,' she said, 'whatever that meant.' Her name was Merili (pronounced 'merrily'). She had a small pointed face, dyed red hair and red-painted fingernails. She was a hairdresser and lived in Toronto.

'When all's said and done,' said Merili, raising her bottle, 'we're all British, right? English, Irish, Welsh, Scots, we're all British and that's where it all started. And that's where it all comes from. Here, a toast, cheers. . .'

We clinked bottles. Merili put her bottle down and rolled her lips, to straighten any blemishes on her cerise-coloured lipstick.

A couple came into the games room. They were both smoking 120-millimetre cigarettes, and they were puffing out the smoke like children having their first illicit drag. They were also very small and very thin.

Merili turned her coiffeured head to the pool table and we watched them begin to play. He broke and the balls scattered across the baize in every direction. The girl, the cigarette drooping ridiculously from her mouth, the sunhat she was wearing equally ridiculously pulled down almost to the bridge of her nose, approached the cue ball. She put her hand on the table, but she couldn't spread out her fingers and form a rest for her cue to run in. Holding it as if she were levering something, she scooped, and flipped the ball over the edge of the table. It landed on the floor with a terrible crash.

Her opponent marked up on his tally the points for a ball out of play. Then he pocketed two striped balls.

The girl's turn came and again she scooped the white onto the floor. He replied by putting another ball into a pocket and his tally rose again.

After the fourth or fifth crash of the ball on the floor, Merili shouted, 'Show her how to do it, for Christ's sake.'

'Ididbutshedidn'tunderstand,' he replied rapidly. He spoke a low, guttural English as if his tongue was stuck to the roof of his mouth.

'They're retarded,' Merili whispered in my ear.

He executed another crisp shot and told me he was from Dublin. His family had emigrated to Toronto when he was four and so he'd lost his accent.

'ButI'mgoingtogetitback,' he said.

He worked in a bar as a pot-boy, and his wife Minnie worked for a Canadian charity called Goodwill.

'They're sweet people,' whispered Merili, 'only they need a little help. No,' she continued more loudly, 'Minnie, *bend*. Let me show you.'

She pushed Minnie into position. The shot was still a scoop but miraculously Minnie pocketed a coloured ball.

'No,' she squealed with delight.

She blushed red and pulled her hat down to cover her face.

★

The next morning Nelson was sitting in the lobby at his desk, taking bookings from those who wanted to go on the fishing safari. He was dark and wiry and very fit, with shoulders slightly hunched from affectation. His current Canadian girlfriend in harlequin shorts which fitted snugly to her body hovered at his side.

'You want to see me?' she said. She had a long face which was very heavily made-up although it was not yet nine o'clock.

'Yes. You wait.' He insolently pointed to the side where she could stand. 'First I work. Later we talk.'

'This had better be good, Nelson,' she said.

He stared at her groin, and then looked at her, and raised his eyebrows up and down, and lasciviously licked his lips.

'Nelson, you're the last word,' she said smirking, and went to the corner where he'd directed her to stand.

I signed up for the safari.

The fishing party assembled in the lobby the following day at nine o'clock.

'Nelson, very, very tired,' Nelson said, 'only three hours sleep.' He was wearing a baseball hat with the Seven-Up logo on it. I think it was then someone made the joke that Nelson had been with his sister all night. Perhaps it was Fred? He was a huge, bald man with a red face, who drove a refuse collection truck in Vancouver.

We climbed into a bus, about a dozen of us, and drove along a straight road, passing scrub, old cabins of weathered clapboard, and flat stretches of grass.

We stopped by the shore and walked out along a pier with huge cracks in the floor and a handrail of rusty hawser.

There would be a tender along presently to take us out to the big fishing boat we could see at anchor. We all sat down on the warm concrete. Joni and Dennis were classical musicians, both Hong Kong Chinese and in their early twenties. The day before they'd gone with a waiter from the hotel to the waiter's home in Camagüey.

Joni said, 'The Cubans are such friendly people. Yesterday, everyone said "Hello" in the street. Everyone smiled. If you smile at anyone in the street in Toronto, they think you're from the loony-house. On every street corner, Pepito held our arms and looked left and right to see if it was safe to cross.'

'We have materialism,' said Dennis. 'We can buy what we want. But what is buying whatever you want? They have something spiritual here which we have lost.'

I was introduced to Ray from Prince Edward Island who told me he didn't like oysters. 'It's a shame really,' he said, 'because two of my brothers-in-law are oyster fishermen. I could get them by the crate.' Lobsters were Ray's bag. He liked them best boiled in seawater.

Joni expressed the hope that there would be a lavatory on board the boat. I was sure there would be.

'Ah, but . . .' It was Vicky, the tiny wife of Fred, the enormous man. '. . . It's different for a lady, you know, we need a different sort of toilet.'

Nelson disappeared and returned with half a dozen lifeguards. They all wore baseball hats, except for one who felt the lack.

'I like your hat,' he said in Spanish to the man who didn't like oysters.

He was speaking about a black baseball hat with yellow emblems on the front. 'I stuck on the designs myself,' said Ray in English.

'It's a very good hat, very pretty,' said the hatless lifeguard.

'The designs look like fried eggs to me,' said Ray in English.

'I don't have a baseball hat,' said the lifeguard pointedly in Spanish, indicating his bare head.

'You want this? Okay,' said Ray, 'but only if we catch some fish.'

'Boy, you got yourself a bargain,' said Fred. 'We get the fish, you get the hat.'

Not understanding a word, the lifeguard, who was called Pedro, just smiled and nodded.

We and the lifeguards were brought out to the boat. It was a flat-bottomed pleasure craft, with a huge, square formica bar in the middle of the deck. It was not a fishing boat; it was a floating gin-palace.

We rode at anchor. Pedro dived into the water and came up with a conch. Another dozen and a half followed.

The engines were started up and we moved away. The sea was smooth, but the boat, with its flat bottom, rolled from side to side. Ralph, a middle-aged man with a diamond flashing from his left ear, announced he only liked to catch fish and hated to eat them.

Pedro was in the poop, holding a conch shell between his legs. With the round end of an old hammer he smashed through the encrusted back, and when the hole was big enough he put a rusty knife in and cut. Everyone clustered around him. He turned the shell over in his hands. The inner lips were smooth, the colour of rhubarb. Pedro slipped his fingers in, and pulled out the organism which lived inside. It looked like a huge slug, was more than six inches long, had feelers at one end, a white fungus-like growth at the other, and horns of roe.

'Ugly-looking sucker,' said Joni.

'Guess that's for lunch,' said Ray.

Sherry, a blonde wife, less than twenty, with a thin brace running across her teeth and perfectly polished nails, said, 'Ugg,' very loudly.

'Are they really for lunch?' asked Dennis enthusiastically, splitting open the creature's black skin with Pedro's knife. The flesh was white and flaky.

Joni said, 'He'll eat anything.'

Dennis said, 'I'll eat it raw.'

'Ugg,' said Sherry again, and her husband Harold, an accountant, led her away.

'Bait,' shouted Nelson, and Dennis sighed.

We anchored about three or four miles down the coast, about halfway between the shore and a reef which was marked by a thin line of white surf.

Fishing lines on hubcaps of polystyrene were handed round. Sherry wrinkled her nose. 'How am I going to put these yucky bits of bait onto the hook?' she asked. Pedro left the cluster of lifeguards in the poop and came and did it for her.

Sherry had the first bite and pulled out a blue tripper fish. The hook had come out through the eye. Pedro came back and, as he ripped it out, excrement the colour of khaki shot from the anus of the fish and spattered across the deck.

She took the newly baited hook from Pedro and dropped it over the side. Together, we all fished on for about fifteen minutes but we caught nothing. Then lunch was laid out on the bar.

'It's fish, folks, in batter with cheese,' said Fred, cutting his open. In his huge hands the knife and fork looked tiny.

'I thought it was conch,' said some wag.

Dennis said, 'It's disgusting.' He pushed his plate away.

Joni whispered, 'I thought you liked fish. Don't make a scene.'

'Not this fish.'

He went up to lie on the sunroof.

Joni said, 'Usually he eats anything fishy.'

'Well I didn't think it was bad,' said Fred when he had finished. 'For nineteen bucks Canadian, you can't complain about this.'

We clustered round the rusting nails and began to fish again. No bites. We complained. They moved us a couple of hundred yards down the coast and we anchored over another piece of sandy seabed, identical to the one we'd left behind.

'Nelson,' shouted Fred from the prow half an hour later, 'I thought this was meant to be a fishing party. We haven't caught a goddamn fish yet.'

There was silence.

'Where's Nelson?' several people asked.

'Nelson!' bellowed Fred.

'Nelson very tired,' came a sleepy voice. He was in a cabin below, curled up on a filthy mattress.

'What a character,' said a voice.

'Throw a pail of water on him,' said Fred.

Someone else suggested the slugs floating in a pail of brine.

We all went on fishing.

A few minutes later Ralph with the earring shouted, 'I've got one,' and landed a grey snapper. For the next half an hour, he pulled one in every few minutes, his pile grew and grew, and then as abruptly as they'd started biting, the fish stopped.

At five the anchor was pulled up and the shore glided past us as we moved up the coast. Several of us sat around the square bar drinking the Chivas Regal miniatures which Fred produced from his pocket. Pedro was called over. Fred gave him two empty miniatures which delighted the lifeguard, and then Ray handed him his baseball hat.

'*Muchas gracias.*'

Pedro carried the hat carefully to the back of the boat and put it down on the engine cover. He took off his teeshirt, stooped down to a bucket and washed his face, under his arms, and his chest. There being no towel, he dried off by shaking himself and standing in the sun. Then he spent several minutes smoothing down his hair with saliva-wetted fingers. He put his teeshirt back on and tied it at the side. His toilette was complete.

Pedro drew himself up to his full height. At that very moment Nelson stepped forward, casually picked up the hat and made as if he was about to put it on his head. Pedro snatched it back and, while Nelson laughed, dusted it all over.

'He sure does love that hat,' said Fred.

'He sure does,' agreed Ralph.

Pedro raised the hat like a crown, settled it on his head and adjusted the peak.

'What do you pay for one of these? Four bucks, five bucks?' asked Fred.

'I don't remember what I paid,' said Ray, 'I may have been given it.'

'Right,' said Fred, 'they give 'em away, don't they?'

Pedro was standing with the other lifeguards showing his hat off. One pointed at the emblem.

'I stuck that on myself, said Ray again.

'Well, now he has a hat like all the other ones,' said Fred, and it was true. Now he had a baseball hat like the others.

We landed at the pier and got onto the bus.

'Not a bad day,' said Fred settling beside me. He reeked of whisky.

The bus bumped off, and Fred fell asleep with the sun slanting across his face.

'He sure does love that hat,' I heard him mumbling. 'He sure does love that hat . . . He sure does love that hat.'

★

On Thursday evening, I was standing at the bar near the cabaret stage. Patti, who was one of the activity leaders employed by the Canadian tour company who hired the resort, was on stage holding the microphone.

'I want couples from the audience for the newlyweds game,' she said, 'and I don't want any women and women, or men and men. I want women and men. This is a clean show.'

After five couples had gone up and been applauded, the men disappeared and the questions started:

'What part of his body would your husband most like to change?'

'What cartoon character is he?'

'What's his favourite expression?'

'What drink is he?' ('A shot of stiff vodka' brought the house down.)

'What part of his body would you most want to change?'

And so on.

I talked to Julian the waiter.

'The way to learn Spanish is to get a dictionary and talk to waiters,' he said. 'They have the most patience.'

Anna walked by. Anna was a young Canadian girl who looked like Lucy in the Peanuts cartoon strip. She was wearing a pink catsuit that clung to her body.

'Very nice,' said Julian, 'but she is no *señorita*. She is like this.'

He glided his fist through an imaginary space in the air, giving a most extraordinary simulation of intercourse.

'In English you say,' and then he said in English, 'fuck. She likes to fuck.'

'*Claro*.'

'Much fuck. Much, much fuck. We Cubans fuck Canadian womens.'

In the sand dunes that day, taking India to the beach, I had stumbled on two couples; the men were Cuban, the women were Canadians. It had been difficult to explain to a six year old what was happening.

'I have a girlfriend in Canada,' he continued, 'but that's love. Anna is different.'

'Okay,' said Patti on stage, 'I'm going to tell a joke. On their first honeymoon night, the husband asks his wife to put on his shorts. She refuses, saying it's kinky. "Too right baby," says the husband, "and don't you forget, I wear the pants around here." Well the wife thinks: Right, I'll get you, buster. She throws her panties to her spouse and she says, "Hey, put these on." "They're too small," he replies, "I'll never get into them." "That's right, buster, and if you go on talking the way you just have, you never will."'

The five male contestants returned. Before leaving earlier, they'd been told to prepare a routine. What they performed now was the chorus of 'Guantanamera' with arms linked and legs kicking in the air. It was a feeble exhibition. I went off to get another beer.

'What character, sir, would your wife say you most reminded her of?' I heard in the distance.

'It must be Superman.'

'Why?' asked Patti, in a mock-bashful accent.

'I do it in the phonebooth.'

It was clearly time to leave.

24

The Quakers

We left Santa Lucia on the northern coast and headed south to the *carretera central* where we turned east. In Victoria de las Tunas, the first large town we came to, a young boy was throwing paper darts at every lorry which hurtled by.

We neared our destination, the city of Holguín, towards evening. On the outskirts there was a wide, shallow river where we saw three or four cars in the water, being washed. There were two Chevrolet DeLuxes, a Ford Custom, and a Pontiac Chieftain 8, all dating from the early Fifties. They were nice cars but common cars—nearly 1,250,000 Chevrolet DeLuxes were produced in 1950—and I'd seen more and more of these types and fewer and fewer of the exotic models, the further east we had got. The east was the poorest part of Cuba, but though it was less likely, I still hadn't given up hope of finding an Eldorado Brougham.

On the outskirts of Holguín, with its stretches of shrub-covered wasteland, its stadium and unfinished nineteen-storey skyscraper, we found the motel El Bosque.

There was no water in our cabin, and a man from the desk came to turn it on. I followed him outside so I could learn where the mains tap was, and saw, against a wall, a pile of discarded 1950s bathroom cabinets. I returned to our bathroom and saw what I hadn't noticed before: there was a new bathroom cabinet and it was exactly the same model from the People's Republic of China, the installation of which we'd been present at in Viñales and other places. It seemed we were synchronous with the tide of bathroom modernisation which was sweeping across the country.

In the centre of town we found single-storey houses from the Spanish era, with paint peeling from the doors and shutters. It was like every other city. We went into the state-owned ice-cream parlour, part of the Coppelia chain. Coppelias were ubiquitous, like the peeling paint and the buckled pan-tiled roofs. Before the revolution, ice cream was imported from the US and Howard Johnson's 28 Flavors was the prestige brand. Fidel had promised to outdo the Yankees with twenty-nine flavours, but on this dismal Sunday afternoon there were only two: vanilla, with or without candied fruit peel.

The elderly couple on the next table started to argue. He had allowed his eyes to linger too long on the young waitress. Our scoops of ice cream came with biscuits crumbled over them. Another identical city, another identical Coppelia, with wobbling metal chairs and voices echoing from the walls as if it was a swimming pool. Cuba seemed to share the quality of claustrophobic homogeneity of the United States, if not its exact form. I found myself wishing for difference, dissent, nonconformity.

We hired a horse-and-cart taxi and toured the town. I have a blurred recollection of US cars, with their shrill, almost effeminate-sounding horns, and the shiny sack under the horse's matted tail, where its olive-green droppings collected.

In the evening we waited under leafy trees as darkness fell. Nearby was the Iglesia de Amigos, the Church of Friends or Quaker meeting house. There was going to be a service. Here was the promise if not of dissent, at least of something different.

At eight o'clock we went in. Pews, rafters, a lectern with a drape reading '*Dios es amor*'. We sat down. Two young men came up and shook our hands. There were about thirty-five of us.

Pastor Ajo appeared, a short, plump man in a suit. We sang 'En La Cruz' and the collection tray was handed round. The choir filed onto the dais. One member was blind behind her enormous dark glasses and her fingers played with the side of her dress as she sang.

The text was Luke 19, verses 28–40. Christ rides down the Mount of Olives on a colt which has never been ridden before. His disciples hail him as the King. Pharisees among the crowds demand Christ rebuke them.

> And he answered and said unto them,
> I tell you that, if these should
> hold their peace, the stones would
> immediately cry out.

'Immodest, yes,' Pastor Ajo agreed, 'at first sight. But three days after he was crucified, Christ rose from the tomb and came before his disciples. He ate fish and a honeycomb. He had risen from the dead as he had said he was going to do.'

For an hour and a half, Pastor Ajo spoke. His theme was man's need for Christ to prove his divinity. But why not faith instead of scepticism? he argued. His audience sat attentively, some with bibles open on their laps at the relevant passages. Once or twice there were calls from the floor for clarification. I wasn't bored for a second.

Afterwards, I talked to Felix. He taught physics in a local night school. Quaker missionaries had originally come to the area in the nineteenth century, he told me, from the United States, and Holguín was the first city to have a Quaker meeting house. Besides themselves and the Roman Catholics, there were also Baptists, Seventh Day Adventists, Evangelists, and Methodists who held a weekly service in English in their cathedral.

The congregation clustered around us.

'What sort of a city is it?' I asked.

'It's a city of parks,' one said. 'It's a city of churches,' said another. 'It's a city of parks and churches,' said a third, and everyone laughed uproariously.

Felix showed me the hymn books which the choir had sung from. Each one had been typed up entirely on tracing paper by the pastor's wife, Clara.

We said goodbye and wandered down the street to a cafeteria. It had no windows, just a door open to the street, the shutter up. Inside steam hissed from an antiquated coffee machine. We went to the back of the queue. The grains were in a muslin container which looked like an upsidedown witch's hat and boiling water was trickling over them. A drunk was staggering about offering everyone waiting a drink from his bottle of *aguardiente* (cheap and highly intoxicating cane brandy), while an angry young man with a broken arm was furiously banging the cast around his arm on the counter.

The straining was finished and the coffee was put into a battered pot and heaps of slightly yellow, sticky sugar were spooned in. Twelve porcelain cups, they were really like outsize thimbles—and they were all the cups they had in this cafeteria—were put onto the counter. They were filled and as we filed forward I read the sign on the wall:

Domingo de la Defense—19 April
A Demostrar una vez más la capicidad combativa del Pueblo Holguíñero

'Sunday of Defence—19 April: to show once more the fighting capacity of Holguin.' This day of Civil Defence would have to involve the CDR, and as there would be no Holguíñero who was not involved in the CDR, this meant everyone. It just so happened the day in question was Easter Sunday. The thirty-five earnest Quakers to whom we had just said goodbye were going to have duties to perform that day, around which their worship would have to be fitted.

Pastor Ajo's talk about faith and scepticism was harmless to my ears but I could see that in a country where religion was a challenge to authority, because it proposed an authority higher than the state, faith could be dangerous.

With the accession to power of the Fidelistas in 1959, relations with the churches were good. Some—not all, but some—churchmen had spoken against Batista. Two clergymen, a Protestant and a Catholic, had served as chaplains with the Fidelistas in the Sierra Maestra. The Catholic Church had certainly not made the mistake it had made in the nineteenth century, during the wars of independence, of identifying with the oppressor.

But as the regime moved increasingly in the direction of socialism, the churches, especially the Catholic Church, became restless. Early in May 1960 a mass held in Havana cathedral to commemorate the victims of communism was broken up by militiamen singing the Internationale. Later in the month the Archbishop of Santiago, Mgr Pérez Serantes, a supporter of Fidel's from the start, a man who had saved his life after the attack on the Moncada Barracks and who had appeared with him publicly in Santiago after victory in 1959, issued a pastoral letter denouncing the restoration of relations with the Soviet Union. As private schools were closed and other centres of opposition were banned, the Catholic Church increasingly became a centre of opposition. In August 1960 the Cuban bishops formally denounced the Castro regime in a pastoral letter. In reply Fidel said, 'Whoever betrays a revolution such as ours betrays Christ and would be capable of crucifying Him again.' On 3 August 1960 six members of the Juventud Católica, together with a Spanish Jesuit, had been captured after a gun battle with the police in which two policemen were killed and the Jesuit wounded. On 4 December the Catholic hierarchy issued another pastoral letter urging Fidel to reject communism. In his reply, Fidel said, 'To be anti-communist is to be counter-revolutionary.' The country's very last independent publication, the Church magazine *La Quincena*, ceased to publish. At this point, miraculously, the crisis petered out. The churches stayed open. The papal delegate, Mgr Cesare Zacchi (who later became the Bishop of Havana), remained. So did the Cuban diplomatic representative in the Vatican.

Relations were not easy, however. In the early Sixties the police made lists of those who went to church. Religious practice came to be seen as no longer antisocial, or anti-revolutionary, but that did not mean it was welcome either. Not a single state enterprise or state farm has been built with a church or a chapel on it, and religious education has been eliminated from the school curriculum. This policy has been so zealously carried out that the terms BC and AD have been replaced with '*Antes nuestra era*' (ANE: 'Before our era'), and '*Después nuestra era*' (DNE: 'After our era'). No practising Catholic can become a member of the Communist Party.

In 1965 Holy Week was re-christened 'Playa Girón Week' and became a period devoted to mass voluntary labour. In 1969, when Cuba was attempting to produce 10,000,000 tons of sugar, the period became known as 'Playa Girón Month'. It has since been modified to the more modest 'Playa Girón *Quince*', or fortnight. Practising Christians have been unlucky with the dates of the Bay of Pigs invasion (17–19 April) falling so close to Easter.

The practice of religion has also been made difficult with straightforward disruption. Streets near churches have been known to be turned into playgrounds or turned over to fiestas at the times of services, with the result that the mass has been drowned out by the noise produced. Licences to repair churches have often been extremely hard to obtain, with the result that numerous churches have had to be closed down. With no new churches being built, there have been fewer and fewer places of worship, leaving many towns with no church and many priests or pastors with no alternative but to hold services in private houses. But this is a criminal offence for which clergymen have been sent to prison.

Changes abroad, however, have forced changes in Cuba. Throughout the Sixties and Seventies Catholics, including priests, in South America became more 'progressive' and militant. There was the Camilo Torres Movement named after the Colombian priest killed by the Colombian army in 1966, which saw no contradiction between the armed struggle and a Christian conscience. Latterly, there has been both the radicalised Church opposition in El Salvador, and the Sandinista government in Nicaragua, with several Catholic clergymen in its ranks. Liberation theology has gained much ground. With Cuba wanting to be seen as the leader of South and Central American revolutionary endeavour, some of the classic communist dogma about religion has had to go. Thus, in 1986 came *Fidel y Religion*, an interview book, in which the most significant of many *volte-faces* was the admission that religion was no longer the opiate of the people.

However, none of this had made much difference to Pastor Ajo and his congregation in practical terms. Easter Sunday was going to be a day of military activity. They were going to have to share it with the state.

Later, as I lay in bed, I kept wondering: What was it that the state was so worried about? Then these considerations evaporated when the telephone rang and a voice at the other end said, 'Do you want to change money?'

I said, 'No,' and put the receiver down.

A few minutes later the voice rang back, and a few minutes after that another voice rang, offering a higher rate.

In the morning the telephone calls resumed. We decided to leave and go south to Bayamo.

25

Bayamo

Somewhere along the *carretera central* we came to a stretch of road about a hundred yards long, on either side of which, for no apparent reason, millions of brown beer bottles had been dumped. The ground was completely covered with shards, so that for a moment I thought I was seeing iodine-coloured ponds. In this wilderness of glass three boys were scavenging. They had collected a dozen or so intact bottles for which they would get five centavos each.

We were travelling across one of the flattest parts of Cuba. There were not even mountains to be seen in the far distance. Two yoked oxen had fallen in the heat. A man prodded them with a stick but they wouldn't stand. The spinning shadow of the wind vane of an artesian well lay across the road. Two girls waved us down and, smiling through the window, told us they wanted to to go Bayamo.

We arrived an hour or two later, and drove down streets with horse-drawn carriages and lorries. We gathered from a butcher that if we wanted a hotel we should go to El Parque. 'Ah, El Parque,' said one of the girls. It's in the centre. Straight on.'

We were facing a T-junction.

'Oh, go right,' she said, 'then left.'

We found ourselves in a maze of side streets. Every pedestrian now gave contradictory directions for El Parque. As we drove I kept seeing a yellow belfry with a cross above the roofs of the houses. Finally, we emerged into a tree-lined square: Céspedes Park.

'There,' said one of the girls pointing.

The Royalton Hotel was beside a church with a yellow belfry —the same belfry which had been on our left throughout our peregrinations. We'd been driving for an hour in a complete circle.

The girls closed the hot doors of the car and smiled and said, '*De nada*,' effusively and went off happily. We went through the shabby doors of the Royalton into the shabby lobby. Here we discovered they had no rooms and, even if they had, rooms for all peso hotels were booked from a central office in another hotel. Enquiries here produced another negative. All the rooms in town had gone.

There was only one solution. We drove back to the Royalton, piled our luggage outside the entrance and waited. The hotel staff came out to stare at us. Soapy water spread along the nearby gutter smelling of mop and disinfectant. Every ten minutes we'd ask the apologetic clerk at the desk if there had been a cancellation. Finally, breakthrough. A woman who had seen us hanging around came and told us that she had just cancelled.

We re-entered the lobby with its antiquated adding machine, registered and went up the stone stairs. All the bedrooms were on a gallery which overlooked a central well and the kitchens. There was an overpowering, steamy smell of old fat and food.

Our room was number 6, with a grey door. It was small, hot, airless. The two bedsteads were buckled, though the sheets were crisp. We ran the shower and air rumbled in the pipes far away, but there was no water. The holes at the back of the lavatory pan, through which a seat should have been attached, had been plugged with filler.

The clerk from the desk appeared in an agitated state. He had forgotten to make a note of my passport number. He took it down three times.

'What time does the water come on?' I asked him.

'Six or seven or something like that. Not until tomorrow now'

'And for how long?'

For a moment I thought he was about to burst out laughing. 'For as long as it lasts,' he said, and slid apologetically away.

Lying reading on the creaky bed, I saw that the bulb in the bedside lamp began to flicker uncertainty, turning yellower and yellower as the voltage dropped. Before I could get across the room, the power cut had started.

I found our brand-new Duracell torch with fresh batteries. We left, locking the door. Down at the desk the kerosene lamps were hissing and the shadow of the apologetic clerk was spreading across the ceiling.

Outside it was pitch dark. I realised I had left my cigarettes in the room. I returned, lighting the way with the torch. With the cigarettes in my pocket, descending the winding stone stairs, it gave out. A rat ran past in the darkness.

Outside again, a Buick crawled around the square, catching in the sweep of its beam the haunches of a couple kissing on a bench, a piece of pink column, a broom resting against a tree.

Mario, the waiter from the restaurant in the Royalton, was drunk. He slurred as he told us where we could find food, 'electricity or no electricity'. I showed him my torch. I explained I had once seen the Prime Minister of Great Britain, Mrs Thatcher, talking about it as a new and great British invention, and how on the dark stairs it had suddenly stopped working.

He looked at me, his eyelids trembling, swaying slightly on the spot, and said perhaps the only word of English he knew: 'Shit.' He then fell over backwards.

We drove through the dark streets. Hurricane lamps swung on the backs of the horse-drawn carriages. The hotel with food, 'electricity or no electricity', was filled with North Vietnamese who chain-smoked and combed their long black hair continuously between courses.

It was several hours before the power came on again. We had

returned and were sitting in Céspedes Park on a stone bench still warm from the sun. Then, ten minutes later, the electricity went off again and everyone jeered. 'That's it for the night,' a man told us, 'no more electricity.' He sounded delighted.

We groped our way up the stairs and passed a restless night on the rickety beds in our sweltering room.

In the morning the tap was still dry. We filled the galvanised pail with drinking water from the plastic barrel in the hall and washed in the shower. The half-bar of red Russian soap left my skin red and smelling of carbolic. The lavatory stank.

After breakfast—tinned tomato juice, coffee, and bread with either butter or *chorizos*: there was nothing else—I went and sat in Céspedes Park. On the next bench was a blind man who tapped his stick on the marble floor. His half-deaf companion held a transistor radio jammed against his ear, playing at full volume. A third man hobbled up, using the sawn-off bottom of a hatstand for a crutch. Then a fourth man appeared, whose right foot had been amputated. Invalids' corner.

The newspaper sellers had their quarter opposite, occupying two benches. At about ten o'clock their newspapers arrived. Two dozen copies each of *Granma* to sell. They loosened the twine around their bundles, putting it in their pockets. In readiness, I got out 10 centavos. But instead of starting to work, they each peeled off a copy, sat on the remainder (the seats were cold now in the morning) and started reading—six of them in a row, all silent. A man came up to buy a paper and was told to go away. When they had finished reading, after half an hour, they went to work. This involved no effort. They all sat with their hands outstretched at different points around the square, and as the day became warmer, I could hear money tinkling into their palms.

We went to the confectioner, queued and twenty minutes later ordered four squares of cake filled with guava paste, ten dry biscuits with thin smears of apricot jam between the halves, and three crumbling, flaking pastry triangles dusted with sugar. No other customers bought in quantities of less than half a kilo and we were a puzzle to the shopkeeper. We also wanted to buy a dry vanilla cake but he couldn't sell us one. The trays hadn't been counted. 'Come back in an hour,' he said. In the dairy next door, our attempt to buy the rest of lunch—a litre of milk—foundered for the same reason. Not until the milk receipt had been checked would they sell. 'Maybe in the afternoon,' the assistant said.

In the afternoon we changed hotel bedrooms; in between carrying suitcases, we watched the hotel kitchen staff at their table at the bottom of the well sifting through huge piles of rice by hand and taking out what they didn't like, including pieces of wood and screws. The new bedroom was the same as the old, tiny and airless.

I went back to Céspedes Park, and sat down to watch. Boys playing football; the fat street-sweeper with the split skirt gathering the yellow blossom which fell from the trees; sparrows making their nest inside a junction box.

We were in the room and waiting for the water to come on at six. The first sign was the tinkling sound of the water closet starting to fill. Next, the tap started to rasp and splutter. Finally, half a dozen thin needles dribbled from the shower head. All over the hotel I could hear shouts of joy mingled with admonishments to get going. In fifteen minutes it was all over. The city was dry again.

On the gallery, the newly showered menfolk gathered to smoke. Their vests were crisply ironed; their hair combed and shiny. There was a smell of soap and scent. Through the open doors of their dark bedrooms—again there was no power—I could see their wives hanging up the just-washed clothes.

★

The people of Bayamo, the Bayameses as they are called in the Cuban national anthem, had a long and distinguished history of resistance to Spanish colonial authority in the nineteenth century.

The first of these must surely be José Antonio Saco (1797–1879). Saco left his home town and went to Havana as a young man. He was a brilliant journalist and hugely popular with the younger Cubans who were discontented with the stagnant state of the country and Spain's rigid control. Saco was the editor of *Revista Bimestre Cubana*, and in a notorious article on Brazil he argued for the abolition of slavery. This was a highly contentious issue at the time; slavery had been abolished in the British Empire and the Cuban oligarchy was terrified that the Jamaicans were going to set the Cuban blacks a very bad example. The slave rebellion in Haiti at the end of the eighteenth century was still vividly remembered by the planter class. Saco wasn't an abolitionist for humanitarian reasons but because he was frightened. His argument was that such a large influx of Africans would eventually lead to black dominance and then to revolution. Therefore slavery had to go.

But Saco's views were not what the planters or what the Spanish administration wanted to hear. Sugar was booming, and sugar needed slaves. Fortunes were being made. To make the situation that little bit more complicated, the importation of slaves had technically been halted in 1820. However, it continued illegally in Spanish colonies, with the Spanish-appointed Captains-General turning a blind eye to the practice because they were receiving a cut from the slavers. It was one of the perks of the post. Saco had to go, the planters clamoured, and go he did, into exile in Paris in 1834. The man who sent him was Captain-General Miguel Tacon. When Tacon left his post and returned to Spain in 1838, one of the many titles he went home laden with was Vizconde de Bayamo. As well as the city's name, he also took home with him one of the largest fortunes any Captain-General had made from turning a blind eye to the illegal slave-trade.

In the early nineteenth century a process of mutual fascination was developing between Cuba and the US. The Cuban oligarchy was looking north because it wanted support with the maintenance of its slave economy. In return, certain elements in the US were looking covetously towards Cuba, charmed by the possibilities of expanding the union to include this Caribbean island with its substantial slave economy.

This convergence of interests took practical shape with the

policy of annexation, *anexionismo*. Under the policy, the US would buy Cuba from the Spanish government, which would make it impossible for the South's greatest fear to come to pass: the creation in Cuba of another negro republic like Haiti. From the point of view of the sugar-producing oligarchy in Cuba, in an uncertain world, and with slavery actively under attack, union with the South looked like the best way of ensuring the old way of life went on. Three attempts were made, but fortune did not smile on the scheme; *anexionismo* aborted, in the first instance because of the truculence of the Spanish government who realised it would be seen as an admission of failure, and on the second and third occasions because of the withdrawal of US support. With the collapse of the scheme, the men of the Junta Cubana in New York, who had been agitating for annexation, inevitably shifted their thinking towards independence. In 1855, one of the junta's members issued a manifesto in which he declared somewhat sourly that, as the US had failed Cuba over the *anexionismo*, there was only one alternative: independence—even if the cost of this was emancipation. It was a proposition which many in Cuba, particularly those belonging to the sugar-producing oligarchy, were not going to view with much charity.

The event which was going to set the painful process in motion happened, as so often in Cuban affairs, abroad. In 1861 the American Civil War broke out, and slaving, which had continued up to this point because a good deal of the illegal slaving had been done on ships sailing under the US flag which the British had been unable to stop and search, effectively stopped as the northern US states agreed to allow the British navy powers of inspection. The last run into Cuba was in 1865.

The consequence for the Cuban economy was painful. The prices charged for slaves rose to astronomical heights, and small landowners found themselves in serious difficulties when it came to getting their cane harvest cut and ground.

In March 1866 elections were held in Cuba for the first time since 1820. The now aged Saco, still in exile in Paris, here re-enters the story. He was elected, the Cubans travelled to Madrid, along with representatives just elected in Puerto Rico, and met the Spanish Colonies Minister, ironically a man named de Castro. The predilection of these men from the colonies was generally towards reform, but Saco now refused to support the idea of abolition, and the Cuban reformers reached no agreement.

Next in the long series of events which would eventually cumulate in Bayamo was the introduction of a new tax in February 1867 by Captain-General Francisco Lersundi. The reformers studied their position. Annexation by the US, which would certainly be a way to escape from the clutches of Spain, was well and truly out; a slave-owning Cuba would never be admitted to the union now. The only way forward was rebellion against Spain. But any revolt presented problems because Spain could simply imitate Abraham Lincoln's tactics, and beat them, as he had beaten the South, with the weapons of emancipation. If Spain declared Cuba's slaves free, she would have an army overnight. Clearly, if white Cuba was going to beat Spain, negro support would have to be obtained. But to do this Cuba's leaders would have to emancipate the slaves themselves, which would undo the wealth of the country. There is no point in having a rebellion if you are the status quo, and to do so will mean the end of your position. The reformers ended up paralysed on the emancipation issue.

But some others were not. The planters of Oriente province in eastern Cuba were isolated. They were poor; they were neglected; the railways hadn't reached them yet. The smaller sugar planters were finding life particularly difficult, with slaves only to be had at exorbitant prices and capital loans unavailable because the people they had traditionally borrowed from were the slavers, and they weren't around any more. These men saw rebellion as a desperate means to halt their decline, even if it meant rushing into the unknown territory of emancipation.

When these ideas were taking shape, Bayamo was a conventional, provincial town. In 1867 it had about 10–12,000 inhabitants, a church, a town hall, a prison and a barracks. Its main square was Plaza Isabella II. That year a Junta Revolucionaria was formed in Bayamo, organised by the masonic lodge. The Junta sent Pedro Figueredo (a man who had already achieved some notoriety by composing a revolutionary march which had been played in the church, the one with the yellow belfry around which we'd circled) to negotiate with the reformers. Help was promised, then withdrawn.

At this moment there occurred an event, one much delayed result of which was that Plaza Isabella II became Parque Céspedes. It was a meeting on a farm called San Miguel de Rompe near Las Tunas of the Oriente rebels, presided over by Carlos Manuel de Céspedes (1819–74). He was a native of Bayamo, aged forty-eight. He had spent a good deal of his younger days in Spain and had participated there in revolutionary activity. He had returned to Cuba in the 1850s; his family owned a small sugar plantation not far from Bayamo.

At the meeting Céspedes made a stirring speech in favour of armed rebellion. Nothing was agreed amongst the putative insurgents, but his star was set to rise. Events abroad began to augur well for the project. In Spain, revolution broke out, and Queen Isabella II fell. Then, on 23 September 1867, revolution broke out in Puerto Rico. The conspirators were still timid, but one Luis Figueredo performed an isolated act by hanging a Spanish tax collector on his plantation. The Junta Revolucionaria went underground. There were meetings, though no decision was reached on the slavery question. A rebellion was planned to start around Christmas. Then the authorities, via the priest of the wife of one of the conspirators, got to hear of what was planned, and Lersundi, the Captain-General, sent word to arrest the plotters.

This proved to be the final prod which was needed. In October 1868 the planters rose against Spain. Céspedes was named as commander for the Bayamo area. One of his first actions was to free the slaves on his plantation and enrol them in his army, already 147 strong. Yet, while on the one hand declaring as he set them free that he believed that men were created equal, at the same time he also declared that abolition should be gradual, and that former slave owners should be compensated. However ambiguous his stance was, he had freed his slaves, and this had the effect of causing men, especially free blacks, to join his forces in large numbers. He had 12,000 troops by the end of October, and with them he captured Bayamo and Holguín. Rebellion flared next around Puerto Principe, now called Camagüey.

A number of leading reformers in the west publicly supported the rebels, but this provoked a counter-reaction, the volunteers, a military association of white Creoles, supported by those larger planters who hadn't joined the reformers' camp. Terrified of emancipation and feeling uniquely Spanish, the Volunteers, who numbered 20,000 infantry and 13,500 cavalry on 1 January 1869, were against negotiations of any kind with the rebels, and believed the only solution was a military one. They ran Havana; they terrorised the Captain-General; they were the nineteenth-century forerunners of the *pieds noirs* and the loyalist paramilitarists of Ulster.

On the rebel side there was schism. Those from around Camagüey, who were mainly cattle ranchers, had little to lose from emancipation and unilaterally freed their slaves. Céspedes, on the other hand, did not want to be forced in this direction. The reformers, raising money for the cause in New York, wouldn't like it. In 1869 he came up with a plan for the future which he hoped would satisfy all parties. The *Reglamento de Libertos* (Rule of the Freed) provided that freed slaves would continue to work for their old masters for eight years, and that besides paying them, those masters would also feed and clothe them. This was not the way to achieve mass support from the slaves, and thus, at the western end of the island, the slaves went on making their masters prosperous.

The military effort of the rebels stagnated until late in 1869, when Céspedes agreed that the only way forward was to destroy the western plantations. The policy provoked terrible retaliation from the Spanish and the Volunteers. The country in the east degenerated into chaos. The Spanish generals in the field now faced the guerrillas in the time-honoured way: with martial law and containment. Oriente province was cut off by an enormous fortified ditch, running across the width of the island at its narrowest point. The fighting dragged on. Céspedes was blamed for alienating the conservatives amongst the rebels by his apparent willingness to risk abolition, and alienating the radicals by his caution. In 1873, the rebels removed him from his position as President of the Republic. A year later he was killed by the Spaniards in an ambush at San Lorenzo, in Oriente.

★

Céspedes had lived in Bayamo in a house overlooking the square which bore his name. It was now a museum. On our last day in Bayamo, we presented ourselves at the front door. The woman who looked after the place was about to lock up; she would not be opening again for some days, she said. We explained we were from Europe in our halting Spanish, and had travelled all the way to Bayamo because of our interest in Céspedes.

'*¿Sabes quien fué Céspedes?*' the old woman said to India.

'*Si*,' said India, who said '*si*' to any question in Spanish she didn't understand, and we were in.

Downstairs, the exhibition was the now familiar assemblage of letters, photographs of dignified, nineteenth-century gentlemen with beards, and maps. The elements were linked together with a commentary which told the story of Céspedes as one of the men who had done the most to stop slavery in nineteenth-century Cuba. There was no mention of the fudge in the statement he made after he liberated his own slaves, or on subsequent occasions. Once again, like Catholics, with their emphasis on possessing the relics, there was also the watch, whip and cigar-holder of the man himself.

Upstairs was more interesting: the great man's furniture was on display there in musty-smelling rooms. Tables and chairs made out of mahogany; two French vases, absolutely hideous; a parlour piano; his huge brass bed with Moorish scenes painted on the headworks and footboards; the earrings and silver hairbrushes of his second wife; examples of the books she embroidered; and his study filled with books on Cuban jurisprudence. Amidst these possessions he spent the last years of his life, growing emaciated, half-blind, fanatically demanding more power and authority, only to discover one day that his presidency had been taken away from him at a meeting to which no one had bothered to invite him.

On the way out, I passed a comment of Fidel's on the wall, in which he described Céspedes as an early opponent of reactionary ideas. I couldn't imagine he would have cared for Cuba as it had developed and it made me laugh. The woman who had let us in watched me curiously from the door as we walked away, while India whispered, 'Why are you laughing?'

There was a statue of Céspedes, father of both Bayamo and Cuba in the square, with '*Nosotros creemos que todos los hombres somos iguales*' ('We believe all men are created equal') of course written underneath. There was another quote at the back of the statue. It was Céspedes' comment on learning that the Spanish authorities had coldly murdered his son: '*Oscar no es mi unico hijo. Soy el padre de todos los Cubanos que han muerto por la Revolucion*' ('Oscar is not my only son. I am the father of all Cubans who have died for the revolution').

*

After the deposition of Céspedes, the war dragged on. Conservatives amongst the rebel forces now conducted a whispering campaign against their best generals: against Antonio Maceo, because he was black and they feared he would institute a negro republic, and against Maximo Gómez, ostensibly because he was a Dominican and not a Cuban national but actually because he supported Maceo.

The Spanish sent in General Arsenio Martínez Campos with 25,000 men. Besides fighting a tough campaign, Campos offered a general pardon, the liberation of those slaves who had fought with the rebels, and freedom for the revolutionary leaders if they agreed to leave Cuba. An armistice was signed on 11 February 1878 at Zanjón. Maceo refused to accept the terms because they did not include the abolition of slavery, and he fought on for three months until he was defeated. Campos allowed him to sail out of Santiago and into exile.

The war was over. It had cost over 250,000 lives and over $300 million. The rebels failed because they had not been able to accept, early enough, that the only way to win was to cross into the prosperous west and lay waste to the rich plantations there. Why did they not want this? Because it would have precipitated abolition, and they believed that abolition would destroy the country's prosperity.

And what of slavery, the source of their difficulties? There is a school of political thinking which argues that difficult progressive measures can only ever really be successfully carried through by a reactionary establishment. ('Only the British Conservative Party can resolve the Irish problem' is an example.) In November 1879 Martínez Campos, who had become Prime Minister in Madrid, passed a law: for the next eight years there was to be a period of *patronato* during which slaves would be paid by their owners; then, in 1888, the institution of slavery would disappear for ever.

The process had already been started. Quite a number of slaves who had fought in the rebel army had been freed. In 1880 there were only about 200,000 slaves in Cuba, against 270,000 free blacks.[1] Six years later, in September 1886, there were only about 26,000 slaves held on the *patronato* because many owners, believing that paying for free labour was cheaper than maintaining their negroes, had released them before the proper day. Slavery had withered, and the same year the *patronato* was abolished two years early by general consent.

The war bankrupted a number of planters. After the agreement at Zanjón, with the world price of sugar falling, they needed to mechanise, but the capital wasn't available. Into this vacuum stepped companies from the US with a voracious appetite for sugar at home. They bought some of the bigger estates, combined their milling functions to create what were called *centrales*, and built the railways on which small landowners

---

[1] There were also about 40,000 Chinese, contract labourers brought in in the mid-century to offset the declining availability of slaves and from which Cuba's Asiatic-looking inhabitants are descended.

could send them their cane. Thus, for the first time time, there appeared a division between those who grew and those who ground; and those planters who metamorphosed into *colonos* found that not only were they saving by not having to mechanise but it was cheaper to employ contract labour for the six months of the year (January–June) when the cane was being harvested, than it was to have slaves all the year round.

The first War of Independence had been fought by the planter class and lost by them. Within a few years of the Treaty of Zanjón, the old oligarchy, families like that of Céspedes, which had been in Bayamo since 1517, only five years after the foundation of the town, began to lose their power and prestige, either because their bankrupt plantations were bought up by US companies, or because they changed from being growers and grinders to being just growers for someone else. Céspedes was surely in one sense lucky that he died when he did. At least he didn't live to see his class become an irrelevance.

★

Olga sat down at our table in the hotel restaurant.

'My mother is that waitress,' she said, waving towards an elderly woman in black. She told us she came often to this place to eat. She detested cooking and it was easier with the two boys. Boris, who was about eight weeks old, was in the pram beside her; Manuel, three years old, was charging around the tables. Her husband was away in Angola, she said. Olga was nineteen with permanently moist pouting lips and black eyes which focused intently as she listened, but gave no indication that she was understanding.

She ate, bending low over her plate of rice and rapidly spooning it up. In the process several grains stuck to her cheeks. Manuel stood in the middle of the floor, a back-to-front baseball cap was on his head. He was stamping his feet.

'How long were you in the aeroplane which carried you to Cuba?' she asked.

'Twenty-four hours.'

She smiled in disbelief and shook her head.

We went out to the Parque Céspedes after dinner. Olga was standing with her children near the bust of Perucho (*sic*) Figueredo, with the words and music of the Himno Nacional written below. She had been waiting for us.

'Where are you going?' she asked shyly.

'For a walk.'

'I'm going to walk too,' she said. 'I live close to the centre.' It was like the invitation a child would offer: guarded, almost non-existent; the best protection against the slight of rejection.

In the main commercial street there was a large department store with rubber balls and plastic toys laid out behind the glass doors in a temporary display. Olga stopped and pointed at the baby clothes in a window. There was a baby's hat for fifteen pesos, an infant's chemise for forty-five. Nearby a *venta libre* (free sale) sign: these were goods off the ration.

'Have you been buying clothes here for your baby?'

'No,' said Tyga, 'they're cheaper at home.'

'Of course,' said Olga, 'free sale goods are so expensive.' She paused and then she said, 'But on the *libreta* in England baby clothes and food and everything else is very cheap, yes?'

'There is no ration in England.'

Her brow furrowed.

'No ration in England?'

'None.'

'None?'

'None.'

'But the free market is so expensive.'

'Not at home. We pay the same prices as you pay on the ration here.'

She was silent and scowled for a moment and then she said, 'Look at those shoes.'

They were Soviet imports with a thin heel, thin soles and thin straps.

'They cost forty pesos and after a week they go bad,' she said, 'and the shoes on the ration are worse.' But a moment later the rage was over and she was telling us how on Tuesdays and Saturdays the horse-drawn carriages gave cheap rides, twenty centavos a go, to children.

We turned into a residential street and stopped in front of what looked like an uncompleted garage. It was built of grey breeze blocks like the house behind.

She lifted one of the slats of the shutter and put her hand through to open the door. She was oblivious of her neighbours sitting outside their front doors.

'*Entra*.'

We found ourselves in a garage-sized room, with a partition down the middle, home-made formica chairs and a stove balanced on a piece of plywood. It was orderly and spotless.

She ran through to the house next door for water.

'I've got three people in my place and they speak English,' I heard her shouting. 'They live in London.'

Two women followed her back and feigned unsurprise at finding us. The woman who introduced herself as Olga's aunt took a bottle and began to feed the baby Boris.

'Look at the size of this one,' she said. 'He's only two months old. Just imagine how big he's going to grow up to be.'

Olga came forward from the stove. 'I never use the breast,' she said. She took hold of her breasts and began to rotate them. 'Aie,' said her aunt, 'it hurts to feed, and powdered milk is much better than what any woman can give. It has vitamins. They tell us at the clinic.'

Olga wanted to know about our flat. Which floor? How many rooms? What kind of a car did we drive? The prices of refrigerators and television sets? The aunt said, 'I have had the snip, so no more children.' Neighbours came in to listen and the baby Boris was handed round, while Olga continued with her questions, oblivious of her son.

Manuel dragged his baseball bat outside. From across the street a big black woman with curlers shouted. Two girls started to knock up a badminton shuttle and the prettiest made sure she stood right in front of our doorway. Manuel fell in the street and the pretty badminton player brought him in and took him into the room behind the partition. I went in to look. It was a tiny room. He was asleep in a hammock, and she was fanning him and humming. There was a home-made silhouette of Mickey Mouse holding a frame with pictures and documents behind it. I bent forward to look. There were Olga, and Manuel, and Boris, and Olga in a dress with a man who I presumed was her husband, and the same man in a uniform, and then I saw in the corner a letter from the army. Olga was a widow, and it wasn't that her husband was in Angola, he'd been killed there and we hadn't grasped that earlier when she had mentioned the country.

The little boy muttered something in his sleep and I left Mickey Mouse and his display and went back next door. Olga had fetched her old, upright fan and it was sending cold air gusting about the room. I wrote down our address and she wrote the Spanish equivalent beside each line: *apartamento* over flat: *calle* beside street: *ciudad* against London: and *pais* against Inglaterra. When she finished she still looked unhappy, so we drew a picture of an envelope with a stamp and wrote out the address, putting Señor and Señora before our names.

We said goodbye and walked back through dark streets, where bicyclists without lights continually flitted past us.

In the square devoted to Céspedes, I sent my family on ahead and stopped to jot down the first verse of the national anthem, which was inscribed on the memorial to its composer:

Al combate corred Bayameses
Que la patria os contempla orgullosa
No temáis una muerte gloriosa
Que morir por la patria es vivir.

To the battle, Bayameses, run
Let the fatherland proudly observe you
Do not fear a glorious death
To die for the fatherland is to live.

The first War of Independence cost 250,000 lives. Two hundred thousand of those were Spanish, and the greatest cause of mortality was not the fighting, but disease and fever. Today, it is not known how many Cuban soldiers have died in Angola fighting on the side of the government against South African-backed rebels. Certainly thousands.

It seemed to me, standing there in the square with the back of the Céspedes memorial a few feet away and Céspedes' melancholy remark on the loss of his son, that from the first War of Independence, through all the wars and revolutions which followed to the present, and a widow living in a house with the dimensions and comfort of a garage with two children, there was an unbroken continuity of sacrifice by the Cubans.

Overhead a beautiful crescent moon hung just above the tops of the palm trees.

26

Another Story of Invasion

We drove out of Bayamo, and the further east we went the hotter and moister the atmosphere became. The glue on the seams of my Aroma cigarettes started to come unstuck. There were hills, their slopes covered with vegetation, their peaks shrouded in mist. Suddenly Santiago de Cuba, the second largest city after Havana, lay spread out below, smog hovering in the air.

We found the old Casa Grande hotel which overlooked another Parque Céspedes, in the centre of town. While we were waiting to book in, young men shamelessly came up, leant on the desk and asked us to change money. The armed policeman ignored them and flirted with every girl whose attention he could attract. We followed a good-looking young black outside. Tyga took the rolled-up copy of *Granma* which he gave her, leant against the hotel wall, and opened it. The pesos were inside. India ran up and down the steps. I handed him the dollars and a second later he had vanished.

In the afternoon we set out for Granjita Siboney, where Fidel and his followers had stayed before the ill-fated attack on the Moncada Barracks on 26 July 1953. It had been a small farmhouse then, which the state had turned into a museum.

'Monuments line the road to the farm,' Tyga read from the guidebook. 'Each is dedicated to a soldier who died, and notes simply and elegantly what his name was and how he died. Displayed in the farmhouse are weapons, uniforms and some personal possessions, including the rebels' shopping lists. The exhibition describes events leading up to and following the assault. There are many newspaper articles as well which describe the capture, torture and murder of the rebels. Six were killed in battle; sixty-eight in cold blood by members of Batista's army, who afterwards left the bodies strewn around the farm giving the impression a pitched battle had been fought. Opening hours. . .'

We never saw a thing because we decided to turn off the road and go to the Playa Siboney instead. It was a pebble beach with fat Soviet men in Nikita Khrushchev hats sitting in the shallows, the warm seawater lapping around their bodies. Their slimmer wives swam slowly in the sea, their sunglasses resting on top of their carelessly piled hair; when they came out they pulled on the back of their bikini bottoms and dropped the sunglasses down. Later in the afternoon some of the Soviets had a party, drinking Coca-Cola and puffing away furiously on Marlboro cigarettes. From the hills behind appeared a thin man, barefoot and in a filthy white suit, like a Mexican peasant in a painting by Diego Rivera. He squatted behind a tree, and every time a Russian had finished with a can and threw it on the ground, he would scurry forward and take it. Nothing gets wasted in Cuba, and in many Coppelias I had seen scoops of ice cream being carried off in empty drinks cans. As far as the Soviets were concerned, the scavenger did not exist.

In the evening we went to the Casa de la Trova. *Trovas*, descended from the medieval ballad, were sung in Cuba throughout the time of Spanish occupation. They were concerned either with love or great historical events. Casas de la Trova existed in every town we visited. Here, *trovadores* both amateur and professional performed for free, singing both the old songs and what were called *trovas nuevas*, songs about life in contemporary Cuba.

The room was small, the seats crowded with spectators. The air was thick with smoke. The lavatory at the back had broken and an evil-smelling puddle spread from under the door. The first act was a seven-piece band, six cadaverous black men in pork-pie hats and a white trumpeter all in cream, a key ring dangling from his belt. During the drummer's solo he kicked on the accented notes, while six lugubrious black faces stared ahead. The block player and the maracas player took it in turns to sing, in clear, sweet voices.

The next act was again a seven-piece—three guitars, double bass, percussion, maracas and block—and again the players of the last two took it in turns to sing. One was a white man with huge cauliflower ears and no teeth who sang side on to the audience as if he were making ready to run away, and the other was an enormous man in a beret, with shining eyes, who sang in a voice of honey, shaking his maracas at an incredible speed and running on the spot.

The effect was electric. A cheer went up from the audience. An unshaven man, very small and very podgy, was leading a pretty young plump girl to the front. Her lips were smothered with thick lipstick. He was a wonderful dancer, which she was not; but as his groin crept closer to hers and his arm slid further along her back, she started to smile and let him lead her while the audience roared. Two young boys near us laughed so much at this extravagant seduction that they fell off their chairs.

*

We awoke to drum majorettes in the street below the hotel balcony, accompanied by a small brass band. Tyga was covered with small, extraordinarily itchy bites: dozens, if not hundreds of them. When the maid appeared, we complained about the bedbugs.

'Oh no,' said the maid, waving her finger. 'There are no bedbugs here. No, no, no. . .'

She was adamant, and hurt. She lifted the mattress and ran her thumb along the ticking around the edges. 'You see, no bedbugs. The mattress is fumigated regularly. The edges also.'

'But she is bitten.'

Tyga lifted her teeshirt to show her swollen belly completely covered with bites.

'Look,' said the maid, more adamant than ever. She indicated that with her I was to turn over the bed. We flipped over the base. There on the underside, scurrying and scrambling about, were at least two dozen cockroaches, long wrigglers the colour of nicotine.

'Cockroaches, yes,' said the maid triumphantly, 'but bedbugs, never.'

★

It was sunny when I went to the bank but on the way back the sky darkened and the atmosphere became heavy. Rain started to spit and then to pour. From our bedroom I looked down into the empty streets, the tarmac glistening like wet liquorice, a few stragglers running with newspapers over their heads. When I put my hand out into it, I could feel the rain was warm.

Half an hour later the sky cleared and the rain stopped. It was as if a whole series of gauzes had been lifted away. I could see the harbour again, and the Soviet ships berthed there. Nearly ninety years before, from the same spot, I would have seen the Spanish fleet of Admiral Cervera. Cervera's orders were to accept or avoid battle with the invading forces as he thought fit. The invading forces were from the US and were known to be greatly superior. Cervera's orders were a nonsense. How did this come about?

The period following the armistice of Zanjón at the end of the first War of Independence saw, in July 1878, the election of forty Cuban deputies to the Madrid Cortés. The introduction of the political process had led to the establishment of two political parties, firstly, what later became the Liberal or Autonomist Party, made up of middle-class Cubans who'd taken little part in the rebellion and had backed Zanjón, and the Constitutional Union Party, whose members, fearing that autonomy would lead to separation, wanted to be certain that Cuba would always be part of Spain: many supporters or ex-members of the Volunteers joined them.

The Liberals, or Autonomists, were obviously the radical party, but they only had seven out of 450 seats in the Cortés. The Constitutional Union Party had the lion's share of Cuba's seats and important connections with commercial interests in Spain. The influx of huge numbers of *peninsulares*, people of Spanish birth, into Cuba ensured that the Constitutional Union Party was the dominant voice.

Six years after Zanjón, nothing radical had happened in Cuba. In March 1884, when sugar prices began to slip, there was discontent. Those with revolutionary tendencies began to recover their nerve. In 1885 their numbers were swelled by an amnesty under which many exiled rebels returned. But a leader was needed.

That person was José Martí, surely the most famous figure in the Cuban pantheon of revolutionary figures. Stepping off the aeroplane in Havana, the very first thing to be seen is his name in large neon letters over the terminal building named after him. Thereafter, there is not a single village, town or city that does not have some principal building or road bearing his name. Extracts from his writings are to be found everywhere: on hoardings, outside Communist Party or Poder Popular buildings, and even in the San Carlos seminary, Havana, one of only two training places for priests in Cuba. From Martí's considerable body of work, it is possible to extract, I believe, statements to support any point of view.

Martí was born in 1853. His father was from Valencia and had become a Havana policeman. His mother was from the Canary Islands. He was classic *peninsulares* stock in other words, yet he gravitated not towards the Volunteers, the *pieds noirs* of the Caribbean, but in the opposite direction.

Martí was fifteen when the first War of Independence started. He sympathised with the rebels and actively supported them through the newspaper he founded, *Patria Libre*, to which he contributed. It was a mistake to let his feelings be so known. In 1869 he wrote a letter to a school friend, accusing him of treachery because he had attended a pro-Spanish parade. For this crime he was sentenced to six years' imprisonment. In 1871 he was allowed to leave for Spain on the condition he did not return to Cuba.

This was a mistake on the part of the authorities because Martí ended up in Madrid which was then a centre of revolutionary ferment. He studied law, moved to Saragossa and got his degree. He also wrote plays on the theme of national independence.

He visited his parents, by now in Mexico, in 1875, and there he remained, acquiring moderate celebrity in the country's literary circles. In 1877 he returned to Havana under a false name. He hated the city, loathing its Hispanic atmosphere as well as the authoritarian nature of the administration. He left and went to Guatemala. There he married the daughter of a Cuban sugar baron, Carmen Zayas Bazán (rather than the daughter of one of the country's ex-presidents with whom he was in love for a while: a more exciting but a less suitable choice). In 1878, at the age of twenty-five, he was allowed to return to Havana openly. Once again he loathed it. Leaving his wife behind, he went first to Spain and then to the US. He was to stay fourteen years during which time he produced prodigious amounts of journalism, busied himself with the activities of exiles and became co-ordinator, fund-raiser and president of the Cuban revolutionary committee in New York.

Martí's achievements in the first instance were organisational. He persuaded Cuban workers in the US to contribute ten percent of their earnings to the cause. He founded the newspaper *Patria* to promote the cause of independence. He founded the La Liga de Instrucción movement which acted as a training school for revolutionaries, first in New York and later extending its activities to Tampa in Florida. He re-organised his followers as the Cuban Revolutionary Party. He persuaded the Cuban exile clubs in the US to agree on a common revolutionary programme called the 'Bases'. He persuaded Maximó Gomez and Antonio

'Titan of Bronze' Maceo to lead the rebel forces when the insurrection eventually materialised.

Hand in hand with these achievements went his ideological work. Through his journalism he created distrust of the Autonomist scheme for freedom within the Empire. Simultaneously he attacked *anexionismo*, in which a considerable number of Cubans living in the US still had faith. With these two out of the way, there was no progressive alternative to independence.

Martí's total opposition to annexation was given impetus by his perception of what was happening in the US. A new mood was sweeping the country, pugilistic, bellicose and imperial. For a hundred years the US had been continuously expanding territorially, but then in 1890 came the massacre at Wounded Knee. This finished off the Indian problem, and sights shifted abroad. Then there was the sheer size of the US. Every year Martí had lived there, 500,000 immigrants had arrived. With 70,000,000 people in 1890 the US already had a population larger than that of any European country. In 1892 the US overtook England as the world's largest producer of steel and was set to become the largest industrial nation on earth. The domestic market could not expand further and therefore the place to expand was abroad.

There were also men coming of age, and more importantly coming to power, who had no direct experience of war or hardship in the way their parents had had in the Civil War. Ambition with this sort of ignorance was a fatal combination. And there was the new journalism or so-called 'yellow press', principally Hearst's *Journal* and Dana's *World*.

Battling for circulation, around 1895 their circulation war reached a critical point. They articulated the new mood of expansionism and gave the US a new collective voice.

Because it suited their republican, democratic, anti-colonial profile, the yellow press, certainly the *World*, the *Journal* and the *Sun*, supported the Cuban revolutionary cause. The information bureau of the Cuban junta in New York was happy to supply these newspapers with sensational information about Spanish perfidy and the virtue of the revolutionary cause. The junta got their views across and the newspapers boosted sales. It was a successful arrangement, but Martí didn't believe for a second that America wasn't capable of becoming Cuba's enemy. He saw that the US was an imperial power on the rise, as Spain was on the decline, and after the takeover of Hawaii in 1893 there were ample grounds for believing that one day it would be Cuba's turn. Martí warned his followers against the US as much as he railed against Spain. Prophetically, he saw Cuba as the bulwark against US expansionism. He expressed his views perhaps best of all in his last, most famous, most quoted and also unfinished letter:

> It is my duty . . . to prevent, through the independence of Cuba, the USA from spreading over the West Indies and falling with added weight upon other lands of Our America. All I have done up to now and shall do hereafter is to that end . . . I know the Monster, because I have lived in its lair—and my weapon is only the slingshot of David.[1]

While Martí was organising in the US, Cuba was not a happy land. Her *peninsulares* seemed not to have learnt anything from the 1868–78 war. Spaniards were favoured at all levels of the administration, and got the jobs. There were hardly any Cubans or *criollos* in the Constitutional Union Party—a revealing fact. There was more and more grumbling about running a country from as far away as Madrid. Incompetence and corruption were on the increase. There was less money around because world sugar prices were coming down. Havana was growing seedy. There was the cost of the ten-year war, an annual interest repayment to Spain of $10.5 million. It was hardly surprising that Cubans felt disenchanted with the motherland.

On the political front, the Conservatives increasingly saw the Liberals as dangerous separatists, whilst those who believed independence was the only solution regarded them as toadies, somewhat the same fate which the Irish Nationalist Party

---

[1] The translation is Hugh Thomas's, taken from *Cuba, or the Pursuit of Freedom*.

suffered when they faced Sinn Fein in the general election in November 1918. Something had to be done, even the Spanish realised that. Sagasta, a Liberal, became Prime Minister at the close of 1892 and the following year offered Cuba a package of reforms, somewhat along the lines favoured by the Autonomists. Military and foreign affairs, justice, finance and public order were to remain the responsibility of Madrid, but public works, communications, health, education and economic production were to be overseen by an autonomous island government. But the offer pleased neither side. Its collapse was a godsend to Martí and the separatists. By 1894 the plans of the revolutionaries were pretty far advanced, and at the end of the year Martí decided the uprising was to start the following spring.

In April 1895 Martí, Gómez, Antonio Maceo and his brother José landed at different points on the Cuban coast.

Early in May they met. Maceo wanted a military junta to exercise control until victory. Martí did not, so nothing was agreed. On 19 May Spanish forces surprised Gómez a few miles south-east of Bayamo, and Martí, prominent on a white horse, was killed. The revolutionary forces had lost their principal civilian leader – the man who had grasped better than anyone (except perhaps Maceo) the dangers posed by the US, even before the war had begun. But his death left the generals in a position of authority, and they were able now to run matters as they wanted without civilian interference.

They organised their forces, numbering between 6,000 and 8,000, into mobile columns, often mounted, which operated independently and lived off the land. The Spanish troops they opposed numbered about 52,000 throughout the island. In Oriente, where everyone supported the rebels, the Spanish just abandoned the countryside to them and stuck to the towns. In mid-October Gómez was able to take the war into the prosperous western part of Cuba.

Avoiding anything like a pitched battle, Gómez, Maceo when he later got through to the west, and their troops destroyed property and cane, US- and Cuban-owned, with abandon. It soon looked as if the 1896 harvest was going to be ruined. A large number of ex-slaves joined the rebel forces and participated in the destruction of the mills and plantations where they had once worked, turning the war from a colonial to a true revolutionary war.

Fanned by the yellow press, there was a growing demand in the US for 'action' without any real sense of what that 'action' was to be. As far as Spain was concerned, troubled at home and vilified abroad, there was only one option, to beat the rebels with a war of terror. The man for the job was Valeriano Weyler, a puritanical Spanish general of German descent. He arrived early in 1896.

The situation was desperate. Weyler decided he would isolate Maceo in Pinar del Rio from Gómez further east. He divided the island into further sections with north–south lines. He re-equipped the *trocha*, the trench dating from the last war. He re-equipped his cavalry with machetes instead of sabres, giving his soldiers the same lightweight weapon as their opponents, and cut the size of his cavalry units to make them self-sufficient. He turned the defence of the towns over to volunteers. He recruited Cuban counter-guerrillas. But to give his forces the same advantages as the enemy wasn't going to be enough to win him the war. He had to rob them of their unique advantage, the support of the population. This led to his most controversial step: the plan to concentrate whole populations within designated 'military areas' into well-defended outposts. As most of the country was a 'military area' this policy was going to have implications for almost everybody. Military commanders were also given extraordinary powers to try, punish or execute whoever contravened his decrees.

From the start, Weyler's policies were pursued energetically. But his strategy was a gift to the information bureau of the junta. A militantly pro-Cuban climate was developing in the US. But this in its turn only made the Spanish more determined than ever to press on, win and then negotiate with the rebels from a position of strength.

On 21 October 1896, Weyler issued his first concentration order. The entire rural population of Pinar del Rio province in the west was given eight days to move into the towns. Anyone outside the concentration areas thereafter would be regarded as a rebel and treated as such. Before the end of the year, Maceo was caught by a Spanish column and killed.

It does not require very much clairvoyance to see where a combination of a ruthlessly fought colonial war, a bellicose yellow press (whose confused reports were giving the impression it was Weyler who was burning the canefields and not the rebels), and an expansionist mood in the US was going to lead. Inevitably, it had to end with US intervention.

All that was lacking from the scenario was the acquisition of power by those with expansionist tendencies. This came about with the inauguration of President William McKinley and the entry into his administration of figures who openly wanted war, such as Theodore Roosevelt. After this had been achieved, the only element wanting was a pretext to declare war on Spain. Before this could come about, history again became unpredictable.

On 28 June 1897, Cánovas, the Conservative Spanish Prime Minister who had replaced Sagasta, was assassinated by a rebel-financed Italian anarchist. Sagasta, the old Liberal Prime Minister, now returned to power. Weyler resigned.

Early in September 1897, the new US envoy to Spain, General Stewart L. Woodford, presented to the Spanish government a long note which stated that unless peaceful measures were undertaken to end the conflict in Cuba, the US would be obliged to take steps. In November Sagasta's administration replied with an announcement of plans to extend the Spanish constitution of 1876 to Cuba. The island would gain universal suffrage and all sorts of other rights.

It was a proposal that should have been on the table at Zanjón. Now it was too late. The initiative had passed to the US. In January 1898, none the less, the first Cuban home-rule government was constituted, its members being old reformists and autonomists. There were riots and disturbances in which a few disgruntled members of the Spanish military participated. General Fitzhugh Lee, the US Consul-General in Havana, a fat man who wore a white suit and a panama hat and who favoured intervention, telegraphed Washington. He reported events as being much worse than they were and falsely suggested that US nationals and interests were threatened. The USS *Maine*, launched in 1890 and the kind of powerful capital ship Roosevelt wanted to see in the new navy, was dispatched to Cuba. She arrived at the end of January 1898. On 15 February 1898 the USS *Maine* blew up or was blown up in Havana harbour. Out of the ship's company of 355, 258 men were killed.

Roosevelt, and Hearst's *Journal*, were in no doubt who had committed the outrage. It was the Spanish. The US enquiry concluded that the explosion was caused by a submarine mine, but would not say who was responsible. The Spanish court of enquiry (with which the US government refused to cooperate) came to the utterly different conclusion that the cause of the explosion was internal. Historical research indicates that the Spanish findings were probably correct. The *Maine* was using a new and highly volatile type of gunpowder which was also badly packed. But the events of the previous years had been building towards intervention and here it was at last: the pretext for intervention.

In the US there were preparations for war, although nothing had yet been decided because the report of the enquiry into the sinking of the *Maine* was still awaited. The yellow press fulminated against Spain and denounced delays, and Hearst's *Journal* announced that come the war they would raise a regiment comprising sporting giants, boxers, football players and a hammer thrower amongst others. The US was utterly transfixed by the *Journal*'s sources of information.

On 28 March 1898 the report of the naval commission of enquiry into the sinking of the *Maine* was delivered to the US Congress. It didn't name names, but the press had been saying the Spanish were monsters for so long and so hard; the only conceivable conclusion was that the Spanish were culpable. On 9 April Sagasta's administration, realising what was looming, acceded to almost all demands previously made by the US as being in their view necessary to secure a lasting peace and prevent US intervention. There would be an unconditional armistice; Weyler's reconcentration orders were to be withdrawn; the *Maine* incident was to be submitted to independent arbitration; and the future of Cuba was to be placed in the hands of the Autonomist government. It was a staggering list of concessions which gave away everything except the right of the US President to determine the constitutional future of Cuba. It should have been acceptable to the US, but the country was for war. On 19 April the House of Representatives and the Senate voted in a resolution which demanded Spain's immediate relinquishment of authority in Cuba. On 25 April the US officially declared war.

The US army was made ready. Roosevelt was given deputy command of one regiment. Fitzhugh Lee, no longer consul in Havana, enlisted as a major-general. A good many of the US architects of this war were going to have a part in it. On 19 May Admiral Pascual Cervera arrived in Santiago harbour with a flotilla of Spanish cruisers, destroyers and torpedo boats: the cream of the Spanish navy. On 29 May the flotilla was spotted, very much to his surprise, by Commodore Schley who had been sent with a squadron of US ships to reconnoitre. With this information, General Miles and the US staff decided to blockade Santiago harbour and land their forces, which were now ready for embarkation, in the Santiago area. On 3 June, a Lieutenant Hobson was sent with the blockship *Merrimac* towards Santiago with instructions to sink it across the narrowest part of the harbour and prevent Cervera and his fleet escaping. In the afternoon the Spanish chief of staff sailed out to the US flotilla and informed them that Hobson's ship had capsized and he was a prisoner. It was a war with some elements of high farce.

On 15 June the US 5th Army Corps embarked at Tampa, Florida: eighty-five officers, 16,000 men and ninety journalists on thirty-two ships. On 22 June there was the first disembarkation of US troops onto Cuban soil at Daiquirí (a village on the coast about sixteen miles east of Santiago). Several hundred Spanish troops nearby did nothing. In the minds of both sides the outcome was inevitable. The US were going to win the war and the Spanish were going to lose it. Both sides were also clear they wanted something quick, simple, and with the honour of both parties maintained. The Cubans, for whose benefit after all the war was being fought, were largely invisible in the scenario, as they were sixty years later during the Cuban missile crisis, which became in the end a duel between the superpowers. Whenever great nations have got involved, it has been Cuba's unvarying fate to be ignored.

From Daiquirí, the US troops marched west and took Siboney, where we had seen the man scavenging Coca-Cola tins on the beach. They arrived on 24 June. The next four days, the US commander in the field, General Shafter, a sixty-three-year-old Civil War veteran, ponderous and dull, spent consolidating his forces, securing his rear and stockpiling supplies. On 30 June he ordered the capture of El Caney, a Spanish position to the north which was going to menace his advance on Santiago de Cuba. Calixto Garcia, the Cuban rebel general in the district, was ordered to advance 4,000 men to help the US forces. Two days earlier he had been visited by none other than William Randolph Hearst himself. Unfortunately, Hearst hadn't got the commission he'd hoped for in the navy and so he'd had to come to Cuba as war-correspondent-in-chief for his newspaper.

On 1 July US troops sallied north towards El Caney, simultaneously striking at the defences which lay due west of Santiago, known as San Juan Hill. There were about 600 Spaniards and two cannon at El Caney and 250 Spaniards at San Juan.

The San Juan position was battered by artillery for about two hours. At nine a.m. 3,000 men were moved up. The Spanish heads were kept down with Gatling fire. One infantry and two cavalry regiments (one black) charged forward. Roosevelt (six pairs of spare spectacles in his pocket) and the Rough Riders followed. One account, by a friend, R. H. M. Ferguson, described Roosevelt as 'revelling in victory and gore'. Hearst was there too, in a straw hat and with a revolver stuck in his belt, taking notes from his own injured reporter, Greelman. The Spanish retired to their next line of defence. The US had captured one of the city's forward defences at a cost of 223 dead,

1,243 wounded and seventy-nine missing. The Spanish tally was 102 dead and 552 wounded. In the eyes of Roosevelt and the US public, it came to be seen as a great victory, an occasion when a young and virile nation, with right on its side, triumphed over an old and feeble one which did not. However, the figures suggest something different. In effect the storming of San Juan cost the US 1,545 men, about ten percent of their effective force. Adding the El Caney Spaniards into the totals, one could say, 700 of the enemy had held up 6,000 US troops and inflicted serious damage. In contrast, the rebels at San Juan suffered a mere ten casualties.

The Spanish should have counter-attacked but, believing the war lost, the decision now made by Captain-General Blanco in Havana was that Cervera had to get his fleet out of Santiago harbour and escape. Blanco's thinking was that whilst Spain would survive the loss of Cuba she would not survive the loss of the prize ships of her navy. Cervera protested. The ships in the US blockade were infinitely superior to his. Blanco overruled him. On 3 July, the Spanish battle fleet sailed out. The plan was to ram one of the blockading ships, the *Brooklyn*, with the *Maria Teresa*. This would break the cordon and the others would slip through. However, this didn't happen. The US fleet, sighting the Spanish ships, got itself into a great tangle in which the *Texas* nearly rammed the *Brooklyn*. The whole of Cervera's squadron slipped through.

If Cervera's boats had been made of steel they'd probably now have made it to Havana (they had a prevailing wind behind them) but they were wooden and powered by steam engines. Fleeing westwards, they ran aground and caught fire, with the exception of the *Colón*, which ran out of coal, had a small battle, then ran aground and caught fire. Hearst visited the naval battleground on his yacht the following day. He collected thirty Spanish sailors as prisoners and gathered they were more frightened of the Cubans than of the US forces. This nonentity of a victory cost the Spaniards 350 dead out of a total of 2,225, and 1,670 prisoners. On the US side the cost was one dead and two wounded.

On land, long and complicated negotiations were continuing with the Spanish commander in Santiago, General Toral. On 14 July Shafter met Toral. If the general capitulated unconditionally, his troops would be allowed to return to Spain. On 17 July the final terms of the surrender were agreed. Santiago and Oriente were to be handed over to the US. After the signing, Shafter and Toral rode together into Santiago and at noon the Stars and Stripes was raised over the Captain's palace. The rebels, who'd been fighting for three years, played no part in the day. Relations between them and the US forces had become increasingly strained in the previous weeks. On 2 July Cuban rebels entrusted with forty Spanish prisoners had cut off their heads. From the start US forces, even more so now they were victorious, had felt more drawn to their chivalrous enemies than to the Cubans. There was also the uncomfortable fact that whilst most of the US forces were white, most of the Cuban forces were black. On the day of Shafter's triumphal entry into Santiago, Cuban troops were not allowed into the city for fear of reprisals, presumably against Spaniards. The local rebel general, Calixto Garcia, had been invited by word of mouth to attend but said no because Spanish municipal officials had not been removed. For Cuba it was not really a fitting climax to thirty-odd years of intermittent civil war. But it was a great day for Roosevelt, who wrote of the US achievement, 'I feel that I now leave the children a memory that will partly offset the fact I do not leave them much money,' and Hearst who, having made ready a printing press to print the *Journal-Examiner* for US troops in Cuba, had had the city covered with posters which read, 'Remember the Maine. Buy the *Journal*'—the Cuban edition of course. The war was over and although, after Santiago, there were more twists and turns to the events, it can be said the island of Cuba now passed into military control of the US. Cuban losses were 300,000 lives, or roughly ten percent of the population,[1] mainly as a consequence of the concentration policy. From

---

[1] The total population was probably about 1,800,000 in 1895. It was down to 1,500,000 in 1899 when the US administration conducted a census.

their force of about 200,000 men the Spanish lost 60,000 lives, or about thirty percent, the majority from yellow fever or other diseases. The number of Spaniards killed outright in battle was 786.

27

The Man from Local Government

A few minutes after the rain had cleared, allowing me to see the harbour where Cervera's ships had anchored, the sun began to shine. In the square below, dedicated to Céspedes, the wet benches began to steam.

The guidebook had mentioned the 'justly famous' Casa de Té and dutifully we decided to pay a visit. It was at the bottom of Aguilera, Santiago's main shopping street, a small room with wobbling tables and a filthy floor. The tea was Russian, stewed black and drunk sweet. I gave a cigarette to an old man. His trousers were tattered and as he begged from table to table his legs caked with dirt showed through.

In the early evening, we closed the shutters of our hotel bedroom and went up to the bar-cum-cabaret on the hotel's roof terrace to see what was there. Stepping out of the lift, we found ourselves in an auditorium in complete darkness except for a couple of waiters with torches setting out tables and chairs. It was completely empty. From the balcony, we looked across the city to the docks lit up with pink sodium lights, and a large white ship along the quayside.

We went to the lobby and slipped outside. The streets were

filled with puddles and the money changers had all vanished. We found a restaurant. The walls were dark wood hung with swords and shields. There was a table but they wouldn't let us sit down because it hadn't been cleared. After forty minutes we cleared the table ourselves, laid it and sat down. The waitress was a thin woman with knobbly knees and dark close-set eyes. We had a furious argument with her. Two Cuban men who were eating in the restaurant sent us each a bottle of beer and India a dish of cheese with guava jam.

On Good Friday morning we went into the enormous cathedral beside the hotel. The original cathedral was started in 1528, and this was the fourth building to occupy the site. The service was in a side chapel. We sat near the back. Young black men in their teens, with their first growth of adolescent beard, slipped into the pew behind us one after the other and asked us to change money. We agreed the third time and passed the dollars and made the transaction through the slot in the back of the seat. One of them went off and lit a candle to the Virgin Mary and then came back and sat through the mass.

The day was not a holiday, but an ordinary Friday. We walked down to the docks and found the vegetable market. It was a large warehouse that stank of rot, selling green and inedible, or red and putrefying, tomatoes and precious little else. We picked a dozen that weren't too badly gone out of the metal baskets into which everything had been tipped and went and joined the back of the queue to pay. About a hundred people were waiting.

In the middle of the warehouse floor an oldish black woman started shouting vituperatively, 'This is shit.'

Around us, everyone touched their heads and said, 'She's mad.'

After half an hour we came to a turnstile, guarded by a woman sitting on a pile of paper bags. Inconceivable as it may seem, she searched everybody's bag in case anyone had helped themselves to the tomatoes, or to the mouldy potatoes or bruised peppers.

Beyond the turnstile our goods were weighed at a battered

scales. We were given a slip. We took this to the cash till and paid. In return we were given a receipt. At the exit sat another woman. We had to give her the receipt before she would let us out onto the street.

Back at the hotel, we were waiting for the lift when a slim young man came up. He was white, with pale blue eyes and an unshaven face.

'Excuse me,' he said. 'Do you mind if I speak with you?'

'Not at all,' Tyga said.

'My name is Jorge, and now I have to say: What is your name? Is that not right?'

He explained he worked in Santiago in the Poder Popular, the local government. He was from Havana, but he'd studied in Santiago which was why he'd ended up working there.

He pointed at Tyga's swollen belly and said, 'I hope I am not being indiscreet but I see you are expecting. My girlfriend,' he continued, 'no, my wife, that's right, is three months expecting. But she is in Havana and I am here. I want to be with another woman and I do not want to be speaking about this matter.'

He smirked and suggested we all took a little rum together, later. Although I didn't like him, I thought it might be interesting and agreed.

He appeared in the hotel lobby at nine o'clock that evening with a slim girl whose breasts were small and whose white teeth rested ever so slightly on her lipstick-covered lower lip. Her name was Nuria. She was a swimwear model.

We went into the street and walked past the Casa de la Trova where crowds were gathering for the evening session. Jorge stopped to shake hands with a young man who he introduced as 'a very good architect'. Nuria had wandered on, and he made a low whistling sound, summoning her to stop. Money changers kept emerging from the darkness and making their signals, and I had to keep shaking my head. A giant of a man, over six foot six, stared at us from a doorway.

'I have something I want to speak to you about,' Jorge said. 'But not now. I will speak about this matter later, when we are seated in the restaurant.'

We found El Baturro and went through the doors from the street into a tiled vestibule. An eighteen year old sat on a chair in the corner. He circled his forefingers around one another and called out, 'Change?' I shook my head. We went through more doors to the restaurant and sat down at a table.

The giant whom I'd noticed in the street sauntered up to Jorge. They started a long, furtive conversation.

'Jorge, the waitress is standing right behind you,' said Nuria suddenly, 'and she's heard every word you've said.'

I realised she thought we spoke no Spanish.

'*Más tarde*,' said Jorge, and the giant stood up, scowled and disappeared. The waitress moved off.

'What was going on?' I asked.

'Oh, he wanted to change money,' said Jorge. 'Of course I have a position, a job in the Poder Popular, and I take a moral view of these matters.' As he continued in this vein I wondered why, if he had such a strong moral view, he had talked to the money changer so earnestly instead of telling him to go away? As I knew from experience, if one said flatly no, they always did.

'I have a very delicate position,' I heard Jorge saying. 'What if at the next table there were colleagues from the office? What if they saw these money changers and me talking? How would I explain what happened at work the next day? One has to be very careful about these things.'

Two enormous policemen carrying guns and nightsticks came through the swing doors of the restaurant. The waitress pointed at Jorge, and Jorge pointed at the corner where the giant in the teeshirt was standing watching us. The policemen ignored this gesture of Jorge's and beckoned him. He got up and went over. He was away speaking to them for some minutes. He returned.

'How did the police get here?' I asked.

Jorge appeared not to understand, so I repeated the question. He said, 'I didn't want you to go back to your country with bad tales about my country, and money changers. And I wanted us to be able to be here and not to be—do you say?—molested.'

'Disturbed.'

'Exactly right,' he said, 'disturbed,' and he laughed and banged on the table, adding, 'Great word, man.'

Then he said, in answer to my question, that he had called the police. But he hadn't left the table to make the telephone call, and when the police had come in, the waitress had pointed at him. It was a very stupid lie. It was obviously she who had made the call.

The two huge policemen walked three money changers including the giant, through the restaurant, past our table and into the filthy lavatory behind us. The door was warped and banged shut with extreme difficulty.

'This matter I wanted to speak to you about, which I mentioned in the street,' said Jorge, 'is that I am not interested in changing. You understand, with my position at the Poder Popular, all I want is to practise my English and make friends.'

The lavatory door banged open and the three money changers were marched by the police through the restaurant and out into the street. The waitress who'd telephoned the police came up to us and laid one wrist over the other. 'They are going to the police station,' she said, 'and then to prison.' She looked grimly at Jorge and stalked off. Later she made her dislike of him abundantly clear by serving us measures of rum which were less than half the usual amount, and then closing the restaurant early to force us out into the street.

We ran into Jorge a couple of times that week coming out of the Poder Popular. He pressed to see us but we declined.

28

The US Naval Station

On a Saturday morning we drove out of Santiago and headed eastwards, intending to return for the city's fiesta in a week's time. We found ourselves in a hilly landscape covered with banana trees and lush vegetation. It was the first time Cuba felt really Caribbean. There were tracks of red earth leading off the highway where black women padded along. There were crowds of staring children. There were shacks made of grey-coloured planks, thatched with palm fronds, which all leant in odd directions as if they were about to fall over. We approached a church nestling at the bottom of a valley under a spreading carob tree. The white and pink paint was flaking off the wooden sides, and at the top of the tiny spire I could see a bell. I slowed down, hoping to hear the sound of voices singing 'Hallelujah', and then as we passed I saw there was rubbish piled in front of the closed front door and a huge padlock and chain stretched across the middle.

Round the next corner we ran into the rear of a huge herd of cattle, from one of the state-owned ranches, being moved along the road. We nosed through the stragglers at the back and pushed on. We expected we would soon come out on the far side, but after twenty minutes of solid progress we were still surrounded. Ahead the humps of the cattle's shoulder blades stretched away like waves for as far as my eye could see.

A lorry honked behind and proceeded with the perilous business of overtaking us. In the back of the lorry there were men with red flags and bottles of *aguardiente*. They laughed and waved at us. I presumed they were volunteer workers on their way to the cane fields. The fortnight of Playa Girón had begun.

The lorry accelerated, the driver furiously honking its horn. The cattle panicked and started to stampede, raising their thin legs in front of us. The gauchos galloping alongside shouted abuse and gesticulated with their hats. The vista of cattle backs stretching ahead now looked like a stormy sea.

We kept close to the wake of the lorry for several miles, slowly making our way through the frantic cattle. We passed finally beyond the head of the herd, and immediately had to slow down again. An articulated lorry had crashed into a house and shed its load of gigantic paper rolls (they were ten feet wide) onto the tarmac. The rescue party were in fine spirits and shouted at us as we passed to take their photographs.

Fifty or so miles from Santiago, we came to Guantánamo, a depressed city of miserable, low houses and railway marshalling yards filled with decrepit rolling stock. On every corner there were either soldiers, police or militiamen. A few miles outside the city, in a flat, desolate, brown landscape filled with brown ponds and abandoned narrow-gauge railway tracks, a huge sign announced that we were nearing the Frontier Zone.

We were about twenty miles north of the US naval base at the bottom of Guantánamo Bay, still the home of 8,000 US personnel.

The reasons for the base's existence arise from the history that followed the Spanish surrender at Santiago. After that anti-climactic occasion General Miles, the US supreme commander, who had not arrived in Cuba until after San Juan and so was feeling somewhat piqued, took a force of volunteers, sailed to Puerto Rico, and began without any orders to do so to conquer the island. (This ran against the explicit wishes of President McKinley.) At around the same time in the Philippines, Spain's largest Pacific colony, a US army of 35,000 disembarked. Finally, on 7 July the cruiser *Philadelphia* was dispatched to take formal possession of Hawaii. Midsummer 1898 was a high point for American imperial expansion.

Meanwhile, in Cuba, Colonel (now acting General) Wood became governor of Santiago. The old Spanish mayor, Leonardo Ros, was reinstated. Galixto Garcia was furious and retired with his troops to the hills. McKinley agreed that, where possible, Spanish officials would remain rather than have their jobs passed over to rebel sympathisers.

McKinley and his cabinet now had to decide what was to be done with their new clutch of possessions. They agreed to keep their forces in the Philippines until the future of the islands was settled; they agreed also that Puerto Rico and other small Spanish island possessions in the Caribbean and the Pacific (including what became Guam) would be ceded to the US; that Spain would drop all claims to Cuba, and that the US would establish an independent Cuban regime. They were bound by the Teller Resolution which had been voted through in April 1898 at the same time as the resolution demanding Spain's immediate relinquishment of authority in Cuba—in effect the US's declaration of war. The Teller Resolution committed the US to an independent, self-governing Cuba and limited her own role to pacification and guidance. The wording had been the suggestion of an old friend of José Martí's, the lawyer Horatio Rubens, a man who should be regarded as one of the real fathers of Cuban independence. Spain agreed to evacuate Cuba by 1 January 1899.

The next four months saw an almost total breakdown of order. It also saw a terrible deterioration in relations between the Cubans and the Americans. The Anglo-Saxons saw their Latin allies as lazy, vicious, greedy and, most importantly, corrupt: therefore not fit to govern themselves. The newspapers, of course, disenchanted because peacetime affairs did not boost sales like war, had a hand in this. Their particular contribution was to depict the Cubans as ruthless attackers of chivalrous Spaniards. However, quite miraculously, the Americans still managed to disarm the Cuban rebels, or transform them into rural guards or policemen.

The US took control of the whole island in January 1899. As at Santiago the year before, the rebels were prohibited from participating in the ceremonies in Havana which accompanied the transfer of power, bar nine Cuban generals who were guests. There were now 24,000 American servicemen on the island. The old Spanish administration, sometimes with the same Spanish officials, remained in place.

The first military governor was General John Rutter Brooke. His regime was generally benign and non-interfering. He was not an annexationist but regarded his job as getting Cuba ready to go her own way, a view directly opposite to that of General Wood in Santiago. He wanted Cuba to be so well governed by the US that the Cubans would clamour for annexation. After various machinations in Washington, in which Roosevelt had a hand, Brooke was replaced by Wood on 29 December 1899.

In April 1900 Wood promulgated a new system for elections with a property qualification which excluded many blacks. In June municipal elections, the first free elections in Cuba, were held. Encouraged by the success of these, Wood decided to organise a national electoral system (for president) and simultaneously frame a constitution which would, among other matters, codify relations between Cuba and the US, possibly giving his country some sort of power of veto over internal affairs. The constitutional convention which followed in the autumn dealt with this and the possible maintenance by the US of a naval base. The idea of buying land for a station at Guantánamo had already been mooted by Admiral Bradford in June 1898.

In January 1901, Secretary of State for War Elihu Root suggested to Wood a novel scheme: the new constitution would give the US the right to intervene to preserve independence and stable government; it would prohibit Cuba from entering into arrangements or treaties which would damage her independence; and grant the US navy stations at certain ports which would facilitate intervention if necessary.

A constitutional conference was convened on the edge of the Zapata swamp. The intention was to combine discussion with a little crocodile shooting. The venue was not all that far from the site of the Bay of Pigs invasion, the illegitimate descendant of the US proposals so many years later. Discussions were equitable, but once they were back in Havana the Cubans denounced Wood. Unmoved, he ploughed on, adding a further provision: if the Cubans didn't keep Havana clean, that too would justify American intervention—confirmation of the eternal correspondence between colonialist rule and hygiene.

In February 1901 Senator Orville Platt of the US Foreign Relations Committee drafted a bill to incorporate Root's suggestions and Wood's proposal. It went through the two houses, and was thereafter known as the Platt Amendment because it had been tacked onto the Army Appropriations Bill. Cuban opinion was not enchanted. In April 1901 the Havana newspaper *La Discusión* published a cartoon which showed Cuba crucified, with the two thieves played by Wood and McKinley and the centurion with the spear as Senator Platt. Wood, unamused, arrested the editor but released him the next day. By means of flattery, cajolement and seduction, the Cuban members of the Constitutional Conference finally accepted the Platt Amendment. On 31 December 1901 the first presidential elections were held. Estrada Palma was elected unopposed. On 20 May 1902 the Cuban flag was hoisted. Wood withdrew.

In November, only six months into genuine independence, the US raised the matter of the bases again. She was constitutionally entitled to them. They were the means by which she would guarantee Cuba's independence. The Americans asked for Guantánamo, Cienfuegos, Bahía Honda and Nipe. Estrada Palma said it would have to be just Guantánamo and Bahía Honda, and the stations would be leased not ceded. Ten years later, the latter was cut out, but the Guantánamo lease was prolonged. The rent to be paid for the forty-five-square-mile site was $2,000 a year, and in the lease document no date was set for re-negotiation. Thus, despite the missile crisis, the Bay of Pigs and everything else, the base was still there in 1987 as we passed within a few miles of it. It was home to 8,000 servicemen, and there is no reason why it won't continue to be in perpetuity.

The base is self-sufficient. It has its own water supply and its own television station—Channel 8. This can be received in Guantánamo and does not go unwatched. The two closest Cuban towns, Boqueron and Caimanera, still provide a few Cuban workers, who go in every day. They are paid in dollars. Residents in these towns have special permits, and non-residents are assiduously kept out. Sailing or swimming through the shark-infested waters to the base is a popular method of emigration: about 3,000 since 1959. Guantánamo and environs, traditionally an area of poverty, has received particular financial attention from the government and extra rations in the case of the two border towns. Workers returning from the enemy's lair have thus been prevented from making unfair comparisons with US standards of living as embodied in this Gibraltar of the Caribbean.

The base occupies the two horns at the bottom of the bay, which makes the water in between American. I only heard one complaint about the base while I was in Cuba, from an Englishman working in Havana. He resented the difficulty of passage through the waterway for the Eastern-bloc merchant marine destined for towns at the head of the bay. Cuban merchant marine is apparently prohibited.

The rent is still paid. In a recent television documentary, Fidel Castro showed the film crew a drawer filled with these cheques. On principle they're uncashed. With an estimated credit of $1,000,000 a day from the Soviet Union, what can a country do with $2,000 a year?

29

The Revolutionary and the Teacher

At Glorieta the road touched Guantánamo Bay at its north-eastern corner, and then started southwards and eastwards towards the last stretch of coast before Europe. A huge sign announced '4 Accidents, 17 Deaths', and the road began to climb. At Tortuguilla, on the other side of the mountains, we saw the Caribbean, and the road turned east. We were on a coastal plain between huge mountains and the sea beating against the lip of rock on the shoreline. The sheets of spray could be seen half a mile away, yet beyond the waters were serene.

At Gajobabo, an old man was exposing himself to the traffic. We turned north and climbed into the mountains along *la farola*, the lighthouse road. This was never part of Machado's central highway but was constructed after 1959 to connect Baracoa on the isolated north-eastern corner with the rest of the island.

The road twisted and turned, hugging the side of the mountains as it climbed. There were long views across forested valleys to green slopes and misty mountain tops. Small landslides had covered the tarmac with stones which caused an eerie pinging to sound in the inner tubes of the tyres.

There were occasional settlements. Yumurí was a collection of wooden shacks, staring children and a man whizzing along the road on a home-made trolley, with castors for wheels which groaned as they spun round. He was transporting a load of firewood. Further on, we saw several more of these trolleys, one with a bath strapped on for carrying water.

We got behind a dusty, crawling bus, with its exhaust backfiring every few seconds. We started to descend from about 1,100 metres and our ears began to pop. At Jobo Dulce we entered a moist valley with plantations of banana trees on either side, their leaves vividly green in the slanting sunlight. At the end of this valley, by the sea, lay Baracoa, city of wooden shacks with corrugated tin roofs and cobbled streets. Christopher Columbus landed here in December 1492 when he was exploring Cuba's northern coast, and planted a cross on the beach. In 1512 Diego de Velázquez founded the city, and for a short while it was the island's capital, until eclipsed by Santiago de Cuba.

Above the city there was an old Spanish fort, built in the 1730s during the War of Jenkins' Ear and subsequently a prison. Its present incarnation was as a motel. We sat in the lobby waiting for the desk clerk to appear. On the television—it was a Cuban programme—Bruce Springsteen sang 'Born in the USA'. Dozens of young men gathered round and watched in mesmerised, adulatory silence. The sun sank behind the ring of mountains and their peaks became purple in the fading light.

I went for a walk. On one of the lower battlement walls, beside the steps leading down to the city, I found a plaque:

Reconstruido en 1900
LEONARD WOOD *Gobernador general de la isla de Cuba*
MAJOR W. M. BLACK USA *Jefe de ingenieros del dpto. de Cuba*
Captain W. H. CHATFIELD USA
Lieutenant J. W. WRIGHT USA *Ingenieros del distrito*

It looked strangely well-kept. The Cubans must have been proud of it. In 1908, the Americans made use of their barracks here and elsewhere again. The second occupation came about in this way.

The provision to allow Cuban sugar into the US on preferential terms, the *quid pro quo* of the Platt Amendment, became law in December 1903. It gave Cuba a 20 percent tariff advantage over other countries, and it was the signal for large investment in sugar. The chance of creating a more balanced economy was once again passed over, and the dominance of American goods was reinforced.

In 1904 came the first free elections for Cuba's Congress. The corruption was shameless: even Martí's heir, the negro writer Juan Gualberto Gómez, polled more votes than were cast for him. Similar skullduggery characterised the run-up to the second presidential elections in November 1905. Palma, the only incorruptible President in Cuba's history until the appearance of Fidel Castro, had amassed considerable funds—$12,000,000 of them —which were in the state exchequer. His supporters, allegedly fearing that the Liberal opposition would vote themselves this money if they got elected, initiated a programme of intimidation which Palma did nothing to stop. The Liberal candidate Gómez withdrew, and Palma was elected unopposed although a third of his votes were faked. As a result there was a threat of insurrection in April 1906 by the disgruntled Liberals, and in came the US Marines, 2,000 of them. They stayed until April 1909 when, in the wake of moderately successful attempts to overhaul judicial, electoral and civil service law, Cuba was deemed fit for self-government again. In the elections before they left, José Miguel Gómez (not to be confused with Gualberto) was elected President.

I brought my family to the bar. The barman was a weedy man with cross-eyes. Because it wasn't yet dark he was refusing to sell beer. The crowd was becoming unruly; ice cubes were thrown; finally, he sensibly agreed. A Cuban mentality was taking hold and we bought double beers and Frescos in case there was a sell-out. We sat down at a table. Before long a man called Alfredo attached himself to us.

He was old and toothless with a protruding chin; he reminded me of Punch. He bought us all drinks. He told us he cut rushes which were made into horses' saddles. It was a very lucrative job. He earned 300 to 400 pesos monthly. He worked twenty days in the month and the other ten days he had off to rest. He drank a bottle of rum a day at work because he was up to his neck in cold water and there were snakes. (There are none in Cuba.) In addition he smoked sixty cigarettes a day, although never cigars which he thought were ugly. He had a grandmother who'd lived until she was 115, so he had no cause to worry about cancer.

Alfredo's revolutionary credentials were impeccable. After Fidel's 1953 attack on the Moncada Barracks he had helped the attackers to hide. Later, he had been a rebel captain with 355 men serving under him. He had been shot twice, once in the stomach, once in the leg. He had the wounds to prove it and wasn't ashamed to show them. Later still, Alfredo had been in prison in Santiago, Guantánamo and Baracoa. The very motel where we were sitting had been a Batista prison, and the last place where he had been held.

'In 1957 they beat me here,' he said. 'In the punishment cell. It's right there, where the desk is now'—he continued pointing through the french doors to the lobby—'that's where they did it. Want another beer? I couldn't walk for a month and I pissed blood for a year.'

After the revolution Alfredo became a policeman. In 1962 he was voted the best policeman in Havana and, as a result, sent to East Germany for a holiday.

In 1982, aged fifty, he had been in Angola as an infantry captain, with 135 men under his command. He loved war.

He had had three wives and six children: four by the third and last wife. She was a revolutionary too, he said, and he loved her the most. It was beautiful when both husband and wife were militant, he said, smiling. Every night he loved his wife as though it were the first night. 'I am the Rudolph Valentino of Baracoa,' he added proudly.

Alfredo's chief ambition was to visit India, he said. The conversation then degenerated somewhat into an enumeration of statistics. Baracoa before and after the revolution: before, twenty-two hospital beds, now 300; before, four doctors, now ninety-two, and thirty-two of them specialists, also twenty-three family doctors for the *campesinos*.

Alfredo's politics became more and more pronounced as he became drunker and drunker. He asked us if we were communists, didn't wait for the answer and embraced us. 'My money is your money,' he said. 'All men are equal. Every time I hear Fidel speak, I get drunk on rum and beer.'

I said goodbye to Alfredo by the plaque to General Wood and the other Americans. He embraced me and then stumbled away down the winding steps to the town, where kerosene lamps glowed in the shack windows, and the pale electric lights on the street corners swayed in the sea breeze.

★

On Antonio Maceo Street in Baracoa there was an *Escuela de Gastronomía*, a school of gastronomy. It took students from all over Cuba and trained them to be chefs, waitresses and barmen. Why it was in a parochial place of 30,000 people and not in a big city, I don't know. Nor did I care, because with the school came a bar. Run by the students, it was open to the public and it never ran out of beer. The clients were exclusively male: peasants, workers, fishermen.

One evening, enjoying a solitary bottle of beer and a glass of *aguardiente* (which was clear coloured, scalded the back of the throat and tasted very like Irish *póitìn*), I met Señor Guy. He was a schoolteacher.

Straight away he asked me what I did, and then told me James Joyce was his favourite author and *Ulysses* his favourite novel. He had just read the new Ellmann *Letters*—a Mexican edition—with its recently discovered, scatalogical additions, the early passionate love letters of James Joyce to his wife Nora Barnacle.

'Very strong,' he said over and over again, emphasising his point by making a fist. His ancestors were French, originally from Haiti, among the thousands of sugar planters who fled the slave revolt of 1791 and landed in Cuba. Their expertise was one of the factors which helped to make the island the world's largest sugar producer in the nineteenth century.

Señor Guy was a short white man, in his thirties. He had a curly beard on his chin which made him look like a troll. His spectacles hung from his neck on a thin leather cord, and as we talked he kept putting his glasses on his nose and then letting them drop again.

'When I was chosen to represent Cuba,' he said, 'in the USSR at a conference on schools, I was very excited. The Soviet Union is the father of Cuba. I grew up with Soviet books, films, goods. But when I arrived there, *aie, aie, aie*, everything was ugly. Houses, people, clothes. East Germany was much more beautiful.'

'*Campañeros*,' a voice shouted, and out of the smoke weaved Alfredo, drunk. For the first time I noticed how his chin curled up to his nose.

He sat down and put his half-drunk bottle of *aguardiente* on the table. Señor Guy looked at the ceiling. Alfredo filled our glasses. We started to drink, heavily. Alfredo began a long and rambling monologue about the economic genius of Cuba. I stared at him without really listening. It was his chin I couldn't take my eyes off. It seemed to be growing like an elephant's trunk, reaching out to his drink and sucking it up, or arching round to his nose. The *campesinos* in the room turned green and purple, and when they moved their hands through the air, yellow sparks shot from their fingers. Dimly, in the midst of it all, I remember Señor Guy whispering in my ear, 'Don't believe a word of it. We export everything and have to bring shit back in. Even our fucking instant coffee comes from Nicaragua.'

'I love Fidel,' cooed Alfredo, his trunk reaching out for a cigarette.

I went on hallucinating from the *aguardiente* for the rest of the evening.

★

The next day Señor Guy didn't have to work and he took us all to the museum. It was the same as the other museums we'd visited; several drawings of Indian aboriginals; a picture of Columbus; a picture of Velázquez; pictures of slaves and their living conditions; a picture of an eighteenth-century *trapiche*, an early, unmodernised sugar mill; memorabilia of the two wars of independence, principally swords and rifles; a cartoon from the time of the Platt Amendment, showing a smirking, malevolent Uncle Sam; a picture of Fidel; pictures of the 'struggle' against counter-revolutionaries; pictures of the benefits of the revolution (a school, a hospital, the chocolate factory). It was the familiar story of inexorable progress from a dark past to a glorious present.

We went outside. The sky was grey.

'Look,' said Señor Guy, pointing at two schoolgirls in the uniform miniskirt. 'Two lovely young Baracoeses,' he continued with eyes shining.

We drove towards the edge of town. The colonial houses with their peeling stucco gave way to wooden shacks. They leant over as if blown by the wind; there wasn't a right angle in sight. Every door and window looked as if it had been drawn by a child. Señor Guy waved at every young woman.

We crossed the wide, brown Macaguani river and drove westwards along the coast. The smell of chocolate wafted from a factory. We passed the place where Antonio Maceo had landed in April 1895, a long beach of black sand. Further on was a tiny school where he had fought his first battle. Señor Guy explained the history mechanically, and we listened without much interest. We turned off the tarmacadamed road and disappeared into a green forest, with the sea to the left crashing on the sandy shore beyond arching coconut trees.

We stopped near the mouth of the river Toa with its greenish waters. Here lived Raphael, an old blue-eyed man, in a thatched hut, guardian of the bust of Maceo which glowered from on top of a pedestal (the general had performed some heroic deed here) and harvester of coconuts. Scuffing up the coarse, charcoal-coloured sand, I turned up pieces of brown pottery and a flat stone with two pinches in it, shaped like a fishing block. The grove had been an Indian settlement. Their artefacts were everywhere.

Above the palms the sky turned black and rain started to fall. Raphael brought us into the parlour of his shack. It was dark. The electricity only came on for an hour in the evening. There was a wooden sofa with twenty or thirty dolls arranged on it, all with plastic bags over their heads. Pinned on the walls there were, among other things, a wooden plaque of a woman in a bikini; a picture of a bowl of fruit cut from a magazine; a large plaster statue of a brightly painted mermaid; half a dozen playing cards, face down, the laminated backs showing; labels steamed from rum and beer bottles; coaster mats; and a flattened-out tin which had once held some type of fish. Outside the tiny, glassless windows, rain tumbled down from the shaggy thatch into the tiny garden where flowers were growing out of discarded kitchen pots and utensils and a trough made out of an old refrigerator.

Raphael gave us a drink made from pine needles and sugar syrup called *pru*. It came from Haiti and had been brought by French planters. It was only drunk in Baracoa. His wife was in hospital; he showed us her photograph. As he told us about his work as a coconut harvester, Señor Guy hissed continuously in my ear, 'And the government exports them all.'

In the car later, Señor Guy said, 'In Cuba it is very hard to buy what you want. You have money but you can't just get a car. It has to be allocated from the workplace. It's crazy.' Then he added wistfully, 'Once upon a time they gave teachers and doctors cars but that's been stopped.'

From this, he went straight on to say, 'I have a sister in Miami. She has a very good life there. She worked for Gillette in Havana and left in fifty-nine. I have seen photographs of her house in Miami: sofas, silverware, pictures on the walls . . . Sometimes she sends money.'

The windscreen wipers screeched as they moved backwards and forwards. Señor Guy seemed to grow morose. Nobody spoke as we bumped along the road past *campesinos* sheltering under old fertiliser bags. Then we came to the outskirts of the town and he waved at a girl and she waved back, and he seemed to become his old self again.

He invited us to his house for supper on Friday; in three days' time. We'd had ten weeks of pizzas and Russian salad pickled in vinegar. We accepted with alacrity.

We saw Señor Guy the next day. We drank some beers together. He repeated the invitation, which was reassuring.

On Thursday we went driving together. Señor Guy said, *en passant,* 'When you come tomorrow, you're going to have tea. Real English tea. I was given it by a visitor from London.'

He made no mention of food. On the other hand, he didn't dis-invite us either. We decided the tea was an extra scrap thrown our way, based on his knowledge, through reading, of the British Isles.

The appointed hour on Friday was nine o'clock. The evening was damp and the streets were empty as we wandered towards his house.

We knocked on the big wooden front door. A dog barked inside. We knocked again and again. Finally, one of us opened the door. There was a front room filled with heavy dark furniture and beyond another room, bordering the patio, where a television glowed and a figure lay asleep on a chair.

'Señor Guy,' I called.

He woke with a start, stood up and apologised.

'Come in, come in.'

The huge door—it stretched fifteen feet to the ceiling—closed behind us. I felt the dog's cold, wet nose bumping my hand. Ominously, there was no smell of food. Or sign of a table. Or the delightful noise of tinkling crockery. We sat down on the rocking chairs.

'My wife will be with us in a moment. She is taking a shower.'

'Yes.'

'Then we will drink tea.'

'Oh, how nice.'

'Real English tea,' he said.

It happened just as he said. Señora Guy appeared with wet hair from the shower and then an old aunt appeared with a tray. I took a cup filled with stewed black tea. Sugar had been added, so much that with the first mouthful some of my fillings began to ache.

'Real English tea,' said the aunt. She was called Mirta.

'Very nice,' I said.

The women led Tyga off to the kitchen to look at the crockery. There was a small boy and India started to play with him. Señor Guy waited for the sound of the women's voices to start, and then went and got a bottle of *aguardiente* from behind a mirror. He threw the tea away and filled our cups with liquor. The first mouthful scorched the back of the throat and made the eyes burn.

'We have many problems here,' he said, 'for instance, you know I invited you to dinner,' he said.

I had been wondering about this.

'Well, no dinner.' He laughed, put his spectacles on his nose and let them fall off again. 'In the shops there was only Russian fish, small pieces of it, and tinned sardines. My wife wasn't going to give you this. We went to the black market to buy meat but the man wouldn't sell. The police were being very vigilant.'

He pulled down an eye.

'Many problems here, many, many problems. For instance, my beard.'

'What about it?'

'There are some people who think it is bad, wrong.'

'Counter-revolutionary?'

'If you like. They don't like it.'

'But Fidel has a beard.'

'That is one of many contradictions in our system.'

I forgot about food and we drank the bottle, laughing all evening.

30

The Eldo

We left Baracoa and retraced our route back along La Farola. Rain was falling again and the mountain tops were obscured by mist. Near the Guantánamo base a bus had broken down by the roadside and the bedraggled passengers were standing in the wet, watching Cuban army personnel carriers manoeuvre across the road. It was still pouring when we reached Santiago, and in the big petrol station on the east side of the city, dozens of bicyclists were sheltering under the forecourt, many of them smoking away furiously.

We went back to the Casa Grande and they gave us a room this time at the side of the hotel, overlooking the Casa de la Trova.

It rained all afternoon, the rain falling on the city in thick silvery needles. It was extraordinary how no one appeared to own a raincoat. It was still raining when we came down from our room in the evening. There were hundreds of people sheltering in the lobby. A young man asked me for a light and I admired his *Playboy* golfing shirt. 'I paid many dollars for it,' he said proudly. 'Do you want to change?'

It was still raining when we ventured out. On the other side of the street, two coatless policemen (did anyone have a coat? I was starting to wonder) smoked in a doorway. They told us the *fiesta* we had come back to the city to see would not be happening because of the rain.

In the streets it was best to walk in the middle of the roads along the worn, glistening tram tracks rather than under the eaves, where the rain plopped down like water from a tap. In Aguilera Street, Saturday-night revellers sheltered by the shop-fronts, while opera, put on by the Poder Popular every Saturday evening, coursed from speakers attached to lamp-posts and buildings. Tickets for *El Atendato* (*The Attentive*) went on sale at the cinema and there was a lot of jostling and ineffectual punching between the men at the head of the queue and young bloods who hadn't waited and were trying to force their way through to the ticket booth. Those waiting in the line which stretched back along the street watched the scuffling develop into a fight without expression, while overhead—what was it doing out in the rain?—fluttered an enormous yellow butterfly about five inches across.

In the Casa de Queso, or House of Cheese, restaurant there were black-and-white photographs of cows on the walls, including a close-up of the udders of a Guernsey and the anus of a Friesian. They had no beer and only one dish: crumbled cheddar served in a glass with tomato purée. After dinner I asked for an ashtray. 'Throw it on the floor,' said one of the waitresses, 'the whole place is an ashtray.'

We woke. It was Sunday morning. There was the depressing atmosphere of Sunday stillness. The only disturbance was the delivery of ice for the hotel. I watched the men pulling the huge blocks, as big as refrigerators, along the filthy pavement.

In the dining room there was only toast and butter, and the butter was rancid. A blind man came in and found a table with some difficulty. Removing his hat, he broke a glass. The old thin waitress was furious. She demanded his purse and removed the money to pay.

'But he's blind,' I said.

'So he should stay at home, shouldn't he?' she shouted back.

We went for a walk in the back streets. We'd come back for the *fiesta* and that had been rained off. It was a mistake to have come. The houses were a tumble of old and decaying colonial and Fifties Florida-style homes. The television was on in every house and a Tom and Jerry cartoon was showing, instantly recognisable from its music. Half a dozen drunks sat outside a closed bar, passing round a bottle of *aguardiente* and tumbling dice on the pavement.

There were doors marked '*Ideologico*', '*Presidente*' and '*Vice-Presidente*' on ev ry block, denoting the homes of CDR officials. They gave a graphic sense of the power and breadth of the organisation. A woman with huge thighs washed her Lada. A baker in flour-covered overalls smoked in a doorway. A young woman with talcum powder between her breasts hurried along.

There was a church at the bottom of a hill. The doors were open and the sound of a limping organ and warbling old voices drifted out. We went in. The congregation was mainly made up of old women in patterned frocks. We took a pew at the back. The priest used a microphone and spoke slowly. He was punctilious but not charismatic. The time for communion approached. Nearly three months of materialism had created a longing for what was opposite. I went up and knelt at the altar rail.

'Are you prepared?' the priest asked sweetly.

'Yes.' Never has a lie come easier.

The priest was called Xavier. After the service he brought us to his house. In the front room thirty parishioners were watching a video of *Joan of Arc* with Ingrid Bergman. We sat in the kitchen. The housekeeper, who was black and fat, gave us hot chocolate made with tinned milk.

Father Xavier was a man in his thirties, with a curly black beard and brown eyes.

I took out my notebook.

'How many priests are there in Cuba?'

'About two hundred.'

'And about the same number of churches?'

'Roughly.'

'That's not enough.'

He shrugged.

'So what do you do?'

'What can we do? I say mass in people's houses.'

'Often?'

He nodded.

'Under current Cuban law that's a serious offence. You could easily go to prison.'

He looked bored. 'I want to show you something,' he said, and brought me out to a garage where there was a 500 cc Triumph motorcycle.

'Some of the parts are not original,' he said, 'but I've been to Havana on her twice.'

On the handlebars hung his old-fashioned helmet with ear-flaps and his goggles which looked pre-war.

I wasn't going to get far with my enquiries about the state of the church in contemporary Cuba, so I switched to the Eldorado Brougham.

'No,' he said, shaking his head, 'I have an idea I know what you mean but I've never seen one.'

We went back to the kitchen. Our cups of hot chocolate sat on the oilcloth-covered table, almost untouched.

'How about some coffee?' Father Xavier suggested. 'Pure, real Cuban.'

'How do you manage to get it?'

'Black market.'

That night, while we lay sleeping in the Casa Grande, someone took a crowbar to the trunk of our Lada. They failed to break open the lock, but made a large dent in the bodywork. We spent the following morning in the police station, getting a statement confirming the attempted robbery. When we returned the car in Havana we would be charged for the damage unless we had this. In the hallway of the police station there were drunks laid out asleep or comatose, and in the lavatory an Italian police motorcycle lay on the floor in bits.

The attempt to break into the car made us mildly apprehensive. At about nine o'clock that evening I looked from the hotel bedroom window. The Lada was parked in a side street. I could see the front but not the back of it.

I went down and moved it to the corner where I knew I would be able to keep an eye on all of it. There was a man in a doorway watching me.

'What happened?' he called over as I got out.

'Thieves.'

He nodded and invited me to have a cigarette. I went over. His name was Herman. He was a militiaman. We talked. I told him about my family.

'Come for a ride,' he said. 'All of you, tomorrow. I have a nice big car.'

'What kind of a car?'

'American.'

'Uh-huh. What type?'

'Nothing special. A '57 Bel Air, four doors, nothing special. But you should have seen . . .'

He looked slightly wistful.

'What?'

'The car before. I had to sell it. A '57 but a Cadillac, an Eldorado.' Impossible, I thought.

I bought him a cigar from the cafeteria on the corner, made him promise to remain in the doorway, and ran up to our room to fetch my *Consumer Guide to Cars of the Fifties*.

I returned and opened the book casually at the Chevrolet section. Herman pointed to a photograph of a 1957 Bel Air sports sedan and nodded.

'This is the car, more or less,' he said. 'I don't have the white and black tyres of course and mine's all one colour.'

He started to thumb back through the book, through the section dealing with early Fifties Chevrolets which led in its turn to the later part of the Cadillac section. I didn't say a word. Herman looked at the pictures of the 1958 Biarritz and the 1959 Sixty Special, with their enormous fins.

He said nothing, turned back a page, and from a dozen pictures of middle-Fifties Cadillacs, his finger went unerringly to a small black-and-white photograph of a 1957 Eldorado Brougham.

'Yes.'

I spent the next half an hour cross-questioning Herman with the aid of my dictionary about the brushed aluminium roof and the Eldorado's extraordinary suspension system. He knew all the answers and kept pointing to the photograph.

When Herman came to take us for the ride the next day, he had his photographs of the car, himself posing proudly beside it. I was ashamed I had doubted him.

We had a nice cruise up to the hills above the city and back again, and then Herman took us to a bar. We adults drank Armenian brandy and India Fresco. Herman had sold the car because its complicated suspension system had kept breaking down and he had reached the point when he could no longer face buying spares on the black market with which to mend it.

I hadn't got to see the car, but the conversation was good enough. I was as close to finding this rarity as I was going to get.

31

The Party Secretary

The next day *Granma* and *Juventud Rebelde* (*Rebel Youth*) were full of one thing, the funeral of Blas Roca, Secretary-General of the old Communist Party of Cuba. 'One of the most human and most generous men I have ever known,' said Fidel in his eulogy.

The Party in which he made his name was founded in August 1925 by communists and socialists from within the big anarchist trade union, the Confederación Nacional Obrera Cubana (CNOC). The early 1930s saw the elimination of anarchists from the union (some even betrayed to Machado's police) which left the Party in control. It was at this time that a young man from Manzanillo, a shoemaker by trade, Francisco Calderío, joined the Party. Later he changed his name to Blas Roca, Blas the Rock.

April 1933 saw the bizarre union of the dictator Machado and the extreme Left. But in the bloody period which immediately followed Machado's fall, it became clear that the Party's pacts with him were a blot on its reputation. The secretary-general who'd concluded them was forced to step down. His replacement was Blas Roca.

Late in 1935, Roca attended a meeting in Moscow of all the

Latin American Communist Parties. With the developing power of Italy and Germany, the new mood was conciliatory. The concept of the Popular Front had found favour. Communists were to seek allies, even amongst the middle classes. However, when the Party's attempts to rally anti-Batista[1] forces into a Popular Front of the Caribbean didn't work, they switched horses and started making overtures to the government. Here they were more successful. In 1937 they were granted permission to organise the Partido Unión Revolucionaria (PUR): openly a front party for the communists.

Batista had been moving leftwards himself. His grandiose three-year plan of 1937 was soon abandoned, but land reform was started in a modest way. This alienated the middle class and the professions, but Batista's eye was on the forthcoming presidential elections. He was tremendously popular with *los humildes*, 'the humble', and now set about getting organised labour on his side. After May 1938 he permitted the publication of the Communist Party daily newspaper, *Hoy*. Shortly afterwards Roca went to confer with Batista, offering him support if he returned the favour by making the Party legal and allowing it the right to reorganise the trades union movement. It was agreed. PUR merged with the Party, the CNOC disappeared and in its place came the Confederación de Trabajadores de Cuba (CTC), in effect, the state trade union. Batista was elected President in June 1940 with strong support from the communists, whose loyalty was rewarded when he brought Party men into the cabinet in 1942.[2] The Party, especially Roca, were very sorry when Batista stepped down in 1944.

Relations between the Party and Batista during the latter's second term of office, after his seizure of power in 1952, were not so serene or mutually beneficial. The communists, like all Cuba's political parties, suffered from the suspension of the 1940 Constitution and the rights it conferred. They did not, however,

---

[1] Batista, though not yet President, was already the power in the land.

[2] One of these was Carlos Rafael Rodríguez who has subsequently become Cuba's vice-president under Castro, a remarkable achievement.

turn to revolution. When Fidel was attacking the Moncada Barracks in Santiago de Cuba in 1953, Blas Roca was in town with communist friends celebrating his birthday. The Party's line on the attack, which must have reflected Roca's view, was that it was 'putschist'.

The remainder of the Fifties saw the Party maintaining a distance from political life, revolutionary and orthodox. With the seizure of power by the Fidelistas in 1959, it found itself in the agreeable position of being untainted by contact of any kind with the second Batista administration.

In the years 1959 to 1961, which saw the establishment of the socialist character of the revolution, many communists, including Roca, played an important role. Power was never fully in their hands, as it lay with the Fidelista 26 July Movement. But the two were amalgamated into what eventually became the Partido Unificado de la Revolución Socialista. PURS, as it was known, was recognised as a fraternal party by the Soviet Union in 1965 and in turn became the new 'Communist Party of Cuba'. Some of the older communists endured these changes. Twenty-one of them, including Blas Roca, made it onto the one hundred-strong Central Committee. None, however, made it to the Politburo or the Secretariat. Those who went to these positions, and got the real power, were 26 July people (although formally they now called themselves communists).

That the Fidelistas were nationalists who, after victory, appropriated the Communist Party is a fact not properly appreciated to this day, particularly in the US. Cuba's current political complexion has come about because, after a revolutionary victory the country needed to attach itself to a strong but distant ally in order to break the influence of a close and powerful force. That is why the colours of the Party were nailed to the mast, so to speak, and room was made for men like Roca.

The later Sixties saw the sometime secretary-general respectable but without the opportunities for exercising his considerable political skills. So he turned in the direction to which so many frustrated politicians have turned: censorship. He was one of those Cuban communists who tried to compel Cuban artists to shun decadent abstract art and adopt the realist-style of the party's Mexican sympathisers such as David Alfaro Siqueiros—a dreadful artist. He also started to become more like an old general. In an interview in the *Daily Telegraph* in 1965, he claimed he was neither afraid of an armed clash with the US nor of nuclear weapons.[1] It is an utterance that lends weight to the theory that, in one part of their souls, the Cuban leaders wanted the US to strike at them in 1962. If it had happened, it would have been the ultimate refutation of US liberalism and goodness, irrevocable proof that the US was, as Martí had said, a monster, and the ultimate martyrdom.

---

[1] Anthony Sylvester, 'Cuba's Lesson for Latin America', *Daily Telegraph*, 11 June 1965.

32

The Fisherman and the Priest

We left Santiago by the *carretera central* in the early hours of the morning when it was still dark, and reached the Sierra Maestra mountains to the north of the city about dawn. '*Evite Accidentes*' ('Avoid Accidents') was picked out with white stones on the first slope. The sun began to rise, lighting up the clouds overhead so they became like mother-of-pearl. The upper reaches were swathed in mist and at the very top we found ourselves in a dense white fog, where we could see nothing of the landscape except the occasional, ghostly palm tree. There were children shivering as they waited for the school bus and a farmer leading a bull along the road with a piece of rope through its nose. In Contra Maestra we saw men cutting cane with machetes. It was our very first sighting of this much-photographed Cuban scene, and we were on our way home.

We stopped at Santa Clara to spend the night with Maria and her family. The television went straight on after dinner and with one eye on the pictures of men with mutton-chop whiskers and women with bustles and long oval faces—it was the old British Victorian maritime saga, *The Onedin Line*—I listened to Gabriel hissing in my ear, 'I am not a communist. I just keep quiet. I work hard. I earn as much money as I can.'

He was jabbing my arm with his finger. I turned round to see him shrugging his shoulders and turning down the corners of his mouth.

'I am not a communist but I say nothing, and now I must have a shower.'

As *The Onedin Line* played on I heard water splashing in the bathroom and Gabriel singing a sentimental Cuban love song.

When I woke up the next morning, the sky outside the window was bright blue. In the living room the oilcloth on the table fluttered. Everyone was asleep. A huge plume of steam hissed from the laundry below the window, and in the kitchen the three chickens we were to have for lunch, their legs tied together with string, clucked forlornly.

Everyone came to the car when it was time to say goodbye. Maria and her mother began to cry quietly. We got into the car and drove off quickly.

We crossed over the ring road circling the city and found the start of the motorway: swathes of glistening tarmac without a central reservation or any markings, wide as an aircraft runway, where huge lorries and their trailers were roaring up and down.

Four or five kilometres further on the *autopista* began. This had replaced the *carretera central* between Santa Clara and Havana, a proper massive motorway with four lanes on either side.

The roadtop was white with patches of oil on it everywhere, daubs on a new canvas. In the distance the surface shimmered like water, continuously receding as we advanced towards it.

The road was empty. It was some time before we saw our first traffic, two bicyclists pedalling furiously on the other side of the reservation. The reflectors on their wheels flashed in the sun. One had a child on his crossbar and the other was carrying a shiny inner tube across his shoulder.

A wooden cross with the word '*Ferrocarril*' loomed up at the roadside. I couldn't place it, and then I had to brake suddenly when I saw running across this pristine, mammoth motorway a railway line. Its tracks stuck a couple of inches above the surface.

Hit at speed they would have been lethal. We stopped, and I looked left and right along the rails into the empty landscape.

We bumped across and drove under an unfinished bridge, a shady archway with three or four men sleeping underneath.

From under the bridge we emerged into the sunlight on the far side. On our right were two dove-grey oxen outside a wooden *bohío*, hitched to a cart loaded with cane. The farmer standing by in his straw hat stared at us as we passed, a figure from a nineteenth-century landscape.

Hours later the city of Havana appeared ahead, a dark, dirty, sprawling shape. Without warning the highway dwindled to two lanes and we found ourselves in a dusty Havana suburb. The road was filled with potholes. Outside little Florida-style bungalows in a leafy street, boys were playing baseball. I was back in the Cuba I was fondest of: the dirty, anarchic meld of the Hispanic and the North American.

The Malecón was like an old friend. I was even pleased to see the memorial to the victims of the *Maine*. We found our way to the Edificio Focsa, a skyscraper completed in 1958 and now disintegrating visibly from the effects of the sea air, like the entire city, only more quickly. We were to be the guests of our new friends, Raoul and Kate, with whom we had stayed in Varadero.

*

On our first afternoon Raoul took me on a literary pilgrimage to Cojimar, a village about eight kilometres east of Havana. Ernest Hemingway had kept his boat, the *Pilar*, there. For twenty years or so Hemingway had lived a few miles away at the Finca Vigía. He had fished out of Cojimar. It may have been used as the model for the village in *The Old Man and the Sea*. And it was where Gregorio Fuentes lived, eighty-seven or eighty-eight years old, sometime master of the *Pilar* and a living, vital connection with the writer.

Cojimar, once separate from the city, was now a part of Havana. We stopped in a quiet suburban street lined with bungalows and little houses.

'There he is,' said Raul.

Through the car window I watched Gregorio Fuentes coming along the pavement. He was an old man in a baseball hat and carrying two shopping baskets.

We climbed out and I was introduced. We shook hands, and his forearm reminded me of a battered leather telescope case. He brought us through a gate and into the tiny garden at the back of his house. There were chairs but he did not ask us to sit down. Nor did he sit himself.

'I am so tired,' he started. 'Visitors are always coming to see me about Hemingway and you're another one. Is there any end to it? Do you know what? Yesterday I had an Italian journalist and he asked me if Hemingway was homosexual. *Aie, aie, aie.*'

I wished I had my family with me. As a family we could have got him talking. Without them I was just another intruder.

Señor Fuentes lit a cigar and pushed it back into his mouth, clamping the end between his teeth.

'Do you want to take my picture?' he asked. He had pulled himself up and looked extremely proud.

He hadn't talked, but at least I could get a very good photograph. I clicked away for several minutes throughout which he maintained the expression. (I shouldn't have bothered. Much later, when I got the photographs back from the developer in London, I discovered the subject's face was lost in a patch of shadow.)

I finished. Gregorio Fuentes turned to Raul.

'Do you know what they want me to do? To go out with parties of tourists. They fish. I talk about Ernest.'

He complained for several minutes, shaking his head. He was under high-level pressure to comply. Even Fidel had asked him.

We returned to Havana in silence, passing sand dunes along the way. There were hundreds of militiamen here, taking it in turns to have a go at using rifles.

The best moment of the afternoon had been seeing Señor Fuentes for the first time, walking slowly down the street with his two shopping baskets and baseball hat. In the evening I returned our Lada.

*

We woke, after our sixth night in the high-rise Focsa, to find the curtains billowing in front of the windows and the blue Atlantic shimmering beyond the Malecón, a mere three blocks away. I could get used to this, I thought.

What was not so agreeable, however, was the lack of water. After twenty-four hours it was still not flowing and the buckets and basins we had filled before the taps had run dry were now almost empty. At least there was water to drink from a huge glass belljar.

We left the tenth-floor flat and went to catch the lift. Three were out of order, and the fourth was too full to take us. Eventually we took the service stairs, tortuous, dark and smelling of the sawdust in a butcher's.

The bus proved as impossible to catch as the lift. We found a taxi. The driver drove with his hand permanently on the horn and shouted 'Shit' through the window at every other driver we overtook. Although he had a meter he didn't turn it on and charged us at what I guessed was four times the normal rate. But in three months it was the only time we were treated like tourists on the street. The last I saw of the driver, he was dragging a woman, who had thought about taking a ride with him and then sensibly changed her mind, towards his cab and shouting, 'Don't worry. I'll get you there.'

In the church we could still hear him as we asked for Father Xavier, the priest from Santiago who regularly came to Havana and had arranged to meet us here.

The Spanish priest in the vestibule pointed with his large cigar. We went through a door and found ourselves in a cloister with Xavier coming towards us.

After greeting us he immediately said, mysteriously, 'There is a dollar problem.'

Miguel, another priest and Xavier's superior, appeared. He looked nervous.

'Miguel has some dollars left in the collection box here by foolish tourists.'

We all smiled at Xavier's joke.

'He wants you to buy some things for a parishioner in the Dollar shop.'

'Of course, what?'

'Shoes,' said Miguel, looking very happy.

He pulled from his pocket a grubby piece of paper with the outline of a foot drawn on it in pencil.

'She's old,' he said to Tyga, 'so not too much of a heel.'

He ran a finger around his lips.

'Lipstick, too. Very strong. Very red.'

He made a fist to emphasise his point.

'And liner, black.'

He ran a finger backwards and forwards along his eyebrows.

But before commerce, the tour. We followed Xavier and Miguel into the church. It was enormous. The pews vanished into a haze of brown. Every inch of ceiling appeared to have been painted with angels, trumpets and clouds, floating in a greenish haze. Staring up, I felt I was standing on an ocean bed staring at the distant surface of the sea, where reflections from the sun were floating and trembling. I was heavy, inert, in fact drowning. Xavier beside me saw it rather differently. 'It almost seems three-dimensional, doesn't it?' he kept saying repeatedly.

Outside in the cloister I wanted to know exactly when the church had been finished.

'Ah,' said the Spanish priest, his body bulging from his shirt, cigars bulging from his breast pocket, 'it's still not finished.'

'A character,' Xavier whispered in my ear.

In the living quarters, in the kitchen, there were salads laid out: the priests' evening meals. Amidst the smell of caster sugar and incense and old paper, which every Catholic place I have been to in the world has had, Miguel slipped me the grubby roll of dollars. At the end of the afternoon he would drive us to the Havana Libre Hotel and in the air-conditioned mall we would do his shopping together.

It was early afternoon and outside the narrow streets were crowded. Peeling balconies, dilapidated buildings and the thick smell of Old Havana: a mixture of putrefying foods that couldn't be identified and the hot, gassy smell of sewer. Xavier led the way, pushing through the crowds. Half a dozen people came up and shook his hand and dozens more called out greetings. He showed us the old F. W. Woolworth's and the small grocery store which had been his family's business until it was nationalised. He explained, sounding bitter for the first time, 'They took it without a cent's compensation.'

The building where the family home was stood on a corner. The ground-level door was open.

'There was a lock but someone stole it,' he said, and smiled. I saw the hole in the wood and remembered the door in Brixton and the round hole where the Yale had been, and a finger hooking through.

We sat in the cramped front room of the third-floor flat drinking coffee with Xavier's mother and his brother Paul. Paul was older and thinner. He was a cinema projectionist.

'So, you live in London,' said Paul. His voice was booming, his English precise.

'Yes.'

'Trafalgar Square?'

'Not exactly. A little way from there.'

'Oxford Street?'

'Quite close to there.'

'It is the principal shopping street, I think?'

'Yes.'

'I know, I have been to London.'

Xavier, who had been following the conversation, shifted in his seat and looked nervously around the room, like one who wants to stop something unfortunate happening.

'Yes, I have been to London.'

Xavier caught my eye and shook his head. It was not true. Paul saw this and smiled.

'With books,' he continued, 'the only means of travel permitted to us Cubans.'

Xavier sighed with relief.

Down in the teeming streets half an hour later, Xavier told us this story:

'When he did his national service, Paul was a sergeant. One of the soldiers in his platoon fell asleep on guard duty. Paul wouldn't denounce the man, so the army sent my brother to prison for two years.'

Only in a country which felt itself under siege, I thought, would such a harsh sentence be passed. Paul wasn't even on duty when the soldier fell asleep.

Back at the church, Miguel was waiting in the cloister. He looked anxious. 'I completely forgot,' he said. 'I have a mass to say at six.'

We only had an hour. We hurtled through the rush-hour traffic in Miguel's dirty, decrepit Volkswagen Beetle, four of us squashed in the back because the front passenger seat was missing.

'This car runs on holy water,' Miguel joked, not unpredictably.

In the shopping mall in the Libre, the atmosphere in the *perfumería* was still and chilled. The middle-aged saleslady had painted nails, a painted face and tightly set hair. I hung back and so did Xavier but Father Miguel followed Tyga across the carpeted floor and leant ostentatiously on the glass-topped counter beside her. A dumb show followed. She looked at one lipstick after another whilst he either shook his head in disapproval or nodded his head in agreement. When the tops came off the bullet-shaped containers and a tentative smear went onto the back of hand or lip, he would squint his eyes and stare closely. Meanwhile the assistant stared at him, with his wrinkled forehead, untidy hair, and the white band around his neck.

The colour was settled on.

'Thank you, this one,' said Tyga.

'Six,' said Father Xavier in a stage whisper, 'buy six.'

It was the same procedure with the eye-shadow, the deodorant which he added suddenly to the list, and later the shoes.

We left the Havana Libre and Miguel became anxious again. Only half an hour to get back to the church and into his robes. He got into his car and sped away, leaving us all standing on the pavement. We watched the black smoke billowing from the exhaust.

We were on the Calle 25 near a Baptist chapel.

'The first church,' said Xavier pointing at it, 'Fidel has entered in twenty years. Jesse Jackson came to Havana. He's a Baptist minister. That's where he spoke, so that's where Fidel had to go.'

We retraced our steps to the Havana Libre and went into one of the dark bars off the lobby. This one had rattan furnishings and the decor was Far Eastern.

Xavier was full of wicked tales, about the Cuban official sent to Canada to buy tractors who returned with snow ploughs; about the prestige Hermanos Ameijeiras Hospital on the Malecón, its valuable surgical equipment being eaten away by the sea air; about the Japanese advisers who, during the construction, had warned about this and been ignored (now the hospital would probably have to be moved); about the pre-built factory from Argentina. The plans to this had been lost and it had had to be assembled using photographs of another factory. Of course, the plant had never worked properly. And there were stories about Fidel. On one of his Howard Hughes-like nightly peregrinations around Havana in his limousine, he had discovered valuable equipment had been dumped in the Havana docks and left for several years. 'Get it moved,' he had said, and it had been, out of sight where he would not be able to see it next time he passed. On another occasion he had summoned a lady journalist in the middle of the night to watch him playing a lengthy game of basketball with his aides before giving his interview.

Returning later from the lavatory Xavier looked downwards and with a smile said, 'I hope there isn't a microphone under the table.'

The achievements of the revolutionary government in the fields of education, housing, nutrition, health and employment he approved of. It was the incompetence and the authoritarian nature of the regime he disliked. But he remained a nationalist.

After his last trip to Rome in 1986, he had gone on to the United States. He had stayed there in a house with several young

American priests. One evening at supper, Xavier noticed a serving mat which was a facsimile of the US coat of arms. There was an eagle and the motto, 'In God We Trust'.

'How strange,' he said, 'to use the emblem of a nation as a rest for hot plates.'

'Watch this, then,' said one of the priests. He dropped the mat on the floor and stamped on it. 'This is what I think of the state, the Presidency, Congress and Capitol Hill, the American dream, Uncle Sam and everything else.'

'I was shocked,' said Father Xavier, leaning across the rattan table in the cold air-conditioned bar. 'No one would do this in Cuba. Everyone loves their country and the flag, even if they hate the state. The flag stands not for government, or communism, but for the land, the nation, us.'

My family returned from the Dollar shop where they had been buying gifts. The bill was settled and we all went into the lobby. It was the evening before May Day. There was a carnival atmosphere. There were girls in tulip dresses with net petticoats and tulle bows in their hair. Their escorts wore box jackets, tightly cut, which shimmered faintly under the neon lights. Xavier talked about Dickens, the Thames and London fog.

'I would give my right arm to visit,' he said.

We parted on N Street and turned up the hill towards the Focsa building.

33

The Notebooks

In the ceiling of the gloomy check-in lounge at José Martí airport a pipe had burst, and a vast rust-coloured puddle covered most of the floor. The atmosphere was saturated with hot-house vapour.

At passport control the man in the uniform told us he was also called Carlo. He was heavily built and had a thick neck. He sat in something like a little garden shed with a slit. We stood in a corridor beside the slit with a mirror overhead and a gate at the end. Never before had Carlo seen the quite legitimate visas which we had stamped in our passports. Telephone calls were made. Higher officials appeared. Minutes turned to an hour. The Czech behind us in the queue whispered mischievously,

'I don't think he knows how to read.'

Eventually we were waved through to the X-ray room. Here one of our suitcases was waiting. Something alarming had shown up on the scanner. It turned out to be a piece of brain coral. No problem. An officer of the Ministry of the Interior took my Billingham camera bag which was my hand luggage and unzipped it by hand.

'Any literature?' he asked.

I gave him my books. Cabrera Infante's *Infante's Inferno*, Julio Iglesias's *In the Fist of the Revolution*, our Cuban atlas, Hugh Thomas's *Cuba, or The Pursuit of Freedom* and Richard Adams's *The Bureaucrats*, a children's book.

The officer carried the books into a side room. We talked to the women who operated the X-ray machines. The officer returned with the books, removed all my diaries from my bag along with some maps, and disappeared into the side room again.

I felt less anxious than I had a few minutes earlier. The diaries which I had filled every day of the trip were not provocative in the way the novel of Cabrera Infante, an exiled Cuban author, was. Taciturn before, I was now quite talkative with the ladies who worked the X-ray machines.

The Ministry of the Interior official returned. He was carrying the single, unfilled notebook which had been among the diaries. He handed it back.

'Please, proceed,' he said.

The next twenty minutes I remember rather like an event seen through a telescope held to the eye the wrong way round.

'I am in Cuba to write. I had permission to come. Can I please have my diaries back?'

'Then where is your accreditation to the Ministry of Foreign Affairs?'

'I don't have any and I was never told I needed it.'

'That is not possible.'

'Our visa, issued in London, was given to allow us to travel round. The embassy knew I was going to write about Cuba.'

'Where is your accreditation?'

'As I said, I don't have any.'

The conversation followed this circular course for a long time until Tyga said angrily, 'This isn't very good publicity for Cuba.'

The Ministry of the Interior official seemed to waver. Then Tyga started to bolt towards the door of the room at the side.

The official caught up with her and stopped her. Policemen appeared. There followed a great deal of shouting and gesturing between Tyga and the official, which I watched. He was angry but he couldn't lose his temper. Not with a woman who was pregnant. She on the other hand was quite at liberty to do so, and did. Finally, it became all too much for the official. He went into the side room and returned with a smaller man who was wearing a grander uniform. The *jefe* was holding my diaries. A still, calm inner voice was saying: Do nothing. Just smile. I hadn't been as careful as I should have been in the diaries. I'd used Father Xavier's real name and described in full our conversation about his illegal masses. I had to get the diaries back.

The *jefe* was shaking with rage. I smiled at him.

'Do you speak Spanish?' he shouted at me.

'Yes.'

'I'm giving these back to you, but I want you to understand that never again will you, as a writer, be allowed to run around our country uncontrolled. I also want you to take note that you have not been in any way molested by us.'

I could feel little balls of his spit landing on my face. I made no attempt to wipe them away.

'But where are the maps?' I heard Tyga saying beside me.

I had noticed their absence too, but the still, small voice was saying: Fuck the maps. Get the notebooks.

I took the pile from the *jefe* and smiled.

'Why thank you,' I said.

'We want our maps,' said Tyga in Spanish.

'Forget them,' I said in English.

As we went through the doors into the departure lounge, our flight to Prague was called.

We got onto a bus and I frantically counted my notebooks. Christ, fifteen, and I thought I'd filled sixteen. I counted again and was relieved to discover I'd missed one out.

As soon as we were airborne I opened a bottle of rum. The drink lulled me to sleep and I dreamt I was wandering around Havana airport in an enormous, brand-new Cuban straw hat and trying to look inconspicuous.

We arrived in Prague full of apprehensions. An overnight visa would be impossible to obtain. The bank would be closed. The central heating would be off. We would have to spend a freezing cold night on incredibly uncomfortable plastic seats in the lounge, until the next day when we could catch a flight to London.

Nothing could have been further from the truth. The visa was a formality obtained in seconds. The bank was open. A bus waited outside to bring us to the hotel. We sped off along a glistening, curving highway. A red flag fluttered from each grey lamp-post.

The Hotel International was enormous, a combination of pseudo-Greek and the Empire State building. In the cavernous, carpeted dining room, tea cups could be heard tinkling. The man behind the desk wore pinstripe trousers, a tie and a jacket. We were expected. An elderly porter in livery appeared and carried our bags to the lift. He spoke English. His daughter lived in Harrow and his son-in-law worked at Kodak in Hemel Hempstead.

Our room on the first floor was panelled with dark wood. Duvets with crisp white covers lay on the beds. There was a mini-bar stocked with champagne and gin; a Sewing Susan with three different colours of thread; a desk with stationery and blotting paper. We turned on the lights, ran the taps, filled our pockets with the free Kleenex. It was then I saw the porter coming towards me, pulling a huge wad of notes out of his pocket. I heard him saying, 'And how much do you want to change, sir? I offer the best rate in the hotel.'

Some things never change.

Unable to sleep, I lay awake all night under the immaculate white duvet. Nearing dawn, the net curtains started to glisten with the first light, and the first tram rumbled along its tracks.

Over the table there was a marble lampshade. It was white with brown streaks in it, and as I stared at it, like a cloud I began to see pictures in it, an Assyrian bow, an eye, a dog resting its head on a paw.

Index